The Art of Concurrency

Clay Breshears

O'REILLY®

Beijing · Cambridge · Farnham · Köln · Sebastopol · Taipei · Tokyo

The Art of Concurrency
by Clay Breshears

Published by O'Reilly Media, Inc., 1005 Gravenstein Highway North, Sebastopol, CA 95472.

O'Reilly books may be purchased for educational, business, or sales promotional use. Online editions are also available for most titles (*http://safari.oreilly.com*). For more information, contact our corporate/institutional sales department: 800-998-9938 or *corporate@oreilly.com*.

Editor: Mike Loukides	**Indexer:** Ellen Troutman Zaig
Production Editor: Sarah Schneider	**Cover Designer:** Karen Montgomery
Copyeditor: Amy Thomson	**Interior Designer:** David Futato
Proofreader: Sarah Schneider	**Illustrator:** Robert Romano

Printing History:
   May 2009:   First Edition.

ISBN: 978-0-596-52153-0

[V]

1241201585

To my parents, for all their love, guidance, and support.

CONTENTS

PREFACE

Why Should You Read This Book?

MULTICORE PROCESSORS MADE A BIG SPLASH WHEN THEY WERE FIRST INTRODUCED. Bowing to the physics of heat and power, processor clock speeds could not keep doubling every 18 months as they had been doing for the past three decades or more. In order to keep increasing the processing power of the next generation over the current generation, processor manufacturers began producing chips with multiple processor cores. More processors running at a reduced speed generate less heat and consume less power than single-processor chips continuing on the path of simply doubling clock speeds.

But how can we use those extra cores? We can run more than one application at a time, and each program could have a separate processor core devoted to the execution. This would give us truly parallel execution. However, there are only so many apps that we can run simultaneously. If those apps aren't very compute-intensive, we're probably wasting compute cycles, but now we're doing it in more than one processor.

Another option is to write applications that will utilize the additional cores to execute portions of the code that have a need to perform lots of calculations and whose computations are independent of each other. Writing such programs is known as *concurrent programming*. With any programming language or methodology, there are techniques, tricks, traps, and tools to design and implement such programs. I've always found that there is more "art" than "science" to programming. So, this book is going to give you the knowledge and one or two of the "secret handshakes" you need to successfully practice the art of concurrent programming.

In the past, parallel and concurrent programming was the domain of a very small set of programmers who were typically involved in scientific and technical computing arenas. From now on, concurrent programming is going to be mainstream. Parallel programming will eventually become synonymous with "programming." Now is *your* time to get in on the ground floor, or at least somewhere near the start of the concurrent programming evolution.

Who Is This Book For?

This book is for programmers everywhere.

I work for a computer technology company, but I'm the only computer science degree-holder on my team. There is only one other person in the office within the sound of my voice who would know what I was talking about if I said I wanted to parse an LR(1) grammar with a deterministic pushdown automata. So, CS students and graduates aren't likely to make up the bulk of the interested readership for this text. For that reason, I've tried to keep the geeky CS material to a minimum. I assume that readers have some basic knowledge of data structures and algorithms and asymptotic efficiency of algorithms (Big-Oh notation) that is typically taught in an undergraduate computer science curriculum. For whatever else I've covered, I've tried to include enough of an explanation to get the idea across. If you've been coding for more than a year, you should do just fine.

I've written all the codes using C. Meaning no disrespect, I figured this was the lowest common denominator of programming languages that supports threads. Other languages, like Java and C#, support threads, but if I wrote this book using one of those languages and you didn't code with the one I picked, you wouldn't read my book. I think most programmers who will be able to write concurrent programs will be able to at least "read" C code. Understanding the concurrency methods illustrated is going to be more important than being able to write code in one particular language. You can take these ideas back to C# or Java and implement them there.

I'm going to assume that you have read a book on at least one threaded programming method. There are many available, and I don't want to cover the mechanics and detailed syntax of multithreaded programming here (since it would take a whole other book or two). I'm not going to focus on using one programming paradigm here, since, for the most part, the functionality of these overlap. I will present a revolving usage of threading implementations across the wide spectrum of algorithms that are featured in the latter portion of the book. If there are circumstances where one method might differ significantly from the method used, these differences will be noted.

I've included a review of the threaded programming methods that are utilized in this book to refresh your memory or to be used as a reference for any methods you have not had the chance to study. I'm not implying that you need to know all the different ways to program with threads. Knowing one should be sufficient. However, if you change jobs or find that what you know about programming with threads cannot easily solve a programming problem you have been assigned, it's always good to have some awareness of what else is available—this may help you learn and apply a new method quickly.

What's in This Book?

Chapter 1, *Want to Go Faster? Raise Your Hands if You Want to Go Faster!*, anticipates and answers some of the questions you might have about concurrent programming. This chapter explains the differences between parallel and concurrent, and describes the four-step threading methodology. The chapter ends with a bit of background on concurrent programming and some of the differences and similarities between distributed-memory and shared-memory programming and execution models.

Chapter 2, *Concurrent or Not Concurrent?*, contains a lot of information about designing concurrent solutions from serial algorithms. Two concurrent design models—task decomposition and data decomposition—are each given a thorough elucidation. This chapter gives examples of serial coding that you may not be able to make concurrent. In cases where there is a way around this, I've given some hints and tricks to find ways to transform the serial code into a more amenable form.

Chapter 3, *Proving Correctness and Measuring Performance*, first deals with ways to demonstrate that your concurrent algorithms won't encounter common threading errors and to point out what problems you might see (so you can fix them). The second part of this chapter gives you ways to judge how much faster your concurrent implementations are running compared to the original serial execution. At the very end, since it didn't seem to fit anywhere else, is a brief retrospective of how hardware has progressed to support the current multicore processors.

Chapter 4, *Eight Simple Rules for Designing Multithreaded Applications*, says it all in the title. Use of these simple rules is pointed out at various points in the text.

Chapter 5, *Threading Libraries*, is a review of OpenMP, Intel Threading Building Blocks, POSIX threads, and Windows Threads libraries. Some words on domain-specific libraries that have been threaded are given at the end.

Chapter 6, *Parallel Sum and Prefix Scan*, details two concurrent algorithms. This chapter also leads you through a concurrent version of a selection algorithm that uses both of the titular algorithms as components.

Chapter 7, *MapReduce*, examines the MapReduce algorithmic framework; how to implement a handcoded, fully concurrent reduction operation; and finishes with an application of the MapReduce framework in a code to identify friendly numbers.

Chapter 8, *Sorting*, demonstrates some of the ins and outs of concurrent versions of Bubblesort, odd-even transposition sort, Shellsort, Quicksort, and two variations of radix sort algorithms.

Chapter 9, *Searching*, covers concurrent designs of search algorithms to use when your data is unsorted and when it is sorted.

Chapter 10, *Graph Algorithms*, looks at depth-first and breadth-first search algorithms. Also included is a discussion of computing all-pairs shortest path and the minimum spanning tree concurrently.

Chapter 11, *Threading Tools*, gives you an introduction to software tools that are available and on the horizon to assist you in finding threading errors and performance bottlenecks in your concurrent programs. As your concurrent code gets more complex, you will find these tools invaluable in diagnosing problems in minutes instead of days or weeks.

Conventions Used in This Book

The following typographical conventions are used in this book:

Italic

> Indicates new terms, URLs, email addresses, filenames, file extensions, pathnames, directories, and Unix utilities.

Constant width

> Indicates commands, options, switches, variables, attributes, keys, functions, types, classes, namespaces, methods, modules, properties, parameters, values, objects, events,

event handlers, XML tags, HTML tags, macros, the contents of files, or the output from commands.

Constant width bold

Shows commands or other text that should be typed literally by the user.

Constant width italic

Shows text that should be replaced with user-supplied values.

Using Code Examples

This book is here to help you get your job done. In general, you may use the code in this book in your programs and documentation. You do not need to contact us for permission unless you're reproducing a significant portion of the code. For example, writing a program that uses several chunks of code from this book does not require permission. Selling or distributing a CD-ROM of examples from O'Reilly books *does* require permission. Answering a question by citing this book and quoting example code does not require permission. Incorporating a significant amount of example code from this book into your product's documentation *does* require permission.

We appreciate, but do not require, attribution. An attribution usually includes the title, author, publisher, and ISBN. For example: "*The Art of Concurrency* by Clay Breshears. Copyright 2009 Clay Breshears, 978-0-596-52153-0."

If you feel your use of code examples falls outside fair use or the permission given above, feel free to contact us at *permissions@oreilly.com*.

Comments and Questions

Please address comments and questions concerning this book to the publisher:

O'Reilly Media, Inc.
1005 Gravenstein Highway North
Sebastopol, CA 95472
800-998-9938 (in the United States or Canada)
707-829-0515 (international or local)
707-829-0104 (fax)

We have a web page for this book, where we list errata, examples, and any additional information. You can access this page at:

http://www.oreilly.com/catalog/9780596521530

To comment or ask technical questions about this book, send email to:

bookquestions@oreilly.com

For more information about our books, conferences, Resource Centers, and the O'Reilly Network, see our website at:

http://www.oreilly.com

Safari® Books Online

 When you see a Safari® Books Online icon on the cover of your favorite technology book, that means the book is available online through the O'Reilly Network Safari Bookshelf.

Safari offers a solution that's better than e-books. It's a virtual library that lets you easily search thousands of top tech books, cut and paste code samples, download chapters, and find quick answers when you need the most accurate, current information. Try it for free at *http://my.safaribooksonline.com/*.

Acknowledgments

I want to give my thanks to the following people for their influences on my career and support in the writing of this book. Without all of them, you wouldn't be reading this and I'd probably be flipping burgers for a living.

To **JOSEPH SARGENT** and **STANLEY CHASE** for bringing *Colossus: The Forbin Project* to the big screen in 1970. This movie was probably the biggest influence in my early years in getting me interested in computer programming and instilling within me the curiosity to figure out what cool and wondrous things computers could do.

To **ROGER WINK** for fanning the flame of my interest in computers, and for his 30-plus years of friendship and technical knowledge. He taught me Bubblesort in COBOL and is always working on something new and interesting that he can show off whenever we get the chance to meet up.

To **BILL MAGRO** and **TOM CORTESE** for being my first manager at Intel and one of my first teammates at the Intel Parallel Applications Center. Working at the PAC gave me the chance to get my "hands dirty" with lots of different parallel codes, to interact with applications and customers from many different technical and commercial areas, and to learn new methods and new threading libraries. It was a "dream come true" job for me.

To **JERRY BAUGH**, **BOB CHESEBROUGH**, **JEFF GALLAGHER**, **RAVI MANOHAR**, **MIKE PEARCE**, **MICHAEL WRINN**, and **HUA (SELWYN) YOU** for being fantastic colleagues at Intel, past and present, and for reviewing chapters of my book for technical content. I've relied on every one of these guys for their wide range of technical expertise; for their support, patience, and willingness to help me with my projects and goals; for their informed opinions; and for their continuing camaraderie throughout my years at Intel.

To my editor, **MIKE LOUKIDES**, and the rest of the staff at O'Reilly who had a finger in this project. I couldn't have done anything like this without their help and advice and nagging me about my deadlines.

To **GERGANA SLAVOVA**, who posed as my "target audience" and reviewed the book from cover to cover. Besides keeping me honest to my readers by making me explain complex ideas in simple terms and adding examples when I'd put too many details in a single paragraph, she peppered her comments with humorous asides that broke up the monotony of the tedium of the revision process (and she throws a slammin' tea party, too).

To **HENRY GABB** for his knowledge of parallel and multithreaded programming, for convincing me to apply for a PAC job and join him at Intel back in 2000, and for his devotion to SEC football and the Chicago Cubs. During the almost 15 years we've known each other, we've worked together on many different projects and we've each been able to consult with the other on technical questions. His knowledge and proficiency as a technical reviewer of this text, and many other papers of mine he has so kindly agreed to review over the years, have improved my written communication skills by an order of magnitude.

And finally, a big heartfelt "thank you" to my patient and loving wife, **LORNA**, who now has her husband back.

CHAPTER ONE

Want to Go Faster? Raise Your Hands if You Want to Go Faster!

> **"[A]nd in this precious phial is the power to think twice**
> **as fast, move twice as quickly, do twice as much work in**
> **a given time as you could otherwise do."**
>
> —H. G. Wells, "The New Accelerator" (1901)

WITH THIS BOOK I WANT TO PEEL BACK THE VEILS OF MYSTERY, MISERY, AND misunderstanding that surround concurrent programming. I want to pass along to you some of the tricks, secrets, and skills that I've learned over my last two decades of concurrent and parallel programming experience.

I will demonstrate these tricks, secrets, and skills—and the art of concurrent programming—by developing and implementing concurrent algorithms from serial code. I will explain the thought processes I went through for each example in order to give you insight into how concurrent code can be developed. I will be using threads as the model of concurrency in a shared-memory environment for all algorithms devised and implemented. Since this isn't a book on one specific threading library, I've used several of the common libraries throughout and included some hints on how implementations might differ, in case your preferred method wasn't used.

Like any programming skill, there is a level of mechanics involved in being ready and able to attempt concurrent or multithreaded programming. You can learn these things (such as syntax, methods for mutual exclusion, and sharing data) through study and practice. There is also a necessary component of logical thinking skills and intuition needed to tackle or avoid even simple concurrent programming problems successfully. Being able to apply that logical thinking and having some intuition, or being able to think about threads executing in parallel with each other, is the art of concurrent and multithreaded programming. You can learn some of this through demonstration by experts, but that only works if the innate ability is already there and you can apply the lessons learned to other situations. Since you've picked up this volume, I'm sure that you, my fine reader, already possess such innate skills. This book will help you shape and aim those skills at concurrent and multithreaded programming.

Some Questions You May Have

Before we get started, there are some questions you may have thought up while reading those first few paragraphs or even when you saw this book on the shelves before picking it up. Let's take a look at some of those questions now.

What Is a Thread Monkey?

A *thread monkey* is a programmer capable of designing multithreaded, concurrent, and parallel software, as well as grinding out correct and efficient code to implement those designs. Much like a "grease monkey" is someone who can work magic on automobiles, a thread monkey is a wiz at concurrent programming. Thread monkey is a title of prestige, unlike the often derogatory connotations associated with "code monkey."

Parallelism and Concurrency: What's the Difference?

The terms "parallel" and "concurrent" have been tossed around with increasing frequency since the release of general-purpose multicore processors. Even prior to that, there has been some confusion about these terms in other areas of computation. What is the difference, or *is* there a difference, since use of these terms seems to be almost interchangeable?

A system is said to be *concurrent* if it can support two or more actions *in progress* at the same time. A system is said to be *parallel* if it can support two or more actions executing simultaneously. The key concept and difference between these definitions is the phrase "in progress."

A concurrent application will have two or more threads in progress at some time. This can mean that the application has two threads that are being swapped in and out by the operating system on a single core processor. These threads will be "in progress"—each in the midst of its execution—at the same time. In parallel execution, there must be multiple cores available within the computation platform. In that case, the two or more threads could each be assigned a separate core and would be running simultaneously.

I hope you've already deduced that "parallel" is a subset of "concurrent." That is, you can write a concurrent application that uses multiple threads or processes, but if you don't have multiple cores for execution, you won't be able to run your code in parallel. Thus, *concurrent programming* and *concurrency* encompass all programming and execution activities that involve multiple streams of execution being implemented in order to solve a single problem.

For about the last 20 years, the term *parallel programming* has been synonymous with message-passing or distributed-memory programming. With multiple compute nodes in a cluster or connected via some network, each node with one or more processors, you had a parallel platform. There is a specific programming methodology required to write applications that divide up the work and share data. The programming of applications utilizing threads has been thought of as concurrent programming, since threads are part of a shared-memory programming model that fits nicely into a single core system able to access the memory within the platform.

I will be striving to use the terms "parallel" and "concurrent" correctly throughout this book. This means that *concurrent programming* and *design of concurrent algorithms* will assume that the resulting code is able to run on a single core or multiple cores without any drastic changes. Even though the implementation model will be threads, I will talk about the parallel execution of concurrent codes, since I assume that we all have multicore processors available on which to execute those multiple threads. Also, I'll use the term "parallelization" as the process of translating applications from serial to concurrent (and the term "concurrentization" doesn't roll off the tongue quite as nicely).

Why Do I Need to Know This? What's in It for Me?

I'm tempted to be a tad flippant and tell you that there's no way to avoid this topic; multicore processors are here now and here to stay, and if you want to remain a vital and employable programmer, you have no choice but to learn and master this material. Of course, I'd be waving my hands around manically for emphasis and trying to put you into a frightened state of mind. While all that is true to some degree, a kinder and gentler approach is more likely to gain your trust and get you on board with the concurrent programming revolution.

Whether you're a faceless corporate drone for a large software conglomerate, writing code for a small in-house programming shop, doing open source development, or just dabbling with writing software as a hobby, you are going to be touched by multicore processors to one degree or another. In the past, to get a burst of increased performance out of your applications, you simply needed to wait for the next generation of processor that had a faster clock speed than the previous model. A colleague of mine once postulated that you could take nine months off to play the drums or surf, come back after the new chips had been released, run some benchmarks, and declare success. In his seminal (and by now, legendary) article, "The Free Lunch Is Over: A Fundamental Turn Toward Concurrency in Software" (*Dr. Dobb's Journal*, March 2005), Herb Sutter explains that this situation is no longer viable. Programmers will need to start writing concurrent code in order to take full advantage of multicore processors and achieve future performance improvements.

What kinds of performance improvements can you expect with concurrent programming on multicore processors? As an upper bound, you could expect applications to run in half the time using two cores, one quarter of the time running on four cores, one eighth of the time running on eight cores, and so on. This sounds much better than the 20–30% decrease in runtime when using a new, faster processor. Unfortunately, it takes some work to get code whipped into shape and capable of taking advantage of multiple cores. Plus, in general, very few codes will be able to achieve these upper bound levels of increased performance. In fact, as the number of cores increases, you may find that the relative performance actually decreases. However, if you can write good concurrent and multithreaded applications, you will be able to achieve respectable performance increases (or be able to explain why you can't). Better yet, if you can develop your concurrent algorithms in such a way that the same relative performance increases seen on two and four cores remains when executing on 8, 16, or more cores, you may be able to devote some time to your drumming and surfing. A major focus of this book will be pointing out when and how to develop such *scalable* algorithms.

Isn't Concurrent Programming Hard?

Concurrent programming is no walk in the park, that's for sure. However, I don't think it is as scary or as difficult as others may have led you to think. If approached in a logical and informed fashion, learning and practicing concurrent programming is no more difficult than learning another programming language.

With a serial program, execution of your code takes a predictable path through the application. Logic errors and other bugs can be tracked down in a methodical and logical way. As you gain more experience and more sophistication in your programming, you learn of other potential problems (e.g., memory leaks, buffer overflows, file I/O errors, floating-point precision, and roundoff), as well as how to identify, track down, and correct such problems. There are software tools that can assist in quickly locating code that is either not performing as intended or causing problems. Understanding the causes of possible bugs, experience, and the use of software tools will greatly enhance your success in diagnosing problems and addressing them.

Concurrent algorithms and multithreaded programming require you to think about multiple execution streams running at the same time and how you coordinate all those streams in order to complete a given computation. In addition, an entirely new set of errors and performance problems that have no equivalent in serial programming will rear their ugly heads. These new problems are the direct result of the nondeterministic and asynchronous behavior exhibited by threads executing concurrently. Because of these two characteristics, when you have a bug in your threaded program, it may or may not manifest itself. The execution order (or interleaving) of multiple threads may be just perfect so that errors do not occur, but if you make some change in the execution platform that alters your correct interleaving of threads, the errors may start popping up. Even if no hardware change is made, consecutive runs of the same application with the same inputs can yield two different results for no more reason than the fact that it is Tuesday.

To visualize the problem you face, think of all the different ways you can interlace the fingers between two hands. This is like running two threads, where the fingers of a hand are the instructions executed by a thread, concurrently or in parallel. There are 70 different ways to interleave two sets of four fingers. If only 4% (3 of 70) of those interleavings caused an error, how could you track down the cause, especially if, like the Heisenberg Uncertainty Principle, any attempts to identify the error through standard debugging techniques would guarantee one of the error-free interleavings always executed? Luckily, there are software tools specifically designed to track down and identify correctness and performance issues within threaded code.

With the proper knowledge and experience, you will be better equipped to write code that is free of common threading errors. Through the pages of this book, I want to pass on that kind of knowledge. Getting the experience will be up to you.

Aren't Threads Dangerous?

Yes and no. In the years since multicore processors became mainstream, a lot of learned folks have come out with criticisms of the threading model. These people focus on the dangers inherent in using shared memory to communicate between threads and how nonscalable the standard synchronization objects are when pushed beyond a few threads. I won't lie to you; these criticisms do have merit.

So, why should I write a book about concurrency using threads as the model of implementation if they are so fraught with peril and hazard? Every programming language has its own share of risk, but once you know about these potential problems, you are nine tenths of the way to being able to avoid them. Even if you inadvertently incorporate a threading error in your code, knowing what to look for can be much more helpful than even the best debugger. For example, in FORTRAN 77, there was a default type assigned to variables that were undeclared, based on the first letter of the variable name. If you mistyped a variable name, the compiler blithely accepted this and created a new variable. Knowing that you might have put in the number '1' for the letter 'I' or the letter 'O' for the number '0,' you stood a better chance of locating the typing error in your program.

You might be wondering if there are other, "better" concurrency implementations available or being developed, and if so, why spend time on a book about threading. In the many years that I've been doing parallel and concurrent programming, all manner of other parallel programming languages have come and gone. Today, most of them are gone. I'm pretty sure my publisher didn't want me to write a book on any of those, since there is no guarantee that the information won't all be obsolete in six months. I am also certain that as I write this, academics are formulating all sorts of better, less error-prone, more programmer-friendly methods of concurrent programming. Many of these will be better than threads and some of them might actually be adopted into mainstream programming languages. Some might even spawn accepted new concurrent programming languages.

However, in the grand scheme of things, threads are here now and will be around for the foreseeable future. The alternatives, if they ever arrive and are able to overcome the inertia of current languages and practices, will be several years down the road. Multicore processors are here right now and you need to be familiar with concurrent programming right now. If you start now, you will be better prepared and practiced with the fundamentals of concurrent applications by the time anything new comes along (which is a better option than lounging around for a couple years, sitting on your hands and waiting for me to put out a new edition of this book using whatever new concurrency method is developed to replace threads).

THE TWO-MINUTE PRIMER ON CONCURRENT PROGRAMMING

Concurrent programming is all about independent computations that the machine can execute in any order. Iterations of loops and function calls within the code that can be executed autonomously are two instances of computations that can be independent. Whatever concurrent work you can pull out of the serial code can be assigned to threads (or cooperating processes) and run on any one of the multiple cores that are available (or run on a single processor by swapping the computations in and out of the processor to give the illusion of parallel execution). Not everything within an application will be independent, so you will still need to deal with serial execution amongst the concurrency.

To create the situation where concurrent work can be assigned to threads, you will need to add calls to library routines that implement threading. These additional function calls add to the *overhead* of the concurrent execution, since they were not in the original serial code. Any additional code that is needed to control and coordinate threads, especially calls to threading library functions, is overhead. Code that you add for threads to determine if the computation should continue or to get more work or to signal other threads when desired conditions have been met is all considered overhead, too. Some of that code may be devoted to ensuring that there are equal amounts of work assigned to each thread. This balancing of the workload between threads will make sure threads aren't sitting idle and wasting system resources, which is considered another form of overhead. Overhead is something that concurrent code must keep to a minimum as much as possible. In order to attain the maximum performance gains and keep your concurrent code as scalable as possible, the amount of work that is assigned to a thread must be large enough to minimize or mask the detrimental effects of overhead.

Since threads will be working together in shared memory, there may be times when two or more threads need to access the same memory location. If one or more of these threads is looking to update that memory location, you will have a *storage conflict* or *data race*. The operating system schedules threads for execution. Because the scheduling algorithm relies on many factors about the current status of the system, that scheduling appears to be asynchronous. Data races may or may not show up, depending on the order of thread executions. If the correct execution of your concurrent code depends on a particular order of memory updates (so that other threads will be sure to get the proper saved value), it is the responsibility of the program to ensure this order is guaranteed. For example, in an airline reservation system, if two travel agents see the same empty seat on a flight, they could both put the name of a client into that seat and generate a ticket. When the passengers show up at the airport, who will get the seat? To avoid fisticuffs and to enforce the correct ratio of butts to seats, there must be some means of controlling the updates of shared resources.

There are several different methods of synchronizing threads to ensure mutually exclusive access to shared memory. While synchronization is a necessary evil, use of synchronization objects is considered overhead (just like thread creation and other coordination functions) and their use should be reserved for situations that cannot be resolved in any other way.

The goal of all of this, of course, is to improve the performance of your application by reducing the amount of time it takes to execute, or to be able to process more data within a fixed amount of time. You will need an awareness of the perils and pitfalls of concurrent programming and how to avoid or correct them in order to create a correctly executing application with satisfactory performance.

Four Steps of a Threading Methodology

When developing software, especially large commercial applications, a formal process is used to ensure that everything is done to meet the goals of the proposed software in a timely and efficient way. This process is sometimes called the *software lifecycle*, and it includes the following six steps:

Specification
> Talk to users of the software to find out what functionality is desired, what the input and output specifications are, and, based on the feedback, formally specify the functionality to be included, a general structure of the application, and the code to implement it.

Design
> Set down more detailed plans of the application and the functional components of the application.

Implement
> Write the code for the application.

Test
> Assure that all the parts of the application work as expected, both separately and within the structure of the entire application, and fix any problems.

Tune
> Make improvements to the code in order to get better performance on target platforms.

Maintenance
> Fix bugs and continue performance improvements, and add new features not in the original design.

The "implement," "test," and "tune" steps may not have hard and fast demarcations between each of them, as programmers will be continually writing, testing, correcting, and tuning code they are working on. There is a cycle of activity around these steps, even when separate QA engineers do the testing. In fact, the cycle may need to go all the way back to the design step if some features cannot be implemented or if some interaction of features, as originally specified, have unforeseen and catastrophic consequences.

The creation of concurrent programs from serial applications also has a similar lifecycle. One example of this is the *Threading Methodology* developed by Intel application engineers as they worked on multithreaded and parallel applications. The threading methodology has four steps that mirror the steps within the software lifecycle:

Analysis
> Similar to "specification" in the software lifecycle, this step will identify the functionality (code) within the application that contains computations that can run independently.

Design and implementation
> This step should be self-explanatory.

Test for correctness
> Identify any errors within the code due to incorrect or incomplete implementation of the threading. If the code modifications required for threading have incorrectly altered the serial logic, there is a chance that new logic errors will be introduced.

Tune for performance

Once you have achieved a correct threaded solution, attempt to improve the execution time.

A maintenance step is not part of the threading methodology. I assume that once you have an application written, serial or concurrent, that application will be maintained as part of the normal course of business. The four steps of the threading methodology are considered in more detail in the following sections.

Step 1. Analysis: Identify Possible Concurrency

Since the code is already designed and written, the functionality of the application is known. You should also know which outputs are generated for given inputs. Now you need to find the parts of the code that can be threaded; that is, those parts of the application that contain independent computations.

If you know the application well, you should be able to home in on these parts of the code rather quickly. If you are less familiar with all aspects of the application, you can use a profile of the execution to identify *hotspots* that might yield independent computations. A hotspot is any portion of the code that has a significant amount of activity. With a profiler, time spent in the computation is going to be the most obvious measurable activity. Once you have found points in the program that take the most execution time, you can begin to investigate these for concurrent execution.

Just because an application spends a majority of the execution time in a segment of code, that does not mean that the code is a candidate for concurrency. You must perform some algorithmic analysis to determine if there is sufficient independence in the code segment to justify concurrency. Still, searching through those parts of the application that take the most time will give you the chance to achieve the most "bang for the buck" (i.e., be the most beneficial to the overall outcome). It will be much better for you (and your career) to spend a month writing, testing, and tuning a concurrent solution that reduces the execution time of some code segment that accounts for 75% of the serial execution time than it would be to take the same number of hours to slave over a segment that may only account for 2%.

Step 2. Design and Implementation: Threading the Algorithm

Once you have identified independent computations, you need to design and implement a concurrent version of the serial code. This step is what this book is all about. I won't spend any more time here on this topic, since the details and methods will unfold as you go through the pages ahead.

Step 3. Test for Correctness: Detecting and Fixing Threading Errors

Whenever you make code changes to an application, you open the door to the possibility of introducing bugs. Adding code to a serial application in order to generate and control multiple threads is no exception. As I alluded to before, the execution of threaded applications may or may not reveal any problems during testing. You might be able to run the application correctly hundreds of times, but when you try it out on another system, errors might show up on the new system or they might not. Even if you can get a run that demonstrates an error, running the code through a debugger (even one that is thread-aware) may not pinpoint the problem, since the stepwise execution may mask the error when you are actively looking for it. Using a print statement—that most-used of all debugging tools—to track values assigned to variables can modify the timing of thread interleavings, and that can also hide the error.

The more common threading errors, such as data races and deadlock, may be avoided completely if you know about the causes of these errors and plan well enough in the Design and Implementation step to avoid them. However, with the use of pointers and other such indirect references within programming languages, these problems can be virtually impossible to foresee. In fact, you may have cases in which the input data will determine if an error might manifest itself. Luckily, there are tools that can assist in tracking down threading errors. I've listed some of these in Chapter 11.

Even after you have removed all of the known threading bugs introduced by your modifications, the code may still not give the same answers as the serial version. If the answers are just slightly off, you may be experiencing *round-off error*, since the order of combining results generated by separate threads may not match the combination order of values that were generated in the serial code.

More egregious errors are likely due to the introduction of some logic error when threading. Perhaps you have a loop where some iteration is executed multiple times or where some loop iterations are not executed at all. You won't be able to find these kinds of errors with any tool that looks for threading errors, but you may be able to home in on the problem with the use of some sort of debugging tool. One of the minor themes of this book is the typical logic errors that can be introduced around threaded code and how to avoid these errors in the first place. With a good solid design, you should be able to keep the number of threading or logic errors to a minimum, so not much verbiage is spent on finding or correcting errors in code.

Step 4. Tune for Performance: Removing Performance Bottlenecks

After making sure that you have removed all the threading (and new logic) errors from your code, the final step is to make sure the code is running at its best level of performance. Before threading a serial application, be sure you start with a tuned code. Making serial tuning modifications to threaded code may change the whole dynamic of the threaded portions such that the additional threading material can actually degrade performance. If you have started with serial code that is already tuned, you can focus your search for performance problems on only those parts that have been threaded.

Tuning threaded code typically comes down to identifying situations like contention on synchronization objects, imbalance between the amount of computation assigned to each thread, and excessive overhead due to threading API calls or not enough work available to justify the use of threads. As with threading errors, there are software tools available to assist you in diagnosing and tracking down these and other performance issues.

You must also be aware that the actual threading of the code may be the culprit to a performance bottleneck. By breaking up the serial computations in order to assign them to threads, your carefully tuned serial execution may not be as tuned as it was before. You may introduce performance bugs like false sharing, inefficient memory access patterns, or bus overload. Identification of these types of errors will require whatever technology can find these types of serial performance errors. The avoidance of both threading and serial performance problems (introduced due to threading) is another minor theme of this book. With a good solid design, you should be able to achieve very good parallel performance, so not much verbiage is spent on finding or tuning performance problems in code.

The testing and tuning cycle

When you modify your code to correct an identified performance bug, you may inadvertently add a threading error. This can be especially true if you need to revise the use of synchronization objects. Once you've made changes for performance tuning, you should go back to the Test for Correctness step and ensure that your changes to fix the performance bugs have not introduced any new threading or logic errors. If you find any problems and modify code to repair them, be sure to again examine the code for any new performance problems that may have been inserted when fixing your correctness issues.

Sometimes it may be worse than that. If you are unable to achieve the expected performance speed from your application, you may need to return to the Design and Implementation step and start all over. Obviously, if you have multiple sites within your application that have been made concurrent, you may need to start at the design step for each code segment once you have finished with the previous code segment. If some threaded code sections can be shown to improve performance, these might be left as is, unless modifications to algorithms or global data structures will affect those previously threaded segments. It can all be a vicious circle and can make you dizzy if you think about it too hard.

What About Concurrency from Scratch?

Up to this point (and for the rest of the book, too), I've been assuming that you are starting with a correctly executing serial code to be transformed into a concurrent equivalent. Can you design a concurrent solution without an intermediate step of implementing a serial code? Yes, but I can't recommend it. The biggest reason is that debugging freshly written parallel code has two potential sources of problems: logic errors in the algorithm or implementation, and threading problems in the code. Is that bug you've found caused by a data race or because the code is not incrementing through a loop enough times?

In the future, once there has been more study of the problem, and as a result, more theory, models, and methods, plus a native concurrent language or two, you will likely be able to write concurrent code from scratch. For now, I recommend that you get a correctly working serial code and then examine how to make it run in parallel. It's probably a good idea to note potential concurrency when designing new software, but write and debug in serial first.

Background of Parallel Algorithms

If you're unfamiliar with parallel algorithms or parallel programming, this section is for you—it serves as a brief guide to some of what has gone before to reach the current state of concurrent programming on multicore processors.

Theoretical Models

All my academic degrees are in computer science. During my academic career, I've had to learn about and use many different models of computation. One of the basic processor architecture models used in computer science for studying algorithms is the *Random Access Machine* (RAM) model. This is a simplified model based on the von Neumann architecture model. It has all the right pieces: CPU, input device(s), output device(s), and randomly accessible memory. See Figure 1-1 for a pictorial view of the components of the RAM and how data flows between components.

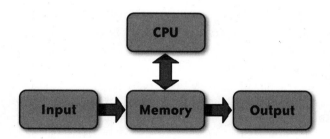

FIGURE 1-1. RAM configuration with data flow indicated by arrows

You can add hierarchies to the memory in order to describe levels of cache, you can attach a random access disk as a single device with both input and output, you can control the complexity and architecture of the CPU, or you can make dozens of other changes and modifications to create a model as close to reality as you desire. Whatever bits and pieces and doodads you think to add, the basics of the model remain the same and are useful in designing serial algorithms.

For designing parallel algorithms, a variation of the RAM model called the *Parallel Random Access Machine* (PRAM, pronounced "pee-ram") has been used. At its simplest, the PRAM is multiple CPUs attached to the unlimited memory, which is shared among all the CPUs. The threads that are executing on the CPUs are assumed to be executing in lockstep fashion (i.e., all execute one instruction at the same time before executing the next instruction all at the same time, and so on) and are assumed to have the same access time to memory locations regardless of the number of processors. Details of the connection mechanism between CPUs (processors) and memory are usually ignored, unless there is some specific configuration that may affect algorithm design. The PRAM shown in Figure 1-2 uses a (nonconflicting) shared bus connecting memory and the processors.

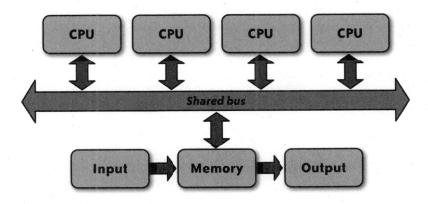

FIGURE 1-2. PRAM configuration with shared bus between CPUs and memory

As with the RAM, variations on the basic PRAM model can be made to simulate real-world processor features if those features will affect algorithm design. The one feature that will always affect algorithm design on a PRAM is the shared memory. The model makes no assumptions about software or hardware support of synchronization objects available to a programmer. Thus, the PRAM model stipulates how threads executing on individual processors will be able to access memory for both reading and writing. There are two types of reading restrictions and the same two types of writing restrictions: either *concurrent* or *exclusive*. When specifying a PRAM algorithm, you must first define the type of memory access PRAM your algorithm has been designed for. The four types of PRAM are listed in Table 1-1.

TABLE 1-1. PRAM variations based on memory access patterns

Memory access parameters	Description
Concurrent Read, Concurrent Write (CRCW)	Multiple threads may read from the same memory location at the same time and multiple threads may write to the same memory location at the same time.

Memory access parameters	Description
Concurrent Read, Exclusive Write (CREW)	Multiple threads may read from the same memory location at the same time and one thread may write to a given memory location at any time.
Exclusive Read, Concurrent Write (ERCW)	One thread may read from a given memory location at any time and multiple threads may write to the same memory location at the same time.
Exclusive Read, Exclusive Write (EREW)	One thread may read from a given memory location at any time and one thread may write to a given memory location at any time.

On top of these restrictions, it is up to the PRAM algorithm to enforce the exclusive read and exclusive write behavior of the chosen model. In the case of a concurrent write model, the model further specifies what happens when two threads attempt to store values into the same memory location at the same time. Popular variations of this type of PRAM are to have the algorithm ensure that the value being written will be the same value, to simply select a random value from the two or more processors attempting to write, or to store the sum (or some other combining operation) of the multiple values. Since all processors are executing in lockstep fashion, writes to memory are all executed simultaneously, which makes it easy to enforce the designated policy.

Not only must you specify the memory access behavior of the PRAM and design your algorithm to conform to that model, you must also denote the number of processors that your algorithm will use. Since this is a theoretical model, an unlimited number of processors are available. The number is typically based on the size of the input. For example, if you are designing an algorithm to work on N input items, you can specify that the PRAM must have N^2 processors and threads, all with access to the shared memory.

With an inexhaustible supply of processors and infinite memory, the PRAM is obviously a theoretical model for parallel algorithm design. Implementing PRAM algorithms on finite resourced platforms may simply be a matter of simulating the computations of N "logical" processors on the cores available to us. When we get to the algorithm design and implementation chapters, some of the designs will take a PRAM algorithm as the basic starting point, and I'll show you how you might convert it to execute correctly on a multicore processor.

Distributed-Memory Programming

Due to shared bus contention issues, shared-memory parallel computers hit an upper limit of approximately 32 processors in the late '80s and early '90s. Distributed-memory configurations came on strong in order to scale the number of processors higher. Parallel algorithms require some sharing of data at some point. However, since each node in a distributed-memory machine is separated from all the other nodes, with no direct sharing mechanism, developers used libraries of functions to pass messages between nodes.

As an example of programming on a distributed-memory machine, consider the case where Process 1 (P1) requires a vector of values from Process 0 (P0). The program running as P0 must include logic to package the vector into a buffer and call the function that will send the contents of that buffer from the memory of the node on which P0 is running across the network connection between the nodes and deposit the buffer contents into the memory of the node running P1. On the P1 side, the program must call the function that receives the data deposited into the node's memory and copy it into a designated buffer in the memory accessible to P1.

At first, each manufacturer of a distributed-memory machine had its own library and set of functions that could do simple point-to-point communication as well as collective communication patterns like broadcasting. Over time, some portable libraries were developed, such as PVM (Parallel Virtual Machine) and MPI (Message-Passing Interface). PVM was able to harness networks of workstations into a virtual parallel machine that cost much less than a specialized parallel platform. MPI was developed as a standard library of defined message-passing functionality supported on both parallel machines and networks of workstations. The Beowulf Project showed how to create clusters of PCs using Linux and MPI into an even more affordable distributed-memory parallel platform.

Parallel Algorithms Literature

Many books have been written about parallel algorithms. A vast majority of these have focused on message-passing as the method of parallelization. Some of the earlier texts detail algorithms where the network configuration (e.g., mesh or hypercube) is an integral part of the algorithm design; later texts tend not to focus so much on developing algorithms for specific network configurations, but rather, think of the execution platform as a cluster of processor nodes. In the algorithms section of this book (Chapters 6 through 10), some of the designs will take a distributed-memory algorithm as the basic starting point, and I'll show you how you might convert it to execute correctly in a multithreaded implementation on a multicore processor.

Shared-Memory Programming Versus Distributed-Memory Programming

Some of you may be coming from a distributed-memory programming background and want to get into threaded programming for multicore processors. For you, I've put together a list that compares and contrasts shared-memory programming with distributed-memory programming. If you don't know anything about distributed-memory programming, this will give you some insight into the differences between the two programming methods. Even if you've only ever done serial programming to this point, the following details are still going to give you an introduction to some of the features of concurrent programming on shared-memory that you never encounter using a single execution thread.

Common Features

The following features are common to shared-memory parallelism and distributed-memory parallelism.

Redundant work

No matter how concurrent an algorithm is, there are still parts that will have to be carried out serially. When the results of those serial computations must be shared, you can perform the computation in one process and broadcast the results out to the other processes that require the data. Sending this information will add overhead to the execution time. On the other hand, if the data used in the computation is already available to other processes, you can have each process perform the computation and generate results locally without the need to send any messages. In shared-memory parallelism, the data for computation is likely already available by default. Even though doing redundant work in threads keeps processing resources busy and eliminates extraneous synchronization, there is a cost in memory space needed to hold multiple copies of the same value.

Dividing work

Work must be assigned to threads and processes alike. This may be done by assigning a chunk of the data and having each thread/process execute the same computations on the assigned block, or it may be some method of assigning a computation that involves executing a different portion of the code within the application.

Sharing data

There will be times when applications must share data. It may be the value of a counter or a vector of floating-point values or a list of graph vertices. Whatever it happens to be, threads and processes alike will need to have access to it during the course of the computation. Obviously, the methods of sharing data will vary; shared-memory programs simply access a designated location in memory, while distributed-memory programs must actively send and receive the data to be shared.

Static/dynamic allocation of work

Depending on the nature of the serial algorithm, the resulting concurrent version, and the number of threads/processes, you may assign all the work at one time (typically at the outset of the computation) or over time as the code executes. The former method is known as a *static allocation* since the original assignments do not change once they have been made. The latter is known as *dynamic allocation* since work is doled out when it is needed. Under dynamic allocation, you may find that the same threads do not execute the same pieces of work from one run to another, while static allocation will always assign the same work to the same threads (if the number of threads is the same) each and every time.

Typically, if the work can be broken up into a number of parts that is equal to the number of threads/processes, and the execution time is roughly the same for each of those parts, a static allocation is best. Static allocation of work is always the simplest code to implement and to maintain. Dynamic allocation is useful for cases when there are many more pieces of work than threads and the amount of execution time for each piece is different or even unknown at the outset of computation. There will be some overhead associated with a dynamic allocation scheme, but the benefits will be a more load-balanced execution.

Features Unique to Shared Memory

These next few items are where distributed-memory and shared-memory programming differ. If you're familiar with distributed-memory parallelism, you should be able to see the differences. For those readers not familiar with distributed-memory parallelism, these points and ideas are still going to be important to understand.

Local declarations and thread-local storage

Since everything is shared in shared memory, there are times it will be useful to have a private or local variable that is accessed by only one thread. Once threads have been spawned, any declarations within the path of code execution (e.g., declarations within function calls) will be automatically allocated as local to the thread executing the declarative code. Processes executing on a node within a distributed-memory machine will have all local memory within the node.

A thread-local storage (TLS) API is available in Windows threads and POSIX threads. Though the syntax is different in the different threaded libraries, the API allocates some memory per executing thread and allows the thread to store and retrieve a value that is accessible to only that thread. The difference between TLS and local declarations is that the TLS values will persist from one function call to another. This is much like *static* variables, except that in TLS, each thread gets an individually addressable copy.

Memory effects

Since threads are sharing the memory available to the cores on which they are executing, there can be performance issues due to that sharing. I've already mentioned storage conflicts and data races. Processor architecture will determine if threads share or have access to separate caches. Sharing caches between two cores can effectively cut in half the size of the cache available to a thread, while separate caches can make sharing of common data less efficient. On the good side, sharing caches with commonly accessed, read-only data can be very effective, since only a single copy is needed.

False sharing is a situation where threads are not accessing the same variables, but they are sharing a cache line that contains different variables. Due to cache coherency protocols, when one thread updates a variable in the cache line and another thread wants to access something else in the same line, that line is first written back to memory. When two or more threads are repeatedly updating the same cache line, especially from separate caches, that cache line can bounce back and forth through memory for each update.

Communication in memory

Distributed-memory programs share data by sending and receiving messages between processes. In order to share data within shared memory, one thread simply writes a value into a memory location and the other thread reads the value out of that memory location. Of course, to ensure that the data is transferred correctly, the writing thread must deposit the value to be shared into memory before the reading thread examines the location. Thus, the threads must synchronize the order of writing and reading between the threads. The send-receive exchange is an implicit synchronization between distributed processes.

Mutual exclusion

In order to communicate in memory, threads must sometimes protect access to shared memory locations. The means for doing this is to allow only one thread at a time to have access to shared variables. This is known as *mutual exclusion*. Several different synchronization mechanisms are available (usually dependent on the threading method you are using) to provide mutual exclusion.

Both reading and writing of data must be protected. Multiple threads reading the same data won't cause any problems. When you have multiple threads writing to the same location, the order of the updates to the memory location will determine the value that is ultimately stored there and the value that will be read out of the location by another thread (recall the airline reservation system that put two passengers in the same seat). When you have one thread reading and one thread writing to the same memory location, the value that is being read can be one of two values (the old value or the new value). It is likely that only one of those will be the expected value, since the original serial code expects only one value to be possible. If the correct execution of your threaded algorithm depends upon getting a specific value from a variable that is being updated by multiple threads, you must have logic that guarantees the right value is written at the correct time; this will involve mutual exclusion and other synchronization.

Producer/consumer

One algorithmic method you can use to distribute data or tasks to the processes in distributed-memory programs is *boss/worker*. Worker processes send a message to the boss process requesting a new task; upon receipt of the request, the boss sends back a message/task/data to the worker process. You can write a boss/worker task distribution mechanism in threads, but it requires a lot of synchronization.

To take advantage of the shared memory protocols, you can use a variation of boss/worker that uses a shared queue to distribute tasks. This method is known as *producer/consumer*. The producer thread creates encapsulated tasks and stores them into the shared queue. The consumer threads pull out tasks from the queue when they need more work. You must protect access to the shared queue with some form of mutual exclusion in order to ensure that tasks being inserted into the queue are placed correctly and that tasks being removed from the queue are assigned to a single thread only.

Readers/writer locks

Since it is not a problem to have multiple threads reading the same shared variables, using mutual exclusion to prevent multiple reader threads can create a performance bottleneck. However, if there is any chance that another thread could update the shared variable, mutual exclusion must be used. For situations where shared variables are to be updated much less frequently than they are to be read, a *readers/writer* lock would be the appropriate synchronization object.

Readers/writer locks allow multiple reader threads to enter the protected area of code accessing the shared variable. Whenever a thread wishes to update (write) the value to the shared variable, the lock will ensure that any prior reader threads have finished before allowing the single writer to make the updates. When any writer thread has been allowed access to the shared variable by the readers/writer lock, new readers or other threads wanting write access are prevented from proceeding until the current writing thread has finished.

This Book's Approach to Concurrent Programming

While writing this book, I was reading *Feynman Lectures on Computation* (Perseus Publishing, 1996). In Chapter 3, Feynman lectures on the theory of computation. He starts by describing finite state machines (automata) and then makes the leap to Turing machines. At first I was a bit aghast that there was nothing at all about push-down automata or context-free languages, nothing about nondeterministic finite-state machines, and nothing about how this all tied into grammars or recognizing strings from languages. A nice progression covering this whole range of topics was how I was taught all this stuff in my years studying computer science.

I quickly realized that Feynman had only one lecture to get through the topic of Turing machines and the ideas of computability, so he obviously couldn't cover all the details that I learned over the course of eight weeks or so. A bit later, I realized that the target audience for his lecture series wasn't computer science students, but students in physics and mathematics. So he only needed to cover those topics that gave his students the right background and enough of a taste to get some insight into the vast field of computability theory.

This is what I'm hoping to do with this book. I don't want to give you all the history or theory about concurrent and parallel programming. I want to give you a taste of it and some practical examples so that you (the brilliant person and programmer that I know you to be) can take them and start modifying your own codes and applications to run in parallel on multicore processors. The algorithms in the later chapters are algorithms you would find in an introductory algorithms course. While you may never use any of the concurrent algorithms in this book, the codes are really meant to serve as illustrations of concurrent design methods that you can apply in your own applications. So, using the words of chef Gordon Ramsay, I want to present a "simple and rustic" introduction to concurrent programming that will give you some practice and insight into the field.

CHAPTER TWO

Concurrent or Not Concurrent?

To get things started, I want to first talk about two design methods for concurrent algorithms, but I want to do it abstractly. Now, before you roll your eyes too far back and hurt yourself, let me say that there will be plenty of code examples in later chapters to give concreteness to the ideas that are presented here. This is a book on the design of concurrent algorithms, and in this chapter I've collected a lot of the wisdom on initial approaches that apply to a large percentage of code you're likely to encounter (it can get pretty dry without code to look at, so be sure you're well hydrated before you start).

In addition, I want to let you know that not every bit of computation can be made concurrent, no matter how hard you try. To save you the time of trying to take on too many impossible things in the course of your day, I have examples of the kinds of algorithms and computations that are not very amenable to concurrency in the section "What's Not Parallel" on page 42. When any of those examples can be modified to allow for concurrent execution, I've included hints and tips about how to do that.

Design Models for Concurrent Algorithms

If you've got a sequential code that you want to transform into a concurrent version, you need to identify the independent computations that can be executed concurrently. The way you approach your serial code will influence how you reorganize the computations into a concurrent equivalent. One way is *task decomposition*, in which the computations are a set of independent tasks that threads can execute in any order. Another way is *data decomposition*, in which the application processes a large collection of data and can compute every element of the data independently.

The next two sections will describe these approaches in more detail and give an example of a problem that falls into each category. These two models are not the only possibilities, but I've found them to be the two most common. For other patterns of computation and how to transform them into concurrent algorithms, read *Patterns for Parallel Programming* by Timothy G. Mattson et al. (Addison-Wesley, 2004). Many of the ideas presented in the next two sections are rooted in material from that book.

Task Decomposition

When you get right down to it, any concurrent algorithm is going to turn out to be nothing more than a collection of concurrent tasks. Some may be obvious independent function calls within the code. Others may turn out to be loop iterations that can be executed in any order or simultaneously. Still others might turn out to be groups of sequential source lines that can be divided and grouped into independent computations. For all of these, you must be able to identify the tasks and decompose the serial code into concurrently executable work. If you're familiar enough with the source code and the computations that it performs, you may be able to identify those independent computations via code inspection.

As I've implied, the goal of task decomposition, or any concurrent transformation process, is to identify computations that are completely independent. Unfortunately, it is the rare case where the serial computation is made up of sequences of code that do not interact with each other in some way. These interactions are known as *dependencies*, and before you can make your code run in parallel, you must satisfy or remove those dependencies. The section "What's Not Parallel" on page 42 describes some of these dependencies and how you might overcome them.

You will find that, in most cases, you can identify the independent tasks at the outset of the concurrent computation. After the application has defined the tasks, spawned the threads, and assigned the tasks to threads (more details on these steps in a moment), almost every concurrent application will wait until all the concurrent tasks have completed. Why? Well, think back to the original serial code. The serial algorithm did not go on to the succeeding phase until the preceding portion was completed. That's why we call it serial execution. We usually need to keep that sequence of execution in our concurrent solutions in order to maintain the *sequential consistency* property (getting the same answer as the serial code on the same input data set) of the concurrent algorithm.

The most basic framework for doing concurrent work is to have the main or the process thread define and prepare the tasks, launch the threads to execute their tasks, and then wait until all the spawned threads have completed. There are many variations on this theme. Are threads created and terminated for each portion of parallel execution within the application? Could threads be put to "sleep" when the assigned tasks are finished and then "woken up" when new tasks are available? Rather than blocking after the concurrent computations have launched, why not have the main thread take part in executing the set of tasks? Implementing any of these is simply a matter of programming logic, but they still have the basic form of preparing tasks, getting threads to do tasks, and then making sure all tasks have been completed before going on to the next computation.

Is there a case in which you don't need to wait for the entire set of tasks to complete before going to the next phase of computation? You bet. Consider a search algorithm. If your tasks are to search through a given discrete portion of the overall data space, does it make any sense to continue searching when you have located the item you were looking for? The serial code was likely written to stop searching, so why should the concurrent tasks continue to waste execution resources in an unproductive manner? To curtail the execution of threads before the natural termination point of tasks requires additional programming logic and overhead. Threads will need to periodically check the status of the overarching task to determine whether to continue or wind things up. If the original search algorithm was to find all instances of an item, each thread would examine all assigned data items and not need to worry about early termination.

You may also encounter situations in which new tasks will be generated dynamically as the computation proceeds. For example, if you are traversing a tree structure with some computation at each node, you might set up the tasks to be the traversal of each branch rooted at the current node. For a binary tree, up to two tasks would be created at each internal node. The mechanics of encapsulating these new tasks and assigning them to threads is all a matter of additional programming.

There are three key elements you need to consider for any task decomposition design:

- What are the tasks and how are they defined?
- What are the dependencies between tasks and how can they be satisfied?
- How are the tasks assigned to threads?

Each of these elements is covered in more detail in the following sections.

What are the tasks and how are they defined?

The ease of identifying independent computations within an application is in direct proportion to your understanding of the code and computations being performed by that code. There isn't any procedure, formula, or magic incantation that I know of where the code is input and out pops a big neon sign pointing to the independent computations. You need to be able to mentally simulate the execution of two parallel streams on suspected parts of the application to determine whether those suspected parts are independent of each other (or might have manageable dependencies).

Simulating the parallel or concurrent execution of multiple threads on given source code is a skill that has been extremely beneficial to me in both designing concurrent algorithms and in proving them to be error-free (as we shall see in Chapter 3). It takes some practice, but like everything else that takes practice, the more you do it, the better you will get at doing it. While you're reading my book, I'll show you how I approach the art of concurrent design, and then you'll be better equipped to start doing this on your own.

> **NOTE**
>
> There is one tiny exception for not having a "magic bullet" that can identify potentially independent computations with loop iterations. If you suspect a loop has independent iterations (those that can be run in any order), try executing the code with the loop iterations running in reverse of their original order. If the application still gets the same results, there is a strong chance that the iterations are independent and can be decomposed into tasks. Beware that there might still be a "hidden" dependency waiting to come out and bite you when the iterations are run concurrently—for example, the intermediate sequence of values stored in a variable that is harmless when the loop iterations were run in serial, even when run backward.

To get the biggest return on investment, you should initially focus on computationally intense portions of the application. That is, look at those sections of code that do the most computation or account for the largest percentage of the execution time. You want the ratio of the performance boost to the effort expended in transforming, debugging, and tuning of your concurrent code to be as high as possible. (I freely admit that I'm a lazy programmer—anytime I can get the best outcome from the least amount of work, that is the path I will choose.)

Once you have identified a portion of the serial code that can be executed concurrently, keep in mind the following two criteria for the actual decomposition into tasks:

- There should be at least as many tasks as there will be threads (or cores).
- The amount of computation within each task (granularity) must be large enough to offset the overhead that will be needed to manage the tasks and the threads.

The first criterion is used to assure that you won't have idle threads (or idle cores) during the execution of the application. If you can create the number of tasks based on the number of threads that are available, your application will be better equipped to handle execution platform changes from one run to the next. It is almost always better to have (many) more tasks than threads. This will allow the scheduling of tasks to threads greater flexibility to achieve a good load balance. This is especially true when the execution times of each task are not all the same or the time for tasks is unpredictable.

The second criterion seeks to give you the opportunity to actually get a performance boost in the parallel execution of your application. The amount of computation within a task is called the *granularity*. The more computation there is within a task, the higher the granularity; the less computation there is, the lower the granularity. The terms *coarse-grained* and *fine-grained* are used to describe instances of high granularity and low granularity, respectively. The granularity of a task must be large enough to render the task and thread management code a minuscule fraction of the overall parallel execution. If tasks are too small, execution of the code to encapsulate the task, assign it to a thread, handle the results from the task, and any other thread coordination or management required in the concurrent algorithm can eliminate (best case) or even dwarf (worst case) the performance gained by running your algorithm on multiple cores.

NOTE

Granularity, defined another way, is the amount of computation done before synchronization is needed. The longer the time between synchronizations, the coarser the granularity will be. Fine-grained concurrency runs the danger of not having enough work assigned to threads to overcome the overhead costs (synchronizations) of using threads. Adding more threads, when the amount of computation doesn't change, only exacerbates the problem. Coarse-grained concurrency has lower relative overhead costs and tends to be more readily scalable to an increase in the number of threads.

Consider the case where the time for overhead computations per task is the same for two different divisions of tasks. If one task divides the total work into 16 tasks, and the other uses only 4 tasks, which scheme would run faster on four cores with four threads? Figure 2-1 illustrates the two task decompositions and their execution with overhead added.

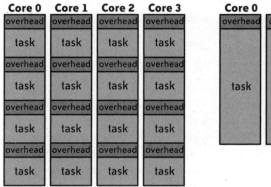
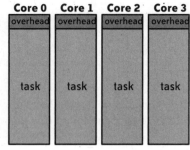

(a) Fine-grained decomposition   **(b) Coarse-grained decomposition**

FIGURE 2-1. Task granularity example

You can imagine that the height of each box in Figure 2-1 represents the amount of time required to execute the associated computation. With many small tasks—each requiring a separate overhead computation—Figure 2-1 (a), the fine-grained solution, will take longer to run than the same work divided into fewer larger tasks, as shown in Figure 2-1 (b), the coarse-grained decomposition. Larger tasks also provide better opportunities for other performance benefits (e.g., reuse of cache, more efficient memory access patterns) that are already part of the serial algorithm.

You will need to strike a balance between these two criteria. For a fixed amount of work, the larger you define your tasks to be, the fewer tasks there will be to assign to threads. You may find that in order to satisfy the second criterion, which is the more important of the two, you will need to define a number of tasks that is fewer than the number of threads. Because reducing execution time is the main reason for writing and running concurrent code, having an application that might not utilize all the cores available is more desirable than having an application that performs worse (takes longer to execute) when using all the cores in the platform.

Finally, don't be afraid to go back and rework your task decomposition. If your initial decomposition does not meet the criteria, you should consider alternate decompositions. Also, if you find that you are not achieving the performance levels you expect, you may need to go back and redefine the tasks, the number of threads to be used, or how those tasks are assigned to threads.

What are the dependencies between tasks and how can they be satisfied?

Two types of dependencies can occur between tasks. The first is order dependency, where some task relies on the completed results of the computations from another task. This reliance can be a direct need to use the computed values as input to the succeeding task, or it may simply be the case that the task that follows will be updating the same memory locations as the previous task and you must ensure that all of the previous updates have been completed before proceeding. Both of these cases describe a potential data race, which we need to avoid.

For example, if you are building a house, putting up the roof involves attaching the rafters to the walls, laying down the decking, and applying the shingles. The dependence between these three tasks is one of execution order. You can't put down shingles until the decking is there, and you can't nail down the decking unless you have the rafters in place. So, instead of hiring three teams to do these three tasks in parallel, you can hire one roofing crew to do all three in the order required (there is parallelism within each of the roofing steps, plus the act of putting on the roof is independent of installing the electrical wiring, the plumbing, and putting up drywall).

To satisfy an execution order constraint, you can schedule tasks that have an order dependency onto the same thread and ensure that the thread executes the tasks in the proper sequence. The serial code was written with the order dependency already taken care of. So, the serial algorithm should guide the correct decomposition of the computations into tasks and assignment of those tasks to threads. Still, even after grouping tasks to execute on threads, there may be order constraints between threads. If regrouping tasks to threads is not an option or will severely hurt performance, you will be forced to insert some form of synchronization to ensure correct execution order.

The second type of dependency is data dependency. Identifying potential data dependencies can be straightforward: look for those variables that are featured on the left side of the assignment operator. Data races require that the variable in question have at least one thread that is writing to that variable. Check for any assignment of values to the same variable that might be done concurrently as well as any updates to a variable that could be read concurrently. Of course, using pointers to reference memory locations can make the identification process trickier. There are tools (covered in Chapter 11) that can assist in finding nonobvious data dependencies in your code.

Solving data dependencies can be more complicated than solving execution order dependencies. In the latter, the sequence of execution within the serial code gives us the solution; in the former, the serial code being written with the assumption of a single-threaded execution leads to the problem.

If you're fortunate enough to have code with no dependencies, sometimes called *enchantingly parallel*, you can skip down to the next section about scheduling. If you're like the rest of us and aren't so fortunate, examine your dependencies to see if they might be removable (recurrences and induction variables) or separable (reduction computations). There are remedies, in many cases, for these dependencies. Those options, as well as a description of these two dependency classes, are discussed in "What's Not Parallel" on page 42.

Now let's go over the two easiest solutions for simple data conflicts between tasks. These are using local variables and adding mutual exclusion code. Consider the pseudocode given in Example 2-1 (if you live in Chicago or New York, substitute some other place like Los Angeles when computing population differences).

EXAMPLE 2-1. *Pseudocode with shared variable*

```
popDiff = abs(Population[MyTown] - Population[NewYork]);
DoSomething(popDiff, MyTown, NewYork);
popDiff = abs(Population[MyTown] - Population[Chicago]);
DoSomething(popDiff, MyTown, Chicago);
```

If we know that concurrent calls to the DoSomething() function are thread-safe (i.e., there are no side effects or dependencies when there is more than one concurrent call to the function), we can assign the first two lines of the example to one thread and the last two lines to a second thread. This will create a data race on the popDiff variable. Since this variable is used only as a temporary or "work" variable, allocating a local copy to each thread will eliminate the problem.

Depending on the threading model that you are using to implement your concurrent algorithm, there can be several ways to create variables that are accessible only to a given thread. In all cases, if you declare a variable within a function that is executed by threads, those variables will be local to the calling thread when they are allocated. Explicitly allocating space from a thread's stack (say with the alloca() function) is another way. OpenMP has the private clause to generate local copies of variables for each thread within the parallel region to which the clause is attached. Both Windows and POSIX threads include a thread-local storage (TLS) API that will allocate memory to hold copies of variables, one per thread, and allow threads to have access only to the copy that is earmarked for that thread.

NOTE

The TLS API is pretty "heavy." I wouldn't recommend using it for things like local work variables within a single routine. Variables that are allocated and accessed via the TLS are persistent across function scopes. If you need local copies of a variable and that variable and its contents need to be available to different functions or disparate calls to the same function executed by the thread, TLS is the mechanism that can give you the private copy and the persistence of value required.

When all else fails, when you don't have the option to make a local copy of a shared variable, when none of the transformations given in "What's Not Parallel" on page 42 can eliminate the data dependency, the only option left is to explicitly provide mutually exclusive access to the shared variable. In most cases a simple lock, or *mutex*, will suffice. In some instances, you can use a less onerous atomic operation. Different threading models will have different options of synchronization objects, and different algorithms will have different protection requirements.

It should go without saying that you will want to use the option that has the lowest impact on performance, since such added synchronization is overhead that was not in the original serial code. This might mean trying several possibilities and even modifying the initial algorithm or data structures to create the chance to use a better synchronization object. It is your job as the programmer to find the best option for each situation you encounter.

How are the tasks assigned to threads?

Tasks must be assigned to threads for execution. Perhaps the more correct way to say this is that threads must know which tasks to execute. In either case, you always want to assure that the amount of computation done by threads is roughly equivalent. That is, the load (of computation) is balanced per thread. We can allocate tasks to threads in two different ways: static scheduling or dynamic scheduling.

> **NOTE**
>
> Under worksharing constructs in OpenMP and the parallel algorithms of Intel Threading Building Blocks (TBB), the actual assignment of tasks to threads is done "under the covers." The programmer can influence that assignment to some degree, though. Even if you use only one of these two threading libraries for your concurrent coding, you should still read through the advice in this section to help you better influence the task assignments in your applications.

In static scheduling, the division of labor is known at the outset of the computation and doesn't change during the computation. If at all possible, when developing your own concurrent code, try to use a static schedule. This is the easiest method to program and will incur the least amount of overhead.

The mechanics and logic of code needed to implement a static schedule will involve each thread having a unique identification number in the range of [0, N–1] for N threads. This number can be easily assigned at the time a thread is created in the order that threads are created (code that can generate unique identification numbers to threads will be part of several implementation examples in later chapters). If tasks are collections of separate, independent function calls or groups of sequential source lines, you can group those calls or code lines into tasks that are assigned to threads through a thread's ID number (e.g., through a `switch` statement). If tasks are loop iterations, you can divide the total number of iterations by the number of threads and assign block(s) of iterations to threads, again through the thread's ID number. You will have to add additional logic to compute the start and end values of the loop bounds in order for each thread to determine the block that should be executed.

When assigning loop iterations into blocks, you need to be sure that each thread doesn't overlap execution of an iteration assigned to another thread and that all the loop iterations are covered by some thread. You won't get the correct results if threads execute an iteration multiple times or leave out the computation of some iterations. An alternative to assigning loop iterations into blocks is to use the thread's ID number as the starting value of the loop iterator and increment that iterator by the number of threads, rather than by 1. For example, if you have two threads, one thread will execute the odd-numbered iterations and the other thread will execute the even iterations. Obviously, you will need to make adjustments to where the loop starts and how to compute the next iteration per thread if the loop iterator doesn't start at 0 and is already incremented by something other than 1. However, the implementation of setting up *N* threads to each do every *Nth* iteration will involve fewer code changes than dividing the iteration set into separate blocks.

Static scheduling is best used in those cases where the amount of computation within each task is the same or can be predicted at the outset. If you have a case where the amount of computation between tasks is variable and/or unpredictable, then you would be better served by using a dynamic scheduling scheme.

Under a dynamic schedule, you assign tasks to threads as the computation proceeds. The driving force behind the use of a dynamic schedule is to try to balance the load as evenly as possible between threads. Assigning tasks to threads is going to incur overhead from executing the added programming logic to carry out the assignment and from having threads seek out a new task.

There are many different ways to implement a dynamic method for scheduling tasks to threads, but they all require a set of many more tasks than threads. Probably the easiest scheduling scheme involves indexing the tasks. A shared counter is used to keep track of and assign the next task for execution. When seeking a new task, a thread gains mutually exclusive access to the counter, copies the value into a local variable, and increments the counter value for the next thread.

Another simple dynamic scheduling method involves setting up a shared container (typically a queue) that can hold tasks and allow threads to pull out a new task once the previous task is complete. Tasks (or adequate descriptions of tasks) must be encapsulated into some structure that can be pushed into the queue. Access to the queue must be mutually exclusive between threads to ensure that threads get unique tasks and no tasks are lost through some corruption of the shared container.

If tasks require some preprocessing before their assignment to threads, or if tasks are not all known at the outset of computation, you may need more complex scheduling methods. You can set one of your threads aside to do the preprocessing of each task or receive new tasks as they arise. If the computation threads *rendezvous* with this extra thread in order to receive the next task for execution, you have a boss/worker algorithm. By placing a shared container to distribute tasks between the threads preparing tasks and the threads executing the task, you get the producer/consumer method. I mentioned these methods briefly in Chapter 1.

Example: numerical integration

Now that you've seen the criteria used to define and implement a task decomposition, let's put those ideas into practice on a very simple application to compute an approximate value of the constant *pi*. We won't worry about the details of how to implement the concurrency with threads, but we can identify the design decisions we need to make, as well as other considerations that we need to take into account to carry through with the implementation.

Numerical integration is a method of computing an approximation of the area under the curve of a function, especially when the exact integral cannot be solved. For example, the value of the constant pi can be defined by the following integral. However, rather than solve this integral exactly, we can approximate the solution by use of numerical integration:

$$\pi = \int_0^1 \frac{4}{1 + x^2} \, dx$$

The code in Example 2-2 is an implementation of the numerical integration midpoint rectangle rule to solve the integral just shown. To compute an approximation of the area under the curve, we must compute the area of some number of rectangles (num_rects) by finding the midpoint (mid) of each rectangle and computing the height of that rectangle (height), which is simply the function value at that midpoint. We add together the heights of all the rectangles (sum) and, once computed, we multiply the sum of the heights by the width of the rectangles (width) to determine the desired approximation of the total area (area) and the value of pi.

I won't create a threaded version of this code, but you're welcome to give it a try on your own based on the task decomposition discussion later.

EXAMPLE 2-2. Numerical integration code to approximate the value of pi

```
static long num_rects=100000;
void main()
{
  int i;
  double mid, height, width, sum = 0.0;
  double area;

  width = 1.0/(double) num_rects;
  for (i = 0; i < num_rects; i++){
    mid = (i + 0.5) * width;
    height = 4.0/(1.0 + mid*mid);
    sum += height;
  }
```

```
  area = width * sum;
  printf("Computed pi = %f\n",area);
}
```

What are the independent tasks in this simple application? The computation of the height for a rectangle is independent of the computation of any other rectangle. In addition, notice that the loop that performs these calculations holds the bulk of the computation for the entire application. The loop is an execution hotspot that you should examine for independent computations.

Are there any dependencies between these tasks and, if so, how can we satisfy them? The two work variables, mid and height, are assigned values in each iteration. If each thread had a local copy, that copy could be used during execution of iterations that are assigned to a thread. Also, the iteration variable, i, is updated for each iteration. Each thread will need a local copy in order to avoid interfering with the execution of iterations within other threads. The sum variable is updated in each iteration, but since this value is used outside of the loop, we can't have each thread work with a local copy that would be discarded after the thread was done. This is a *reduction*, and you'll find tips on solving such situations later in the section "What's Not Parallel" on page 42. The quick and dirty solution would be to put a synchronization object around the line of code updating sum so that only one thread at a time will write to the variable.

How should you assign tasks to threads? With loop iterations as tasks, we can assign blocks of iterations to threads based on an assigned ID number. Alternatively, we can have threads execute alternating iterations based on the number of threads. Because there are no indexed array elements in the loop, and thus no cache issues, I would recommend the latter approach.

The final piece to consider is adding the results of all the individual loop computations together and storing them in a location that you can print from. This will depend directly on how the reduction operation on sum is handled.

Data Decomposition

Before I get started on data decomposition, I want to make sure that you haven't skipped down to this section without reading the previous section on task decomposition. There is a lot of good stuff in that section and I want to make sure you've covered it and absorbed it. Many of the things that are covered there will apply directly to data decomposition, and I won't likely repeat them here. So, even if you think you will only ever be working on data decomposition solutions for the rest of your programming career, be sure to read the section on task decomposition. You'll get a better understanding of the problems that are shared between the two decomposition methods.

When you start to examine a serial application for transformation into an equivalent concurrent solution, the first feature of the computations you might identify is that the execution is dominated by a sequence of update operations on all elements of one or more large data structures. If these update computations are independent of each other, you have a situation where you can express the concurrency of your application by dividing up the data structure(s) and assigning those portions to threads, along with the corresponding update computations (tasks). This method of defining tasks based on assigning blocks of large data structures to threads is known as *data decomposition*. In Mattson's *Patterns for Parallel Programming*, this is called "geometric decomposition."

How you divide data structures into contiguous subregions, or "chunks," of data will depend on the type of data structure. The most common structure that falls into the data decomposition category is an array. You can divide arrays along one or more of their dimensions. Other structures that use an array as a component (e.g., graph implemented as an adjacency matrix) can be divided into logical chunks as well. It will all depend on what the computations are and how independent the processing is for each chunk.

I would add list structures to the set of decomposable data structures, but only if there is an easy way to identify and access sublists of discrete elements. In a linked list implementation this would require index pointers that reference alternate entry points into the list. For example, given a linked list of people arranged alphabetically, the first person whose name starts with a new letter of the alphabet would be referenced with an external pointer for that letter. If the concurrent version of the code needs to set up these external references as part of its overhead, make sure the amount of computation is sufficient to eclipse the additional overhead time. Otherwise, consider a different approach in either the data structure or how you implement the concurrency.

However you decide to do it, the decomposition into chunks implies the division of computation into tasks that operate on elements of each chunk, and those tasks are assigned to threads. The tasks will then be executed concurrently and each task will update the chunk associated with it. Data within an assigned chunk is readily available and safe to use, since no other tasks will be updating those elements. On the other hand, the update computations may require data from neighboring chunks. If so, we will have to share data between tasks. Accessing or retrieving essential data from neighboring chunks will require coordination between threads.

As with task decomposition, load balance is an important factor to take into consideration, especially when using chunks of variable sizes. If the data structure has a nice, regular organization and all the computations on that structure always take the same amount of execution time, you can simply decompose the structure into chunks with the same number of elements in some logical and efficient way. If your data isn't organized in a regular pattern or the amount of computation is different or unpredictable for each element in the structure, decomposing the structure into tasks that take roughly the same amount of execution time is a much less straightforward affair. Perhaps you should consider a dynamic scheduling of chunks to threads in this case.

The next sections outline the key elements that every successful data decomposition solution must account for. It will also address some thoughts on how to deal with sharing of neighboring data to best assure a load balance across computations on data chunks. The three key elements you need to consider for any data decomposition design are:

- How should you divide the data into chunks?
- How can you ensure that the tasks for each chunk have access to all data required for updates?
- How are the data chunks assigned to threads?

Each of these elements is covered in more detail in the following sections.

How should you divide the data into chunks?

Partitioning the global data structure into chunks is at the heart of a data decomposition design. The mechanics for doing this will depend mainly on the type of data structure you are decomposing. For concreteness, I'll deal with one- and two-dimensional arrays as examples. The ideas here can be applied to other structures with a little ingenuity on your part.

Since each chunk of data will have an associated task, many of the same criteria that we had when defining tasks for task decomposition can be applied to the chunks of data decomposition. Specifically, make sure you have at least one chunk per thread (more is probably better) and ensure that the amount of computation that goes along with that chunk is sufficient to warrant breaking out that data as a separate chunk (now, aren't you glad you read the task decomposition section before starting into this section?).

With arrays of elements, you can divide the data into chunks at the individual element level, at the row or column level, as groups of rows or columns, or blocks of nonoverlapping subranges of rows and columns. Figure 2-2 shows a 4×4 array divided into chunks in several different ways.

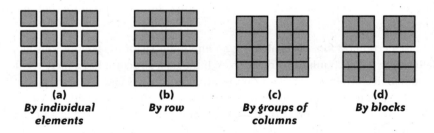

(a)	(b)	(c)	(d)
By individual elements	**By row**	**By groups of columns**	**By blocks**

FIGURE 2-2. Array decomposition examples

The amount of computation required by the associated task will be in direct proportion to the number of elements in a chunk. As stated before, this is known as the granularity of the computation and is exactly like what we had when we were considering how to define tasks.

However, data decompositions have an additional dimension that you must consider when dividing data structures into chunks. This other dimension is the *shape* of the chunk.

The shape of a chunk determines what the neighboring chunks are and how any exchange of data will be handled during the course of the chunk's computations. Let's say we have the case that data must be exchanged across the border of each chunk (the term *exchange* refers to the retrieval of data that is not contained within a given chunk for the purpose of using that data in the update of elements that are in the local chunk). Reducing the size of the overall border reduces the amount of exchange data required for updating local data elements; reducing the total number of chunks that share a border with a given chunk will make the exchange operation less complicated to code and execute.

Large granularity can actually be a detriment with regard to the shape of a chunk. The more data elements there are within a chunk, the more elements that may require exchange of neighboring data, and the more overhead there that may be to perform that exchange. When deciding how to divide large data structures that will necessitate data exchanges, a good rule of thumb is to try to maximize the volume-to-surface ratio. The volume defines the granularity of the computations, and the surface is the border of chunks that require an exchange of data. Figure 2-3 illustrates two different divisions of the same 4×8 data structure into two chunks. Both chunks have the same number of elements (16), but the scheme on the left has eight elements that share a border, whereas the scheme on the right has only four. If updates to each chunk relied on accessing data in the other chunk across the border, the division shown on the right would require fewer overall exchanges.

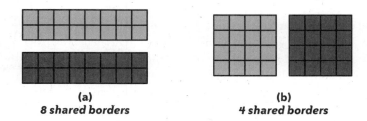

(a)
8 shared borders

(b)
4 shared borders

FIGURE 2-3. Volume-to-surface ratio examples

Irregular shapes may be necessary due to the irregular organization of the data. You need to be more vigilant with chunks of irregular shapes to ensure that a good load balance can be maintained, as well as a high enough granularity within the chunk to lessen the impact of unavoidable overheads.

You may need to revise your decomposition strategy after considering how the granularity and shape of the chunks affect the exchange of data between tasks. The division of data structures into chunks influences the need to access data that resides in another chunk. The next section develops ideas about accessing neighboring data that you should consider when deciding how to best decompose a data structure into chunks.

How can you ensure that the tasks for each chunk have access to all data required for updates?

The updating of elements within a data chunk is typically the overwhelming source of computation within concurrent algorithms that use a data decomposition scheme. Not unheard of, but not as interesting, are applications that only read data from large structures. Even in these cases, before an application has the ability to read it, the data must be created and the elements of the data structure holding any data must be updated. I suspect that for applications that simply input the data and then use it only for reference to support other computations, task decomposition would be the better method for concurrent design.

If a chunk itself contains all the data required to update the elements within the chunk, there is no need to coordinate the exchange of data between tasks. A more interesting case occurs when some data that is required by a given chunk is held within a neighboring chunk. In that case, we must find efficient means to exchange data between these nearby chunks. Two methods for doing this come to mind: copy the data from the nearby chunk into structures local to the task (thread), or access the data as needed from the nearby chunk. Let's look at the pros and cons of each of these.

The most obvious disadvantage for copying the necessary data not held in the assigned chunk is that each task will require extra local memory in order to hold the copy of data. However, once the data has been copied, there will be no further contention or synchronization needed between the tasks to access the copies. Copying the data is best used if the data is available before the update operation and won't change while being copied or during the update computations. This will likely mean some initial coordination between tasks to ensure that all copying has been done before tasks start updating.

The extra local memory resources that are allocated to hold copied data are often known as *ghost cells*. These cells are images of the structure and contents of data assigned to neighboring chunks. For example, consider the division of data shown in Figure 2-3 (b). If the update computation of an individual element required the data from the two elements on either side of it in the same row, the whole column from the neighboring chunk bordering the split would need to be accessible. Copying these data elements into ghost cells would allow the element to access that data without interfering in the updates of the neighboring chunk. Figure 2-4 shows the allocated ghost cells and the copy operation performed by each thread to fill those cells.

Another factor to consider when thinking about copying the required data is how many times copying will be necessary. This all depends on the nature of the update computation. Are repeated copies required for, say, an iterative algorithm that refines its solution over multiple updates? Or is the data copy only needed once at the outset of the computation? The more times the copy has to be carried out, the greater the overhead burden will be for the update computations. And then there is the matter of the amount of data that needs to be copied. Too many copy operations or too much data per copy might be an indicator that simply accessing the required data directly from a neighboring chunk would be the better solution.

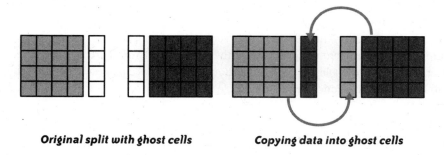

Original split with ghost cells   **Copying data into ghost cells**

FIGURE 2-4. Using ghost cells to hold copied data from a neighboring chunk

Accessing data as needed takes full advantage of shared memory communication between threads and the logic of the original serial algorithm. You also have the advantage of being able to delay any coordination between threads until the data is needed. The downside is that you must be able to guarantee that the correct data will be available at the right time. Data elements that are required but located within a neighboring chunk may be in the process of receiving updates concurrently with the rest of the elements in the neighboring chunk. If the local chunk requires the "old" values of nonlocal data elements, how can your code ensure that those values are not the "new" values? To answer this question or to know whether we must even deal with such a situation, we must look at the possible interactions between the exchange of data from neighboring chunks and the update operation of local chunk elements.

If all data is available at the beginning of tasks and that data will not change during the update computation, the solution will be easier to program and more likely to execute efficiently. You can either copy relatively small amounts of data into ghost cells or access the unchanging data through shared memory. In order to perform the copy of nonlocal data, add a data gathering (exchange) phase before the start of the update computations. Try to minimize the execution time of the data-gathering phase, since this is pure overhead that was not part of the original serial code.

If nonlocal data will be accessed (or copied) during update computations, you will need to add code to ensure that the correct data will be found. Mixing exchange and update computations can complicate the logic of your application, especially to ensure correct data is retrieved. However, the serial application likely had this requirement, too, and the solution to the need for accessing correct data concurrently should simply follow the serial algorithm as much as possible.

For example, if you are modeling the distribution of heat from a source through a metal plate, you can simulate the plate by a two-dimensional array of current temperatures at discrete spatial locations. At each time step of the computation, the new value of each discrete location is the average of the current temperature and the temperature of some set of neighboring cells. Since this calculation will update the current temperature of a cell and skew the results of other cells that use this cell's value, the serial code will have a new and old plate array. The values in the old array are used to update the new values. The roles of the plate arrays are switched for the next time iteration. In the concurrent version of this application, the old plate is read (only) to update the current temperatures in the new array. Thus, there is no need for synchronization to access old data and there should be minimal changes to the serial source in order to implement this concurrent solution.

How are the data chunks (and tasks) assigned to threads?

As with task decomposition, the tasks that are associated with the data chunks can be assigned to threads statically or dynamically. Static scheduling is simplest since the coordination needed for any exchange operations will be determined at the outset of the computations. Static scheduling is most appropriate when the amount of computations within tasks is uniform and predictable. Dynamic scheduling may be necessary to achieve a good load balance due to variability in the computation needed per chunk. This will require (many) more tasks than threads, but it also complicates the exchange operation and how you coordinate the exchange with neighboring chunks and their update schedules.

Being the sharp reader that you are, you have no doubt noticed that in most of the discussion over the last four pages or so I have used the term "task" rather than "thread." I did this on purpose. The tasks, defined by how the data structures are decomposed, identify what interaction is needed with other tasks regardless of which thread is assigned to execute what task. Additionally, if you are using a dynamic schedule of tasks, the number of tasks will outnumber the total number of threads. In such a case, it will not be possible to run all tasks in parallel. You may then come up against the situation where some task needs data from another task that has not yet been assigned to execute on a thread. This raises the complexity of your concurrent design to a whole other level, and I'm going to leave it to you to avoid such a situation.

Example: Game of Life on a finite grid

Conway's Game of Life is a simulation of organisms that live and die within cells arranged as a grid. Each grid cell is either empty or hosts a living organism. Occupied cells are called "alive," while empty cells are "dead." (See Figure 2-5 for an example of a portion of a grid with live and dead cells.) The simulation charts the births and deaths of the organisms through successive time steps or generations. For more information, see *Wheels, Life, and Other Mathematical Amusements* by Martin Gardner (Freeman & Co., 1983) or the tens of millions of words written and pictures drawn since the first computer simulation was written.

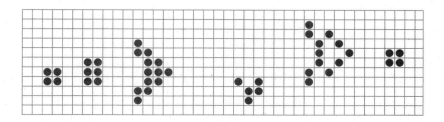

FIGURE 2-5. Game of Life example; black dots represent "live" cells

The state of cells can change from one generation to the next according to the following rules:

- The neighbors of a cell are the eight cells that border the given cell horizontally, vertically, and diagonally.
- If a cell is alive but has one or fewer neighboring cells alive, or has four or more neighboring cells alive, the cell will die of starvation or overcrowding, respectively, in the next generation.
- Living cells with two or three living neighbors will remain alive in the next generation.
- If a cell is dead and has exactly three neighboring cells that are alive, there will be a birth and the dead cell will become alive in the next generation. All other dead cells will remain dead in the next generation.
- All births and deaths take place at exactly the same time. This means that a cell that will be killed is still counted to help give birth to a neighboring cell.

In theory, the grid should be unbounded, but with only finite memory available in computer platforms, the size of the grid "universe" is usually restricted. Still, a very large two-dimensional array can hold current and successive generations of a simulation. The computations to decide whether any cell lives, dies, or is born is independent of the computations of any other cell. Thus, with the very large two-dimensional array and the update of elements in that array, the Game of Life simulation is an excellent candidate for a data decomposition design.

Example 2-3 shows serial code for updating the status of each cell into the next generation from the current generation. I assume that Grid is a data structure that is essentially a two-dimensional array that can hold the values of the user-defined constants ALIVE and DEAD. The grid array has rows indexed by 0 to N+1 and columns indexed by 0 to M+1. The extra rows and columns, whose cells are not considered for update in the given routine, can be thought of as boundary cells of the "universe" that are always dead (think of it as a wall of poison that can't be breached). By adding these boundary cells, I remove the need to deal with the grid edges as a special case. After computing the neighbor count for a cell, the disposition of that cell in the next generation is decided based on the rules just given. As with the task decomposition example, I won't create a threaded version of the code, but you're welcome to give it a try on your own based on the discussion that follows.

```
void computeNextGen (Grid curr, Grid next, int N, int M)
{
  int count;
  for (int i = 1; i <= N; i++) {
    for (int j = 1; j <= M; j++) {
      count = 0;
      if (curr[i-1][j-1] == ALIVE) count++; // NW neighbor
      if (curr[i-1][j]   == ALIVE) count++; // N neighbor
      if (curr[i-1][j+1] == ALIVE) count++; // NE neighbor
      if (curr[i][j-1]   == ALIVE) count++; // W neighbor
      if (curr[i][j+1]   == ALIVE) count++; // E neighbor
      if (curr[i+1][j-1] == ALIVE) count++; // SW neighbor
      if (curr[i+1][j]   == ALIVE) count++; // S neighbor
      if (curr[i+1][j+1] == ALIVE) count++; // SE neighbor

      if (count <= 1 || count >= 4)
        next[i][j] = DEAD;
      else if (curr[i][j] == ALIVE && (count == 2 || count == 3))
        next[i][j] = ALIVE;
      else if (curr[i][j] == DEAD && count == 3)
        next[i][j] = ALIVE;
      else next[i][j] = DEAD;
    }
  }
  return;
}
```

What is the large data structure in this application and how can you divide it into chunks? I've already given away the fact that we can divide the grid into chunks whose tasks can be assigned to threads. What is the best way to perform the division? Refer to Figure 2-5, but think bigger. Groups of rows or groups of columns or blocks seem the most natural divisions. You should anticipate the question of which exchanges of data each potential division strategy will entail and let that influence your answer.

Other factors to consider are the layout of the grid in memory, which may be anticipated within the serial code already, and how each division scheme might adversely affect the given layout. The amount of new code and line changes needed to transform the source code can be a factor influencing your decision. Dividing by rows would require modifications to the i loop, dividing by columns would require modifications to the j loop, and using a block division would require you to modify both the i and j loops.

For a chosen data decomposition, what exchange of data between tasks is required and how will this be accomplished? Since you need access to all eight neighbors of a given cell, if any neighbor cells are in a different chunk, there will need to be some form of data exchange. However, the code uses the curr grid for counting neighbors and is read-only. Each task can simply access the data when it is needed without fear of getting the wrong value or causing a data race with another task. On the other hand, if the rules of computing the next generation allowed us to make changes within the same grid that was being used to count neighbors, it might be better to copy data from other chunks into local ghost cells. If not, the results of your concurrent code may be different than the serial version.

How should you distribute the data chunks to tasks? Since you can determine the amount of computation for any grid cell and any collection of cells at design time, a static distribution will work well. In fact, I would recommend that the number of chunks be equal to the number of threads available.

What are the dependencies between tasks? This is a question that comes from our discussion of task decomposition and goes beyond the exchange of data needed between chunks. The answers to this question are derived from the serial code and the modifications necessary (from all the previous design decisions you've made). The count is a temporary work variable, so a local copy per thread takes care of that. Each thread will also need a copy of the two loop iteration variables. The global arrays are safe, since curr is only read and the updates to the elements in the next grid will not overlap.

Concurrent Design Models Wrap-Up

There often aren't clear, discrete steps to follow when developing a task or data decomposition solution. When considering how to answer the design element questions for your chosen design model, some of the decisions you make will be based on answers to questions that follow and answers that have come before. I hope you got that sense from the discussion of each example given. Even though I had to write down the questions sequentially, you may need to consider more than one thing at a time to devise an efficient concurrent solution.

DESIGN FACTOR SCORECARD

For most of the algorithms that are discussed and analyzed in Chapters 6 through 10, I will include a "Design Factor Scorecard" to discuss the concurrent algorithm and its implementation on four key factors. These factors are taken from Mattson's *Patterns for Parallel Programming* where they are used as criteria concurrent programmers need to keep in mind when designing and implementing parallel applications through the parallel programming patterns that are presented. For our purposes, I've redefined these terms slightly from how Mattson et al. originally used them. My interpretations of these terms are given shortly.

It is my contention that programmers of concurrent algorithms should keep each of these factors in mind, along with their relative importance to each other and the tradeoffs between stressing one factor over another when designing and implementing concurrent algorithms. The merits and tradeoffs possible for the algorithms and code given in later chapters will also be presented in the Design Factor Scorecard section after the descriptions of each algorithm presented.

Efficiency

Your concurrent applications must run quickly and make good use of processing resources. With regard to a concurrent algorithm, efficiency will examine the overhead computations that you must add to ensure a correct execution, how alternative arrangements of threads or organizations of tasks might work better or worse, and what other problems there could be with the performance of the threaded application.

Simplicity

The simpler your concurrent algorithms are, the easier they will be to develop, debug, verify, and maintain. In terms of concurrent code based on a serial version, discussions of simplicity will focus on how much extra code you have to add to achieve a concurrent solution and how much of the original structure of the serial algorithm remains.

Portability

One of the goals of this book is to be as agnostic as possible with regard to available threading models and which models are used to implement the solution algorithms presented. Portability discussions will examine the tradeoffs that you could encounter if you used a different threading model from the one used in this text. While this book is primarily dedicated to the design and exploration of multithreaded codes, one of the options discussed under portability will be distributed-memory variations of the algorithms.

Scalability

Because the number of cores will only increase as time passes, your concurrent applications should be effective on a wide range of numbers of threads and cores, and sizes of data sets. Scalability refers to what you should expect with regard to how a given concurrent algorithm will behave with changes in the number of cores or size of data sets.

My Two Cents' Worth on the Factors

For me, scalability is the most important of these four factors, with efficiency a close second. This means that I will typically try to design a concurrent algorithm that will maintain its level of performance as the number of cores and threads increases to the detriment of a simpler or more portable algorithm. In order to gain that scalability, the algorithm and its implementation must be efficient, so that is my secondary goal.

There have been many times when the scalability of a concurrent application I've written has peaked and flattened out. This was usually due to the requirements of the algorithm and the paraphernalia provided by the threading model being used. In these cases, I would ask myself if it is worth the extra work to try to discover an alternative (which may not exist) that might scale better, or to rewrite the whole thing in terms of a different threading or design model. These are some of the tradeoffs you face when tackling concurrent algorithms.

What's Not Parallel

In the chapters and pages that follow, we're going to explore quite a few things that can be executed concurrently. Before we get to those, though, I want to impress upon you that not everything can be executed in parallel. I don't want you wasting time beating your head against the wall, endlessly poring over this book and others on parallel algorithms, or pestering friends and colleagues (or me) with phone calls in the wee hours of the morning trying to enlist them in your search for a parallel solution, especially when there isn't one.

NOTE

One of the more famous illustrations of a situation that cannot be made parallel is cited in Fred Brooks's 1995 book, *The Mythical Man-Month: Essays on Software Engineering* (Addison-Wesley Professional). The nine-month gestation period for a human is a serial process—you can't get a baby in one month by assigning nine women to the job.

On the other hand, if you wanted to raise a baseball team of players from cradle to Wrigley Field in the shortest amount of time, you could employ 9 women (10 if you want a designated hitter). This would give you a newborn starting lineup after nine months. Asking one woman to do all the work would require about nine years, barring twins and such, and the pitcher (firstborn) would be starting her Little League career when the right fielder (ninth-born) was just arriving.

Algorithms with State

The first example of code that cannot be executed concurrently is algorithms, functions, or procedures that contain a *state*. That is, something kept around from one execution to the next. For example, the seed to a random number generator or the file pointer for I/O would be considered state. Algorithms with state cannot be made directly concurrent, and whenever you encounter such code, a red flag should go up when you are considering concurrency. However, you may be able to take steps to render the code thread-safe, which may be sufficient.

You can make state-filled code thread-safe by adding some form of synchronization or writing the code to be reentrant (i.e., it can be reentered without detrimental side effects while it is already running). The former option will serialize all concurrent executions of the synchronized code (and add unnecessary overhead when not called concurrently), while the latter option may not be possible if the update of global variables is part of the code.

If the variable(s) holding the state does not have to be shared between threads, you can use TLS to overcome this dependence. Using TLS, each thread would have a separate copy of the state variable(s) (accessed in exactly the same way across all threads) to ensure there are no data races on the variable(s). Thus, each thread can have a different random number seed and use the same code to generate a separate stream of numbers that will not interfere with any other thread's seed.

Recurrences

Recurrence relations within loops feed information forward from one iteration to the next. Prime examples of this are time-stepping loops and convergence loops. No matter how many tea leaves we read, tarot cards we consult, or Magic Eight Ball apps we write, we can't parse out future time steps to multiple threads for concurrent execution.

A simple code example of a recurrence is given in Example 2-4. The recurrence shown is the read access of the a[i-1] element that was computed in the previous iteration.

EXAMPLE 2-4. Recurrence relation on array access

```
for (i = 1; i < N; i++)
  a[i] = a[i-1] + b[i];
```

Unfortunately, most recurrences cannot be made concurrent. Prefix sum is a special case of a recurrence that can be made to run concurrently (see Chapter 6 for more details on concurrent algorithms for prefix scan).

If you've got a recurrence relationship that is a hotspot in your code, look for a point "higher" in the call tree that would include execution of the recurrence. Thread there, where possible.

Induction Variables

Induction variables are variables that are incremented on each trip through a loop. Most likely, these are index variables that do not have a one-to-one relation with the value of the loop iterator variable. Example 2-5 shows a code segment with two induction variables, i1 and i2.

EXAMPLE 2-5. Induction variables

```
i1 = 4;
i2 = 0;
for (k = 1; k < N; k++) {
  B[i1++] = function1(k,q,r);
  i2 += k;
  A[i2] = function2(k,r,q);
}
```

As this code stands, even if the calls to function1() and function2() are independent, there's no way to transform this code for concurrency without a few radical alterations to the serial source. Specifically, you would need to replace the array index increment expressions with a calculation based solely on the value of the loop iterator variable.

Without much strain on your brain, I'm sure you can see that you could rewrite the first statement in the loop as shown in Example 2-6.

EXAMPLE 2-6. Solution for first induction variable increment

```
B[k+4] = function1(k,q,r);
```

The second is a bit trickier. Take a moment to see whether you can figure it out on your own. I've put the solution at the end of the next paragraph.

A worse case than the code shown in Example 2-5 are induction variables that have a conditional increment. As an example, say you want to search through a list and copy out all items that have some property, such as all recording artists who released more albums than Pink Floyd. We'll assume that the list is implemented with some random access data structure; otherwise, if we use a linked or pointer-based data structure, we've already got problems about how to efficiently access data concurrently. Now, the loop index variable is running through the full set of data items and the induction variable is only incrementing when we find an item that matches our criterion in order to store it in a second array (indexed by the induction variable). There is no closed-form relation between the value of the loop index and the value of the induction variable.

Did you figure out how to set up the second induction variable form from Example 2-5? It is simply the sum of the integers from 1 up to the current value of k. Thus, you can use the code in Example 2-7 in a concurrent version of the loop.

EXAMPLE 2-7. Solution for second induction variable increment

```
i2 = (k*k + k)/2;
A[i2] = function2(k,r,q);
```

This is a contrived example, of course. Your situations may not be so neat and clean, though I hope they are.

Reduction

Reductions take a collection (typically an array) of data and reduce it to a single scalar value through some combining operation. To remove this dependency, the operation must be both associative and commutative, such as addition, multiplication, or some logical operations. The loop in the code fragment shown in Example 2-8 will find the sum of all elements of the c array as well as the largest (maximum) element in the array.

EXAMPLE 2-8. Reduction code

```
sum = 0;
big = c[0];
for (i = 0; i < N; i++) {
  sum += c[i];
  big = (c[i] > big ? c[i] : big); // maximum element
}
```

At first glance, the loop cannot be made to execute concurrently. Each element, in turn, is added to the running total and compared to the largest element found so far, replacing that largest found element as needed. This is all done in the order of the incrementing index variable i. However, notice that the results would be exactly the same (within limits of rounding and truncation) if the loop were run in reverse order (I mentioned this idea of running a loop in reverse as a good initial test that the loop may be capable of concurrent execution earlier in this chapter).

Taking advantage of the associativity of the operator(s) involved will allow you to create a concurrent version of the reduction algorithm. Divide the loop iterations among the threads to be used and simply compute partial results (`sum` and `big` in the preceding example) in local storage. Next, combine each partial result into a global result, taking care to synchronize access to the shared variables. Of course, if you're threading your loop with OpenMP or Intel TBB, you just need to make use of the `reduction` clause or `parallel_reduce` algorithm.

Loop-Carried Dependence

The final example of code that poses a problem to our efforts to write concurrent applications is known as loop-carried dependence. This dependence occurs when results of some previous iteration are used in the current iteration. Typically, this situation will be evidenced by references to the same array element on both the left- and righthand sides of assignments and a backward reference in some righthand side use of the array element. Obviously, the iterations of such loops are not completely independent. Example 2-9 shows a code fragment that updates corresponding elements of the a and b arrays, but the update of a elements relies on previously updated elements from the b array.

EXAMPLE 2-9. Loop-carried dependence code

```
for (k = 5; k < N; k++) {
  b[k] = DoSomething(k);
  a[k] = b[k-5] + MoreStuff(k);
}
```

Dividing such loop iterations into tasks presents the problem of requiring extra synchronization to ensure that the backward references have been computed before they are used in computation of the current iteration. Recurrence is a special case of a loop-carried dependence where the backward reference is the immediate previous iteration. There is no way to efficiently execute such loop iterations concurrently, since waiting for the backward references to be resolved can require a hefty amount of synchronization.

For example, if your backward reference spans five iterations (as in Example 2-9), you can divide up the loop iterations into chunks with five iterations in each chunk. Once the first iteration of the first chunk has completed, the first iteration in the second chunk can start, since the dependence of the first iteration of the second chunk (iteration #6) has been satisfied. You can daisy-chain loop chunks and threads like this, but it will all need some major code modifications and synchronization to ensure that all prerequisite dependences have been satisfied before execution can start on each separate iteration.

Not-so-typical loop-carried dependence

The loop in the code fragment given in Example 2-10 cannot be made parallel because wrap is carried from one iteration to the next. This is loop-carried dependence that doesn't follow the typical format involving obvious backward references, since the backward references are "hidden" in the wrap variable.

EXAMPLE 2-10. Atypical loop-carried dependence

```
wrap = a[0] * b[0];
for (i = 1; i < N; i++) {
  c[i] = wrap;
  wrap = a[i] * b[i];
  d[i] = 2 * wrap;
}
```

Fortunately, you can restructure this simple case to define wrap before use in each iteration and create a loop whose iterations can be executed concurrently. This is possible because you can assign the proper value of wrap based solely on the value of the loop iterator variable. Example 2-11 shows the results of this code restructuring.

EXAMPLE 2-11. Modified loop-carried dependence

```
for (i = 1; i < N; i++) {
  wrap = a[i-1] * b[i-1];
  c[i] = wrap;
  wrap = a[i] * b[i];
  d[i] = 2 * wrap;
}
```

Disregarding the code used to implement the loop repetition (initializing, incrementing, and testing the loop iterator), you will notice that the modified code is now executing *4N* statements, as opposed to the *3N+1* needed in Example 2-10.

Rewriting an existing algorithm to something less efficient in order to get a better chance of concurrency may be necessary. Don't use something that is too far afield of the original, though. Less efficient serial algorithms will tend to add overhead (as seen when comparing the number of statements in the loop bodies in the previous examples).

CHAPTER THREE

Proving Correctness and Measuring Performance

THIS CHAPTER TAKES A LOOK AT TOPICS RELATED TO THE FINAL TWO STEPS of the threading methodology. The first is knowing when your concurrent algorithms will run correctly or at least have a good idea that you've done a good job of designing an error-free concurrent algorithm. The second topic covers some of the ways you can measure how well your concurrent code is executing in parallel. Finally, I've put in a little history review (don't worry—it's short, it's related to the topic of this book, and it never hurts to know where you've been to have a clue about where you might be going).

Verification of Parallel Algorithms

In his 2006 book *Principles of Concurrent and Distributed Programming*, Second Edition (Addison-Wesley), M. Ben-Ari defines an abstraction for formally verifying the correctness and other properties of concurrent algorithms. Unlike other theoretical abstractions in computer science that deal with hardware (e.g., PRAM), Ben-Ari's abstraction deals with how concurrent programs execute. I don't want to get into all the details and justifications for this abstraction here. I recommend that you read Ben-Ari's book for that and for another good resource in concurrent algorithm design. I want to cover just enough for you to understand the principles and the basic idea of the concurrency abstraction and how to prove concurrent algorithms are correct.

For those of you who haven't immediately curled up into a fetal position or flopped onto the floor kicking and screaming at the thought of formal proofs of algorithms (and for those of you who did but have now picked the book up again), let me assure you that I consider this a vital part of concurrent algorithm design and it's probably not as bad as you think. The more time you spend creating correct concurrent algorithms from the get-go, the less time you will spend chasing down errors that only show up on those Thursdays when the dates are prime numbers. This is a great example of the phrase, "An ounce of prevention equals a pound of cure."

Some potential concurrency errors are going to be obvious and you can avoid them easily. Other errors are going to be subtler and may only show up under very rare and very particular circumstances. Do you need to deal with those rare "corner" cases? Yes, you do. Having a familiarity with Ben-Ari's methods and practicing them whenever you are designing concurrent algorithms will sharpen your skills to identify the potential corner cases that your colleagues overlook. Besides, I make use of Ben-Ari's technique throughout the later chapters of this book and if you haven't read the following sections, you won't know what I'm talking about.

The first part of the concurrent abstraction is that *programs are the execution of atomic statements*. An atomic statement is one that cannot be divided into smaller instructions or that cannot be interrupted until the statement is completed. The bottom line is that there is some granularity of executable code at which even the operating system is unable to interrupt and must wait before it can affect the process that is executing that atomic statement. For purposes of the concurrent abstraction, there are different levels of atomicity we might choose to work with. These range from individual machine code instructions to assembly language code to individual source lines of a high-level language. We can choose the level of atomic execution that makes the most sense, is easiest to work with, and fits with the algorithm we are abstracting. In most cases you can stay at the individual source-line level. There won't be many situations that require you to consider the algorithm that has been broken down to the assembly-language level.

The next part of the concurrent abstraction is to understand that *concurrent programs are interleavings of atomic statements from two or more threads*. I find it easier to assume my concurrent algorithm is executing on a single core. That way, I know the operating system will be swapping the threads in and out of the processor in some interleaved fashion. Plus, dealing with the temporal relationship of two threads executing in parallel on different cores quickly becomes a headache whose cost is nowhere near the value of the payoff methodology.

Operating systems schedule threads in a nondeterministic way, so we cannot predict the exact execution sequence of the atomic statements of multiple threads for any execution, nor can we guarantee that the same order seen from one run will be repeated in the next run or ever again. Thus, to prove or verify any desirable properties of a concurrent algorithm (such as correctness), *we must show that the desirable property holds for all interleavings of atomic statements from two or more threads.*

If you pause a moment and think about this, you'll realize that you will be confronted with a geometrically growing number of interleavings that must be verified. For example, if you have two threads, T0 and T1, each with two statements, s1 and s2, there are six different interleavings of these atomic statements. Figure 3-1 shows the interleavings of these four atomic statements.

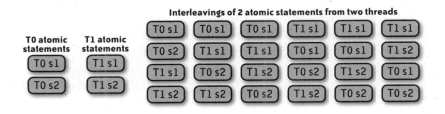

FIGURE 3-1. Interleaving two statements within each of two threads

With two threads, three statements per thread yields 20 distinct interleavings, and four statements each would require verification of 70 interleavings. And this is with only two threads. Imagine the number of interleavings using three, four, or eight threads. What is a programmer to do?

Typically, you will find that of the many different possible interleavings, only a few are relevant in proving that the algorithm under consideration has the desired properties. In the set of interleavings enumerated in Figure 3-1, it may be that we only have to be concerned in those cases where T0 s1 immediately precedes T1 s2. There is only one case where this happens (fifth from the left). You will need to have good reasons for not considering any interleaving that you do not formally verify, of course. You cannot bypass them with some hand-waving, and you can't just sweep them under the carpet because they seem too numerous or difficult.

The final part of the concurrent abstraction is to assume that statements from a thread will eventually be selected for inclusion in an interleaving. This is the *fairness* property of the abstraction. When running multiple processes, every process is given a quantum of time by the operating system to execute statements on the processor. Priority of execution associated with processes may keep a process from getting into the CPU as frequently as many of the others in the system, but the operating system is fair and will give some sliver of time to each process, eventually. Thus, the abstraction enforces the idea that threads will be allowed to proceed at some point, even if it is for a single atomic statement. While the current status of the computation may not allow any thread to do any useful computation, as in the case where the state of other threads and values may prevent a thread from breaking out of a spin-wait loop, that will be a property of the algorithm, not a defect in the concurrent abstraction being used.

To recap, here are the four parts of Ben-Ari's concurrent abstraction that we can use to verify that concurrent algorithms have desirable properties:

- Programs are the execution of atomic statements.
- Concurrent programs are the interleavings of atomic statements from two or more threads.
- All possible interleavings of atomic statements must be shown to retain whatever property we are hoping to verify within a concurrent algorithm.
- No thread's statements may be (unfairly) excluded from any arbitrary interleaving.

Ben-Ari goes into much more formal depth in justifying the properties of his abstraction. He shows how you can use state diagrams and (interleaving) scenarios as tools to formally verify the properties of concurrent algorithms. Even if you're not into formal proofs of algorithms, I recommend reading the chapters from Ben-Ari's text (see if you can get one from your local library if you don't want to shell out the bucks for your own copy) to get a more complete idea about verifying concurrent algorithms.

The next sections of this chapter will develop a solution to a well-known problem in concurrent programming to show you how you can use this concurrent abstraction. I will make several attempts at writing a valid solution, but as you'll see, each will be missing some of the required properties. I may be playing somewhat fast and loose with the granularity of what constitutes an atomic statement in the analyses of each algorithmic attempt. Still, there should be enough detail and rigor to convince a knowledgeable person that the algorithm attempts have the potential to fail for the reasons cited and that the final solution algorithm will work in all possible cases.

Example: The Critical Section Problem

A *critical section* is a portion of code from a concurrent algorithm where shared variables are accessed and an update of these variables is involved. Thus, to avoid a data race on the shared variables, all accesses, read or write, must be restricted to allow only a single thread to execute code in the critical sections at a time. The Critical Section Problem is an exercise to develop a means for mutual exclusion that doesn't use any synchronization objects or primitives that might be defined within a threading model. I prefer the term *critical region* to denote such regions of code, especially since there is a Windows threading object called CRITICAL_SECTION that can be used for enforcing mutual exclusion in a critical region. I like to avoid confusion between terms whenever I can. While I use the classic name for the problem, I will refer to these code segments as critical regions for the rest of the book.

Proposed solutions to the problem must prove that the following two properties hold in all circumstances:

1. The code enforces mutual exclusion. Threads are disallowed from entering the critical region when another thread is occupying the critical region. Plus, if there are multiple concurrent requests to enter the critical region and no other thread is currently executing within the region, only one requesting thread must be allowed to enter the critical region.

2. If a thread is not executing within the critical region, that thread cannot prevent another thread seeking entry from entering the region.

What follows is a step-by-step development of successive algorithms to a solution known as Dekker's Algorithm. Ben-Ari devotes a whole chapter to demonstrate the use of his concurrency abstraction by reworking an initial attempt to derive Dekker's Algorithm. There are some differences between the attempted solution algorithms he describes and the ones I give here.

I will only consider the case with two threads competing for the critical region, since Dekker's Algorithm is defined only for two threads and it keeps things simple. One thread will be executing the ThreadZero() function, and the other will execute the ThreadOne() function. In my analysis of the examples, I shall refer to these threads as T0 and T1, respectively.

In the solution pseudocode examples, the critical regions will be represented as calls to the functions CriticalRegionZero and CriticalRegionOne. I shall assume that both regions access the same shared variables and must be executed in a mutually exclusive way. When a thread is not within the critical region, there are other computations to be done (OtherStuffZero, OtherStuffOne).

The purpose of this exercise is not to develop a solution to the Critical Section Problem. We can easily employ an appropriate synchronization object to limit the number of threads entering a critical region of our code. The development of code that eventually leads to Dekker's Algorithm is used to illustrate M. Ben-Ari's methods of verifying the correctness of concurrent algorithms.

First Attempt

Example 3-1 shows the first attempt at an algorithm that will enforce mutual exclusion on entering a critical region.

EXAMPLE 3-1. First attempt

```
int threadNumber = 0;

void ThreadZero()
{
  while (TRUE) do {
    while (threadNumber == 1) do {} //spin-wait
    CriticalRegionZero;
    threadNumber = 1;
    OtherStuffZero;
  }
}

void ThreadOne()
{
  while (TRUE) do {
    while (threadNumber == 0) do {} //spin-wait
    CriticalRegionOne;
    threadNumber = 0;
    OtherStuffOne;
  }
}
```

The first attempt makes use of a global variable, threadNumber, to announce which thread may enter the critical region. The value of this global is initialized to 0 to allow T0 first access to the critical region. Before entering the region, a thread first checks to see whether it is allowed to enter, based on the value stored in threadNumber. If it is, the thread proceeds into the critical region and, upon exit, updates the threadNumber variable with the value that allows the other thread entry. If the value of threadNumber doesn't match, the thread enters a spin-wait loop until the other thread has executed the critical region and changed the value of threadNumber.

Assuming a single core with two threads that are swapped into the processor, we can see that an execution trace for this example could proceed as shown here:

1. T1 arrives at while loop.

2. T1 waits, since threadNumber == 0.

3. T0 arrives at while loop.

4. T0 proceeds, since threadNumber == 0.

5. T0 enters critical region.

6. T0 exits critical region and sets threadNumber = 1.

7. T1 enters critical region.

Here's your first chance to try out an interleaving on your own. What happens if T0 starts execution first on the CPU and enters the critical region? Will T1 gain access to the region while T0 is executing there? Close the book (be sure to mark your place), go get a snack or something to drink, and ponder that situation before returning to see my analysis.

Welcome back.

If T0 starts first, even if it only executes the start of the while loop before T1 is allowed to execute in the processor, T1 will hit the spin-wait loop. In fact, this is the scenario for any interleaving that starts with T0 and T1 is allowed to execute before T0 has set threadNumber. After the shared variable is set, T1 will be given access to the critical region and T0 will be blocked.

Mutual exclusion is guaranteed. Only one thread at a time is allowed into the critical region, while the other thread will not be allowed into the region until the thread already executing within the region has finished and reset the threadNumber flag to the appropriate value.

What about the case where T1 enters the critical region, does the assigned computation, exits the critical region, and then needs to get back into the critical region before T0 has had the chance to make a pass through the critical region? T1 will not be able to reenter the critical region until T0 has completed the execution of OtherStuffZero, gone through the critical region, and reset the threadNumber flag. We now have the case where one thread that is not in the critical region can prevent another thread from entering. This violates the second property a correct solution must have.

In fact, the circumstances created by the simple solution proposed in Example 3-1 force a lockstep alternation of allowing threads to enter and exit the critical region. Any thread that attempts to deviate from that rigid alternation is stymied and must execute the spin-wait until the other thread has changed the value of the threadNumber flag. Compounding this problem is the possibility of one thread terminating (whether by design, by accident, or by foul play) before the other. If the surviving thread attempts to enter the critical region without the dead thread having a chance to change the value of the threadNumber flag, this will create a deadlock on the surviving thread.

This is not an acceptable state of affairs. Let's see if we can do better in the next attempt.

Second Attempt

To get around the problem of the lockstep execution requirement of the first proposed solution to the Critical Section Problem, the second solution uses a global flag, one per thread, to denote when a thread is executing within the critical region. Example 3-2 shows the pseudocode for the second attempt.

EXAMPLE 3-2. Second attempt

```
int Thread0inside = 0;
int Thread1inside = 0;
```

```
void ThreadZero()
{
  while (TRUE) do {
    while (Thread1inside) do {}  // spin-wait
    Thread0inside = 1;
    CriticalRegionZero;
    Thread0inside = 0;
    OtherStuffZero;
  }
}

void ThreadOne()
{
  while (TRUE) do {
    while (Thread0inside) do {}
    Thread1inside = 1;
    CriticalRegionOne;
    Thread1inside = 0;
    OtherStuffOne;
  }
}
```

As in the code for the first attempt, two threads each execute one of the two functions given. The two status flags, Thread0inside and Thread1inside, indicate when the corresponding thread is executing within the critical region. Before attempting to enter the critical region, a thread checks on the status of the other thread. If the status flag indicates the other thread is already within the critical region, the thread attempting entry executes a spin-wait until the thread within the critical region exits and resets its status flag. If the other thread's status flag doesn't indicate that the thread is running code in the critical region, the thread attempting to enter the critical region will set its own status flag, execute code in the critical region, and then reset the status flag to show that it is no longer inside the critical region.

This version solves the lockstep problem: T1 can enter and exit the critical region any number of times unless T0 is already in the critical region. If a thread is within the critical region, its status flag will indicate this fact and the other thread attempting to enter will be kept out until the thread in the region exits and resets its status flag.

While mutual exclusion is enforced if one thread is already in the critical region, a problem worse than the possibility of starvation is that this algorithm cannot guarantee mutual exclusion in the general case. Consider the following interleaving of executions between the two threads, T0 and T1, which demonstrates how two threads can be allowed to enter into the critical region at the same time:

1. T0 tests Thread1inside in while conditional.

2. T0 finds Thread1inside == 0 (conditional is FALSE).

3. T1 tests Thread0inside in while conditional.

4. T1 finds Thread0inside == 0 (conditional is FALSE).

5. T0 enters critical region.

6. T1 enters critical region.

This interleaving forces us to conclude that the second proposed solution will not keep two threads out of the critical region. One obvious fix is to disallow a thread from accessing the while loop conditional evaluation whenever the other thread is running the while loop test within its own function.

Third Attempt

The previous attempt used what I would call "selfish" threads. Before entering the critical region, a thread sets its status flag announcing that it is proceeding into the critical region. The only cooperation between the threads is checking the status of the other selfish thread before barreling into the critical region. The third attempt uses more genteel threads that take into account the other thread's intention to enter the critical region. Example 3-3 shows the pseudocode for the third attempt.

EXAMPLE 3-3. Third attempt

```
int Thread0WantsToEnter = 0;
int Thread1WantsToEnter = 0;

void ThreadZero()
{
  while (TRUE) do {
    Thread0WantsToEnter = 1;
    while (Thread1WantsToEnter) do {}  // spin-wait
    CriticalRegionZero;
    Thread0WantsToEnter = 0;
    OtherStuffZero;
  }
}

void ThreadOne()
{
  while (TRUE) do {
    Thread1WantsToEnter = 1;
    while (Thread0WantsToEnter) do {}
    CriticalRegionOne;
    Thread1WantsToEnter = 0;
    OtherStuffOne;
  }
}
```

In this attempt, each thread declares the desire to enter the critical region by setting the appropriate desire flag. However, before proceeding into the critical region, the thread first checks on whether the other thread wants to enter the critical region. If so, the first thread will enter a spin-wait loop until the second thread has executed the critical region—satisfying the desire to enter the region—and resets its desire flag. Otherwise, finding that the other thread is not interested in entering the critical region, a thread will proceed into the critical region and reset its desire flag after exiting the region.

Hold your horses there, buckaroo! Isn't this just the second attempt algorithm with a different name for the status flag? No, but I'm not surprised if you thought that. Go back to Example 3-2 and look closely. The difference between the second and third attempts is the order of the setting of a thread's status flag and the testing of the other thread's flag. In the second attempt, the spin-wait while test came before the setting of a thread's flag; in the third attempt, the status flag is set before the spin-wait while conditional checks the other thread's flag.

To illustrate how this algorithm is intended to execute, let's assume we have T1 executing OtherStuffOne. When T0 wishes to enter the critical region, it first sets ThreadOWantsToEnter to 1 and then examines the value of Thread1WantsToEnter to find that T1 has not announced any desire to enter the critical region. T0 will proceed into the critical region. Should T1 finish with the other computations and require access to the critical region, it will set Thread1WantsToEnter to 1 and then examine ThreadOWantsToEnter, which it finds to also have the value 1. This will put T1 into the spin-wait loop until T0 exits the critical region and resets ThreadOWantsToEnter to 0.

> **NOTE**
> The desire flag will be set to 1 not only when a thread wishes to enter the critical region, but also while the thread is executing in the critical region. Since threads cannot know whether a desire flag is merely the announcement of intent or denotes that the other thread is currently executing in the critical region, they must assume that it means the latter and that the other thread is executing in the critical region.

Mutual exclusion is enforced when a thread is in the critical region, and threads are free to enter and leave the critical region in any order that their execution will take them. As you should have guessed by now, there is a problem and I hope you've already seen it. If not, the following interleaving shows how this attempt can run into trouble:

1. T0 sets ThreadOWantsToEnter = 1.
2. T1 sets Thread1WantsToEnter = 1.
3. T0 tests Thread1WantsToEnter in while conditional.
4. T0 finds Thread1WantsToEnter == 1 (conditional is TRUE).
5. T0 executes spin-wait.
6. T1 tests ThreadOWantsToEnter in while conditional.
7. T1 finds ThreadOWantsToEnter == 1 (conditional is TRUE).
8. T1 executes spin-wait.

This situation reminds me of the two gophers, Mac and Tosh, from the Warner Brothers cartoon shorts of the 1940s and '50s. These rodents were overly polite to everyone and to each other. For example, whenever they both wanted to pass through a door, they would take turns trying to get the other to precede them. This was done by alternately cajoling the other with phrases like, "After you," and, "No, I must insist, you first."

The threads T0 and T1 can both state the desire to enter the critical region before testing the intentions of the other thread. In that case, both threads will go into their spin-wait loops and never have the chance to reset the desire flag that will release the other thread. This is a classic deadlock situation. Each thread is waiting for an event (the reset of the desire flag of the other thread) that will never occur.

To avoid a deadlock situation, we must deny one of the four necessary conditions of a deadlock (see the sidebar "Four Necessary Conditions Required to Allow Deadlock") from occurring. To solve this problem, we need to find a way to break out of the spin-wait loop that caused the problem in the first place. The fourth attempt at a solution will take this approach.

FOUR NECESSARY CONDITIONS REQUIRED TO ALLOW DEADLOCK

To have the potential for deadlock between two or more threads and the set of resources that are required by each, four conditions must be met. In a paper titled, "Sequencing tasks in multiprocess systems to avoid deadlocks" (in *Conference Record of 1970 Eleventh Annual Symposium on Switching and Automata Theory*), E. G. Coffman, Jr. and A. Shoshani first enumerated these four conditions as follows:

Mutual exclusion condition
   Individual resources are either available or they are held by no more than one thread at a time.

Hold and wait condition
   Threads that are already holding some resources may attempt to hold new resources.

No preemption condition
   Once a thread is holding a resource, that resource can only be removed when the holding thread voluntarily releases the resource.

Circular wait condition
   A circular chain of threads requesting resources that are held by the next thread in the chain can exist.

To prevent the possibility of deadlock from occurring, one of these conditions must not be allowed to exist. There are many different ways to prevent one or more of these conditions. A text on operating systems theory should have some discussion about deadlock and how you can prevent it.

Fourth Attempt

The fourth attempt has the same polite threads from the previous algorithm, but it removes the "hold and wait" condition of deadlock that was plaguing the third attempt. Example 3-4 shows the pseudocode for two threads with the deadlock breaking modifications.

EXAMPLE 3-4. Fourth attempt

```
int Thread0WantsToEnter = 0;
int Thread1WantsToEnter = 0;

void ThreadZero()
{
  while (TRUE) do {
    Thread0WantsToEnter = 1;
    while (Thread1WantsToEnter) do { // not quite a spin-wait
      Thread0WantsToEnter = 0;
      delay(someRandomCycles);
      Thread0WantsToEnter = 1;
    }
    CriticalRegionZero;
    Thread0WantsToEnter = 0;
    OtherStuffZero;
  }
}

void ThreadOne()
{
  while (TRUE) do {
    Thread1WantsToEnter = 1;
    while (Thread0WantsToEnter) do {
      Thread1WantsToEnter = 0;
      delay(someRandomCycles);
      Thread1WantsToEnter = 1;
    }
    CriticalRegionOne;
    Thread1WantsToEnter = 0;
    OtherStuffOne;
  }
}
```

As in the previous algorithm, when a thread seeks to enter the critical region, it sets the associated desire flag and then checks the status of the desire flag for the other thread. If that other thread does not wish access to the critical region, the original thread proceeds. However, if the other thread does want to enter the critical region (or is in the critical region already), the original thread will enter the while loop. This does not simply perform a spin-wait as we have seen in all the attempts so far. Instead, an iteration of the while loop resets the thread's desire flag, delays the thread for some random number of cycles, sets the desire flag to 1, and retests the status of the other thread's desire flag in the while condition.

With this modification, if the two threads set their associated desire flags and then check on the status of the other flag, the threads will not wait in deadlock. One of the threads should be given a shorter delay time before setting its desire flag and finding the other (still delayed) thread not yet wanting to enter the critical region. Of course, there is the chance that the random delay will be exactly the same for each thread each time the thread is delayed and we would be back in the same situation as the third attempt. The probability of such an event occurring would be about the same as two independent and fair roulette wheels hitting exactly the same sequence of results each time they are spun.

As with the third attempt, mutual exclusion is enforced when a thread is in the critical region and threads are free to enter and leave the critical region in any order that their executions will take them. I avoid the circumstances leading to deadlock using a random arbitration of which thread should be allowed to proceed into the critical region. Still, this variation contains a problem that is detrimental to the execution of threads within this algorithm. The following interleaving of thread executions demonstrates this potential dilemma:

1. T0 enters critical region.
2. T1 sets `Thread1WantsToEnter` = 1.
3. T1 finds T0 in critical region.
4. T1 resets `Thread1WantsToEnter` = 0, and delays.
5. T0 exits critical region.
6. T0 quickly performs `OtherStuffZero`.
7. T0 gains access to critical region.
8. T1 sets `Thread1WantsToEnter` = 1.
9. T1 tests `Thread0WantsToEnter` in `while` conditional and finds T0 in critical region.
10. T1 resets `Thread1WantsToEnter` = 0 and delays.
11. T0 exits critical region.
12. T0 quickly performs `OtherStuffZero`.
13. T0 gains access to critical region.

Are you starting to get the hang of this interleaving analysis? Before you saw my interleaving, did you figure out that it is possible for one thread to keep the other out of the critical region indefinitely? Such behavior is known as *starvation*. This interleaving can go on indefinitely, stranding the unlucky T1 in a perpetual state of starvation.

Does this violate the required properties of a correct solution? Not really. This starvation and mistreatment of T1 is not the fault of T0, but is a direct result of the adverse scheduling by the operating system. While I would agree that such starvation of one thread by this algorithm is extremely unlikely, it is still possible, and it is a situation that we should try to avoid if at all possible.

When analyzing threaded algorithms and the correctness of the interactions between threads within that algorithm, you cannot assume anything about execution speed. Multiple processors within a symmetric multiprocessor system may not all have the same clock speed, and future multicore processors may not contain homogeneous core elements within the same package. Not to mention that the amount of computation assigned to a thread can be different from that given to another thread. Thus, you must examine *all* possible execution interleavings of threads in order to demonstrate that you have a correct concurrent algorithm.

Dekker's Algorithm

Our final attempt is known as Dekker's Algorithm. Rather than relying on the polite nature of threads or a capricious random function to break the tie when two threads wish to enter the critical region, the algorithm bestows a "favored" status on the thread to be allowed entry and acts as a tiebreaker (like the possession arrow in basketball, for my sports-minded readers). Example 3-5 gives the pseudocode for this solution to the Critical Section Problem.

EXAMPLE 3-5. Dekker's Algorithm

```
int favored;
int ThreadOWantsToEnter, Thread1WantsToEnter;

void ThreadZero()
{
  while (TRUE) do {
    ThreadOWantsToEnter = 1;
    while (Thread1WantsToEnter) do {
      if (favored == 1) {
        ThreadOWantsToEnter = 0;
        while (favored == 1) do {}  // spin-wait
        ThreadOWantsToEnter = 1;
      }
    }
    CriticalRegionZero;
    favored = 1;
    ThreadOWantsToEnter = 0;
    OtherStuffZero;
  }
}

void ThreadOne()
{
  while (TRUE) do {
    Thread1WantsToEnter = 1;
    while (ThreadOWantsToEnter) do {
      if (favored == 0) {
        Thread1WantsToEnter = 0;
        while (favored == 0) do {}
        Thread1WantsToEnter = 1;
      }
    }
    CriticalRegionOne;
```

```
        favored = 0;
        Thread1WantsToEnter = 0;
        OtherStuffOne;
    }
}
```

For all the previous attempts, we only had to show that one case led to a dilemma in order to show there was a problem with the algorithm. To show that Dekker's Algorithm gives a correct solution, we must examine all possible interleavings of thread execution and show that each one will lead to a desired outcome. For this algorithm, we can take all of the possible situations between threads and condense them into the four cases listed next. Since the code for each thread is algorithmically the same, we can restrict our analysis to one thread dealing with the status of the other thread and know that the analysis of cases where the roles are reversed will be the same.

Case 1

If there is no conflict for entry into the critical region, Dekker's Algorithm will allow a thread to enter as needed, just as the three previous attempts did. For example, if T0 is ready for access to the critical region, it sets Thread0WantsToEnter to 1 and checks Thread1WantsToEnter. If the desire flag for T1 is 0 (determined by the middle while condition test), T0 skips the body of the middle while loop and enters the critical region.

Case 2a: T0 is the favored thread

For this case, we assume that T1 is executing in the critical region and T0 wishes entry. T0 first sets Thread0WantsToEnter to 1. When it finds that the value of Thread1WantsToEnter is 1, T0 will check the favored toggle. When the value is 0, T0 is the favored thread. T0 will not execute the body of the if statement, but will wait for T1 to exit the critical region and reset its desire flag. After that has happened, T0 will exit the middle while loop and proceed into the critical region. Since Thread0WantsToEnter has been set and remains set while T0 does a spin-wait, T1 will be prevented from entering the critical region until after T0 has taken advantage of the favored status and completes execution in the critical region.

Case 2b: T1 is the favored thread

This case also assumes that T1 is executing in the critical region and T0 wishes entry. T0 first sets Thread0WantsToEnter to 1. When it finds that the value of Thread1WantsToEnter is 1, T0 will then check the favored toggle. When the value is 1, T1 is the favored thread and T0 resets its desire flag before entering the spin-wait loop waiting for T1 to set the favored toggle upon exit from the critical region. Once T0 has exited the spin-wait and set Thread0WantsToEnter to 1, T1 would not be allowed to enter the critical region until T0 has reset its desire flag after taking advantage of the favored status and executed the critical region code.

Case 3

If both threads wish to enter the critical region at the same time, both threads will set their respective desire flags. If T1 is the favored thread, upon entering the middle while loop, T0 will execute the body of the if statement and reset its desire flag. By turning off its own flag, T0 allows T1 (the favored thread) to skip the if statement and exit the middle while loop into the critical region. When it leaves the critical region, T1 sets the favored toggle to 0. T0 may then proceed from the spin-wait on favored and into the critical region when Thread1WantsToEnter has been reset.

What about indefinite postponement?

The fourth solution attempt suffered from indefinite postponement when a thread, having exited the critical region, quickly executed other computations and reentered the critical region before the random delay of the other thread had elapsed. Could T1 keep T0 from entering the critical region? The only way that this can happen is if T1 is allowed to execute and T0 is not. However, this situation violates the fairness criteria of Ben-Ari's concurrent abstraction. Thus, at some point we must allow T0 to execute the next atomic statement. When this next statement is the evaluation of the while conditional expression of (favored == 1), the result will be false and T0 will then break out of the spin-wait and set its desire flag. Once this happens, T1 will not be allowed back into the critical region, since T0 has shown a desire to do so and T1 is not the favored thread. The following interleaving shows one possible execution that demonstrates this.

Current status:

```
Thread0WantsToEnter == 0
Thread1WantsToEnter == 1
favored == 1
T0 was last executing while (favored == 1) do {}
T1 is executing CriticalRegionOne
```

1. T1 exits critical region.

2. T1 sets favored = 0 and resets Thread1WantsToEnter = 0.

3. T1 executes OtherStuffOne.

4. T1 sets Thread1WantsToEnter = 1.

5. T1 tests Thread0WantsToEnter in while conditional.

6. T1 enters critical region.

7. T0 tests favored toggle in while conditional.

8. T0 finds favored == 0.

9. T0 sets Thread0WantsToEnter = 1.

10. T1 exits critical region.

11. T1 sets favored = 0.

12. T1 resets Thread1WantsToEnter = 0.

13. T1 executes OtherStuffOne.

14. T1 sets Thread1WantsToEnter = 1.

15. T1 tests Thread0WantsToEnter and finds T0 wishing to enter the critical region.

16. T1 resets Thread1WantsToEnter = 0.

17. T1 loops in spin-wait until (favored == 1).

18. T0 enters the critical region.

At some point, T0 must be given the chance to resume execution of at least one atomic statement. When T0 is able to execute, it finds the favored toggle has been set in its favor and it can set its desire flag to inform T1 that T0 is ready to enter the critical region. From this interleaving we can conclude that a thread cannot indefinitely postpone another thread from entering the critical region.

What Did You Learn?

Dekker's Algorithm was used here to solve the Critical Section Problem. One of the obvious drawbacks to Dekker's Algorithm is that it is only defined for two threads. Plus, there are better algorithms to solve this problem, such as Lamport's Bakery Algorithm and Peterson's Algorithm. The latter is simpler than Dekker's Algorithm and even has a variation that works for multiple threads. Besides, all threading models and libraries have synchronization objects that can enforce mutual exclusion between any number of threads. Thus, Dekker's Algorithm was not the main point of the preceding exercise.

The point of all of this was to show you how to identify concurrency errors or demonstrate correctness using the concurrency abstraction of Ben-Ari and the interleaving of atomic statement executions between the two threads. I hope that you tried the interleaving analysis on your own for each solution attempt before reading about the faults that each attempt contained. Some of these were subtle, particularly in the starvation case. This is not something that a software tool would be able to identify, and this is why the interleaving analysis is important and can assist you in designing correct concurrent solutions before we ever attempt to alter a line of code.

I'll be using the interleaving analysis during the discussions and implementation of several algorithms in the later chapters of this book. You might want to practice your analysis skills as you cover a new algorithm, especially those codes for which I don't have analysis already.

There Are No Evil Threads, Just Threads Programmed for Evil

It is tempting to anthropomorphize (ascribe human attributes to) threads when trying to determine how they will interact with each other. I do it with both serial and parallel codes and data structures. It can make analysis a little easier to wrap your mind around. Just don't go too far with it. If you start giving them too many human passions and frailties, you could start thinking that a thread will maliciously try to sabotage your application's execution. As with any program, threads will only do what you tell them to do (not necessarily what you want them to do). Don't program evil threads.

Performance Metrics (How Am I Doing?)

Once you have coded an algorithm, you will want to know how well that code will execute. The faster an application runs, the less time a user will need to wait for her results. Also, shorter execution time gives the user the chance to run larger data sets (e.g., a larger number of data records, more pixels, or a bigger physical model) in an acceptable amount of time. For serial applications, you can measure an application's speed using a stopwatch. Simply time the run from start to finish.

After you've made optimizations to the code (for example, rearranged the execution order of statements, used a more efficient memory access scheme, or replaced a critical algorithm with a more efficient one) and rebuilt the application, by simply comparing execution times from the two versions you can see whether there was any serial execution improvement. It is the same with concurrent programs.

The time taken to execute is your paramount concern in developing parallel solutions. When doing comparisons, elapsed time is always the final judge of whether the concurrent code is better than the serial one. If you've taken the time to modify your company's flagship application to run on multiple cores and the execution time is slower than the original, you shouldn't expect too much in the way of a Christmas bonus. However, after reading this book, if you are able to make a positive change to the application and the parallel version runs faster, how can you communicate how much faster your concurrent application now performs (and enhance your bonus prospects)? You could report two execution figures—serial execution time and parallel execution time on the same input data set—to your manager. Managers, being the busy people that they are, will be happier if you give them one number instead of two. One such number that offers a tangible comparison of serial and parallel execution time is *speedup*.

Speedup

Simply stated, speedup is the ratio of serial execution time to parallel execution time. In the past I've seen this ratio expressed as both a percentage and as a multiplier. I prefer stating speedup figures as a multiplier, since using percentages can lead to confusion (and your goal is to make clear to your manager the superiority of your programming skills and accomplishments, not confuse him). For example, if you stated that your parallel execution is 200% faster than the serial code, does it run in half the time of the serial version or one third of the time? Is 105% speedup almost the same time as the serial execution or twice as fast? Is the baseline serial time 0% speedup or 100% speedup? On the other hand, if you said your parallel application had a speedup of 2×, it is clear that it took half the time (i.e., you could have run the parallel version twice in the same time it took the serial code to execute once).

When computing speedup, be sure to use the best serial algorithms and code to compare against. In later chapters, we'll see cases where an inferior serial algorithm is easier to transform into a concurrent version. Even if this is the case, you must use the faster serial algorithm for your speedup calculations. Who would voluntarily use a less-than-stellar serial application when a better one was available? I assume that any big software project you undertake to parallelize will already use the very best serial algorithms available. Even if it doesn't, the best serial code is still the bellwether application version against which your efforts are going to be considered.

Be aware that speedup can (and should) change with the number of cores employed by the application. You can get a feeling for the scalability of your code by noting how the speedup changes as you make more cores available. Examples of speedup performance are graphed in Figure 3-2. Perfect speedup (solid line) occurs when the computed speedup number is equal to the number of cores (e.g., 4× speedup on four cores). For an application that scales well, the speedup should increase at or close to the same rate as the amount of cores employed increases (the dashed line in Figure 3-2). That is, if you double the number of cores, the speedup should double. If your speedup figures fail to keep up (dotted line), your application doesn't scale well on the data sets you have been measuring.

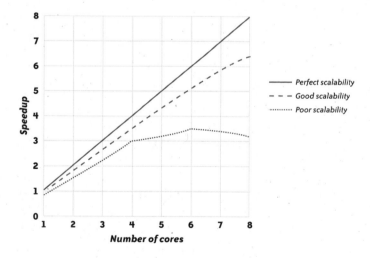

FIGURE 3-2. Example speedup curves

In very rare circumstances, you may find that the speedup of your application exceeds the number of cores. This phenomenon is known as *superlinear speedup*. If you run into this, suspect that you have made some error. First, double-check the timings of both the serial and the concurrent applications. Next, make sure that your applications are performing the desired computations correctly and getting the expected results. Finally, ask yourself whether you are testing your application with a data set whose size is typical, as opposed to one that simply tests specific functionality.

The typical cause for superlinear speedup is that the data set has become small enough per core to fit into local cache. When you ran the serial application, the data had to stream through cache and the processor had to wait while cache lines were fetched. If the data was reused, the cache lines that were evicted previously had to be reread, causing the processor to wait once more. When the data is divided into chunks that all fit into the cache on a core, there is no waiting for reused cache lines once they have all been placed in the cache. Thus, the use of multiple cores can eliminate some of the overhead associated with the serial code executing on a single core. Data sets that are too small—smaller than a typical data set size—can give you a false sense of performance improvement.

Amdahl's Law

Before starting any parallelization project, you may wish to estimate the amount of performance increase (speedup) that you can realize. Without actually writing any concurrent code, you can use Amdahl's Law to give you an upper bound on the speedup you can attempt to achieve. To use Amdahl's Law, you will need to know what percentage of execution will be able to run in parallel and what amount of code must run in serial. Since this is only an estimate, you don't need to have exact figures. If you have an idea about which functions should execute mostly concurrent, you can use a profiler report (from a typical data set) with a breakdown of percentages of execution time per function. Once you have the percentage of parallel execution time and, consequently, serial execution time, just plug the values into the formula.

There are several formulations of Amdahl's Law, but I prefer this one:

$$Speedup \leq \frac{1}{(1 - pctPar) + \dfrac{pctPar}{p}}$$

where *pctPar* is the percentage of execution time that will be run in parallel, and *p* is the number of cores on which to run the parallel application. To compute speedup, the formula has taken the serial execution time and normalized it to 1. The time of the parallel execution is estimated in the denominator to be the percentage of serial time (*1 – pctPar*) and the percentage of execution that can be run in parallel divided by the number of cores to be used (*pctPar/p*). Figure 3-3 shows several speedup curves using this formula on different numbers of cores with varying percentage amounts of parallel execution. Notice that the curve for 75% parallel execution is only approaching 3× speedup at 8 cores.

By arbitrarily increasing the number of cores available, you can lower the amount of execution time required for the parallel sections of your code as much as you want. If we assume infinite numbers of cores are available, the parallel execution time could be essentially zero. With this assumption, Amdahl's Law gives us an upper bound on the speedup we might expect to achieve from the parallelization of a serial application. With zero parallel time, the formula turns into the reciprocal of the serial percentage; thus, 75% parallelism can get no more than 4× speedup (on an infinite number of cores). This illustrates the fact that the speedup of a concurrent application is ultimately dependent on the portion of serial execution. This is why you will want to parallelize as much of the code as possible.

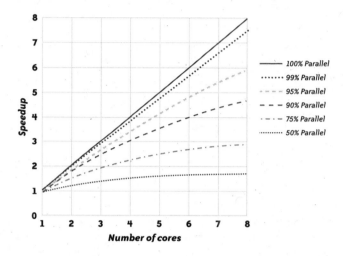

FIGURE 3-3. Estimated speedup curves for different amounts of percentage of parallel execution time using Amdahl's Law

Amdahl's Law has received quite a bit of criticism for the way it ignores real-world circumstances like concurrency overhead (communication, synchronization, and other thread management) and not having processors with infinite numbers of cores available (yet). Other parallel execution models have been proposed that attempt to make reasonable assumptions for the discrepancies in the simple model of Amdahl's Law. Still, for its simplicity and the understanding by the user that this is an upper bound, which is very unlikely to be achieved or surpassed, Amdahl's Law is a pretty good indication of the potential for speedup in a serial application.

Gustafson-Barsis's Law

Besides not taking into account the overheads inherent in concurrent algorithms, one of the strongest criticisms of Amdahl's Law is that as the number of cores increase, the amount of data handled is likely to increase as well. Amdahl's Law assumes a fixed data set size for any and all numbers of cores used. This is reflected in the assumption of the serial percentage remaining the same. But what if you had eight cores and were able to compute a data set that was eight times the size of the original? Does the serial execution time increase? Even if it does, will the time of the serial portion in the concurrent code be the same fraction of overall execution time as it would be if you ran this larger data set using the serial application? Perhaps more to the point, can the larger data set even be run on a single core system?

The Gustafson-Barsis Law, also known as *scaled speedup*, takes into account an increase in the data size in proportion to the increase in the number of cores and computes the (upper bound) speedup of the application, as if the larger data set could be executed in serial. Where Amdahl's Law is a tool for predicting the amount of speedup you could achieve by parallelizing a serial code, Gustafson-Barsis's Law is used to compute the speedup of an existing parallel code. The formula for scaled speedup is:

$$Speedup \leq p + (1 - p)s$$

where *p* is the number of cores, and *s* is the percentage of time the parallel application spends in serial execution for the given data set and number of cores. For example, if the total execution time for a parallel application is 1,040 seconds on 32 cores, but 14 seconds of that time is for serial execution on 1 of those 32 cores, the speedup of this application over the same data set being run on a single thread (if it were possible) is:

$$Speedup \leq 32 + (1 - 32)(0.013) = 32 - 0.403 = 31.597$$

NOTE

Could you have used Amdahl's Law to compute this speedup estimate? If we take the serial execution percentage of 1.3%, the equation for Amdahl's Law yields 22.808 = 1/(0.013 + (0.987/32)). However, this is a false computation, since the percentage of serial time is relative to the parallel time of the 32-core execution, not the potential parallel time.

If you multiply the number of seconds (1,026) for parallel execution on 32 cores, you find that the total amount of work done by the application takes 1,026*32+14 = 32,846 seconds. The nonparallel time (14 seconds) is 0.0426% of that total work time. Using that figure, Amdahl's Law calculates a speedup of 1/(0.000426 + (0.999574/32)) = 31.582.

If you want to see the derivation of the Gustafson-Barsis Law, you can go to John L. Gustafson's original paper, "Reevaluating Amdahl's Law" (*Communications of the ACM*, 1988) or Michael J. Quinn's book, *Parallel Programming in C with MPI and OpenMP* (McGraw-Hill, 2004).

Efficiency

Related to speedup is the metric of *efficiency*. Whereas speedup gives us a metric to determine how much faster our parallel applications are versus their serial brothers, efficiency tells us how well we are utilizing the computational resources of the system. To calculate the efficiency of your parallel execution, take the observed speedup and divide by the number of cores used. This number is then expressed as a percentage.

For example, if you have a 53× speedup on 64 cores, your efficiency is 82.8% (53/64 = 0.828). This means that, on average, over the course of the execution, each of the cores is idle about 17% of the time.

You may be tempted to take this metric and think that if you ran the application on 17% fewer threads and fewer cores, the efficiency would approach 100% without adversely affecting the execution time. This might work, but it really depends on why the application isn't getting full use out of the cores. Using fewer threads means dividing the data into larger chunks, and larger granularity can improve performance. Fewer threads would mean less contention on synchronization objects and less time sitting idle waiting to be given the turn to update shared variables. However, if the threads executing the parallel work are sitting idle waiting for results from the thread running serial portions of the code, you probably won't get any efficiency gain (and will likely see an increase in execution time) from running on fewer threads (cores).

There are just too many causes and effects and different ways that threads running on cores can interact to even begin to generalize what you should expect to happen if you increase or decrease the number of threads running the application. You'll just have to try a few different situations for your application, take the measurements, and interpret the results with your knowledge of how the application works and how it was threaded.

One Final Note on Speedup and Efficiency

Throughout this discussion of metrics, I assume that you are using one thread per core. If your application overloads the system with more threads than cores, you need to use the number of threads (in place of "cores") in all the previous formulas. There can be performance benefits (though usually minor) when you overload the system with threads. Of course, Intel processors with Hyper-Threading (HT) technology are designed to support multiple threads per core.

Your measurements of speedup and efficiency will tell you whether the utilization of more threads than cores is worthwhile. If your execution time remains almost the same with two threads per core and no change in the data set, your speedup will also stay about the same. Your efficiency will be halved, though. This is telling you that even if the physical cores are cranking at nearly 100%, the threads are only being used half the time (where threads may have been nearly fully utilized when there was only one thread per core). If hardware utilization is more important to you, and the execution time is not suffering, not having all threads as busy as possible may not be a detriment.

Review of the Evolution for Supporting Parallelism in Hardware

The following paragraphs take a roughly chronological tour of processor and platform innovations that have led us to multicore processors. Being a self-described "software guy," I tend to drift off when programming books or presentations go on about hardware details for long. So, I won't take much time to cover this topic. It won't hurt my feelings if you skip it.

While it does nothing expressly parallel, out-of-order execution allows processors to execute instructions whose arguments are ready to be used regardless of where the instructions were within the serial code. After the execution, a reordering buffer "retires" instructions in the order in which they were originally written. All of this was built into the hardware of processors to get faster execution of instructions. The foundation for data flow parallelism is the idea of initiating execution of instructions based on the readiness of arguments, rather than on sequential order.

Multiple execution units launch two or more instructions at the same time, if those instruction's arguments are ready for use. Execution units are typically designed for specific types of instructions, such as integer or floating-point computation, memory access, or conditional expression evaluation. Intel HT Technology took advantage of the fact that not all execution units within a serial processor would be used at the same time. If a thread didn't have any integer computations available, the operating system scheduler was free to allow another thread that did have a pending integer computation to use the free integer execution units. To the system and the user, HT appeared as a second "logical" processor in the system.

Streaming SIMD Execution (SSE) technology adds special registers to the processor that hold multiple data elements at the same time. The multiple items are used in a single computation via a single instruction and in the time it takes to execute that instruction. Each item in the register, of course, is used in the same operation. For example, with a four-wide SSE register set, you can load four integers into one SSE register, another four integers into another SSE register, and add the two registers together storing the corresponding four results into a third SSE register. This type of execution is also known as *vector parallelism.*

Symmetric multiprocessing (SMP) allows you to install multiple physical processors (chips) onto a motherboard, which are then able to share memory and other system resources. Multiple threads from a single process can be executed on the multiple processors. A thread will have exclusive access to the cache available on the processor in which it is executing, as well as the shared memory of the platform. SMP is more of a support feature of platforms and operating systems than it is a processor technology.

Most recently, multicore processors have been rolled out with multiple processors built into the chip. Increasing the speed of the clock that drives execution of instructions within the processor requires higher power consumption and the generation of more excess heat from the chips. If clock speeds had continued at the pace of doubling every 18 months or so, it was hypothesized that the heat generated by processors would have approached that of a rocket exhaust—clearly not a sustainable path to better and better performance. So, rather than increase the speed of the processor's clock, the extra chip real estate that has come from further miniaturization of processor components has been devoted to installing additional processors. Thus, lowering the clock speed and adding a second processor core lowers both the amount of heat produced and the power required to run the multiple cores overall. It also provides a path to keep increasing application performance, and that path to future performance goes through concurrent programming and parallel execution.

CHAPTER FOUR

Eight Simple Rules for Designing
Multithreaded Applications

SINCE IT IS RIGHT THERE IN THE TITLE OF THIS BOOK, THE FOLLOWING SENTENCE shouldn't come as any surprise: *Concurrent programming is still more art than science*. This chapter gives eight simple rules that you can add to your toolkit of threading design methods. I've tried to organize the rules in a semichronological way, but there's no hard and fast order to the rules. It's like being confronted with, "No running by the pool," and, "No diving in the shallow end." Both good ideas, but not diving can come before not running or vice versa.

By following these rules, you will have more success in writing the best and most efficient threaded implementation of your applications. You may recognize some of these, since I've mentioned a few of them in previous chapters. In upcoming chapters, when discussing the design and implementation of specific algorithms, I'll try to drop in a relevant reference to one or more of these eight rules to show that they're not just here to fill out an extra chapter.

Rule 1: Identify Truly Independent Computations

I've already covered this first rule seven ways to Sunday, but since it's the crux of the whole matter, it bears repeating at least one more time. You can't execute anything concurrently unless the operations that would be executed can be run independently of each other. I can easily think of different real-world instances of independent actions being performed to satisfy a single goal. Consider, for example, a DVD rental warehouse. Orders for movies are collected and then distributed to the workers, who go out to where all the disks are stored and find copies to satisfy their assigned orders. When one worker pulls out a classic musical comedy, it does not interfere with another worker who is looking for the latest science fiction masterpiece, nor will it interfere with a worker trying to locate episodes from the second season of a popular crime drama series (I assume that any conflicts resulting from unavailable inventory have been dealt with before orders were transmitted to the warehouse). Also, the packaging and mailing of each order will not interfere with disk searches or the shipping and handling of any other order.

There are cases in which you will have exclusively sequential computations that cannot be made concurrent; many of these will be dependencies between loop iterations or steps that must be carried out in a specific order. A list of common situations was covered earlier in "What's Not Parallel" on page 42.

Rule 2: Implement Concurrency at the Highest Level Possible

There are two directions you can take when approaching the threading of a serial code. These are *bottom-up* and *top-down*. When initially analyzing your code, you are looking for the computational hotspots that account for the most execution time. Running those portions in parallel will give you the best chance of achieving the maximum performance possible.

In a bottom-up approach, you consider threading the hotspots in your code directly. If this is not possible, search up the call stack of the application to determine whether there is another place in the code that can execute the hotspots in parallel. If your hotspot is the innermost loop of a nested loop structure, examine each successive layer of loop nesting, from the innermost to the outermost, to see whether that level can be made concurrent. Even if it is possible to employ concurrency at the hotspot code, you should still look to see whether it would be possible to implement that concurrency at a point in the code higher up in the call stack. This can increase the granularity of the execution done by each thread.

To illustrate this rule, consider threading a video encoding application. If your hotspot is the computation of individual pixels, you can look to parallelize the loop(s) that deal with each pixel computation within a single frame of video. Looking further "up" from this, you might find that the loop over the frames of video can be executed concurrently by independently processing groups of frames. If the video encoding application is expected to process multiple videos, expressing your concurrency by assigning a different stream to each thread will be the highest level of possible concurrency.

The other approach to threading is top-down, where you first consider the whole application and what the computation is coded to accomplish (all the parts of the application that combine to realize that computation). While there is no obvious concurrency, distill the parts of the computation that still contain execution of the hotspot into successively smaller parts until you can identify independent computations.

For the video encoding application, if your hotspot is the computation of individual pixels, the top-down approach would first consider that the application handles encoding of multiple, independent video streams (which all include the pixel computations). If you can parallelize the application there, you've found your highest level. If not, working "down" to the individual pixel will take you through frames within a single stream and then to pixels within a frame.

The objective of this rule is to find the highest level where concurrency can be implemented so that your hotspot of code will be executed concurrently. This is all predicated on the belief that "higher" levels in the layers of your algorithms will equal more (independent) work, much like the way that layers of a parfait accumulate mass the higher up in the glass you go. Placing concurrency at the highest possible level around a hotspot is one of the best ways to achieve that all-important coarse-grained division of work to be assigned to threads.

Rule 3: Plan Early for Scalability to Take Advantage of Increasing Numbers of Cores

As I'm writing this, quad-core processors are becoming the default multicore chip. The number of cores available in future processors will only increase. Thus, you should plan for such processor increases within your software. *Scalability* is the measure of an application's ability to handle changes, typically increases, in system resources (e.g., number of cores, memory size, bus speed) or data set sizes. In the face of more cores being available, you must write flexible code that can take advantage of different numbers of cores.

To paraphrase C. Northcote Parkinson, "Data expands to fill the processing power available." This means that as the amount of computational power increases (more cores), the more likely it will be that the data to be processed will expand. There are always more computations to be done. Whether it is increasing the model fidelity in scientific simulations, processing an HD stream instead of standard video, or searching through multiple and larger databases, if you are given additional processing resources, someone will always have more data to process.

Designing and implementing concurrency by data decomposition methods will give you more scalable solutions. Task decomposition solutions will suffer from the fact that the number of independent functions or code segments in an application is likely limited and fixed during execution. After each independent task has a thread and core to execute on, increasing the number of threads to take advantage of more cores will not increase performance of the application. Since data sizes are more likely to increase than the number of independent computations in an application, data decomposition designs will have the best chance for scalability.

Even though an application has been written with threads assigned to independent functions, when the input workload increases, you may still be able to utilize more threads. Consider building a grocery store where there are a finite number of separate tasks to be done. If the developer buys adjacent land and the floor space of the store to be built is doubled, you can expect extra workers to be assigned within some of those tasks. That is, extra painters, extra roofers, extra floor tilers, and extra electricians can be used. Therefore, you should be aware of the data decomposition possibilities that can arise from increased data sets, even within solutions that have been decomposed by tasks, and plan for the use of extra threads on extra cores.

Rule 4: Make Use of Thread-Safe Libraries Wherever Possible

If your hotspot computations can be executed through a library call, you should strongly consider using an equivalent library function instead of executing handwritten code. Even for serial applications, it's never a good idea to "reinvent the wheel" by writing code that performs calculations already encapsulated by optimized library routines. Many libraries, such as the Intel Math Kernel Library (MKL) and Intel Integrated Performance Primitives (IPP), have functions that are threaded to take advantage of multicore processors.

Even more important than using threaded library routines, though, is ensuring that all library calls used are thread-safe. If you have replaced the hotspot in your serial code with a call to a library function, it may still be the case that some point higher in the call tree of your application can be divided into independent computations. When you have concurrent computations executing library function calls, especially third-party libraries, routines that reference and update shared variables within the library may cause data races. Check the library documentation for the thread-safety of any library you are using within concurrent execution. When writing and using your own library routines that will be executed concurrently, be sure the routines are reentrant. If this is not possible, you will need to add synchronization in order to protect access to shared resources.

Rule 5: Use the Right Threading Model

If threaded libraries are insufficient to cover all the concurrency of an application and you must employ user-controlled threads, don't use explicit threads if an implicit threading model (e.g., OpenMP or Intel Threading Building Blocks) has all the functionality you need. Explicit threads do allow for finer control of the threading implementation. However, if you are only parallelizing compute-intensive loops or don't need the extra flexibility you can get with explicit threads, there's probably no reason to do more work than necessary. The more complex the implementation, the easier it will be to make a mistake and the harder it will be to maintain such code later.

OpenMP is focused on data decomposition methods, especially targeted to threading loops that range over large data sets. Even if this is the only type of parallelism that you can introduce into an application, there may be external requirements (such as engineering practices dictated by your employer or management preferences) that will prohibit your use of OpenMP. In that case, you will need to implement your threading with an approved (explicit) model. In such a situation, I recommend that you use OpenMP to prototype the planned concurrency and estimate the potential performance gains, possible scalability, and how much effort will be needed to thread the serial code with explicit threads.

Rule 6: Never Assume a Particular Order of Execution

With serial computations, it is easy to predict the statement that will be executed following any other statement in a program. On the other hand, execution order of threads is *nondeterministic* and controlled by the OS scheduler. This means that there is no reliable way of predicting the order of threads running from one execution to another, or even which thread will be scheduled to run next. This is done primarily to hide execution latency within an application, especially when run on a system with fewer cores than threads. If a thread blocks because it needs memory that is not located in cache or to process an I/O request, the scheduler will swap out the blocked thread and swap in a thread that is ready to run.

Data races are a direct result of this scheduling nondeterminism. If you assume that one thread will write a value into a shared variable before another thread will read that value, you may be right all of the time, you may be right some of the time, or you may be right none of the time. Sometimes, if you're lucky, the order of thread execution remains unchanged on a specific platform each and every time you run an application. Every difference between systems (bit locations on the disk or memory speed or frequency of the AC power coming out of the wall sockets) has the potential to alter the thread schedule. Code that relies on a particular order of execution among threads that is enforced through nothing more than positive thinking may be plagued by problems such as data races and deadlock.

From a performance perspective, it is best to allow threads to run as unencumbered as possible, like greyhounds or thoroughbreds in a race. Don't try to enforce a particular order of execution unless it is absolutely necessary. You need to recognize those times when it is absolutely necessary, and implement some form of synchronization to coordinate the execution order of threads relative to each other.

Consider a relay race team. The first runner starts off running as fast as possible. However, to successfully complete the race, the second, third, and anchor runners must wait to receive the baton before they can begin to run their assigned portions of the race. The baton passing is a synchronization between consecutive runners that controls the order of "execution" between stages in the race.

Rule 7: Use Thread-Local Storage Whenever Possible or Associate Locks to Specific Data

Synchronization is overhead that does not contribute to the furtherance of the computation, except to guarantee the correct answers are produced from the parallel execution of an application. Synchronization is a necessary evil. Even so, you should actively seek to keep the amount of synchronization to a minimum. You can do this by using storage that is local to threads or using exclusive memory locations (such as an array element indexed by thread ID).

Temporary work variables are rarely shared between threads, and should be declared or allocated locally to each thread. Variables that hold partial results for each thread should also be local to threads. Combining the partial results into a shared location will require some synchronization. Ensuring that the shared updates are done as infrequently as possible will keep the amount of overhead to a minimum. If you are using explicit threads, you can use the available thread-local storage APIs to enable the persistence of data local to threads from one threaded region to another or from one threaded function call to the next execution of the same function.

If local storage for each thread is not a valid option and you must coordinate access to shared resources through synchronization objects (such as a lock), be sure to properly associate (or "attach") locks to data items. The easiest way to do this is to have a one to one (1:1) relationship of locks to data items. If you have multiple shared variables that are always accessed together, use a single lock to allow exclusive access to all critical regions involving these variables. In later chapters, I'll discuss some of the tradeoffs and alternative synchronization techniques that you can employ, especially if you have to protect access to a large collection of data (for example, an array of 10,000 items).

However you decide to associate locks with data items, never associate more than one lock to a single data object. Segal's Law states, "A man with a watch knows what time it is. A man with two watches is never sure." If two different lock objects—say, lockA and lockB—protect access to the same variable, one part of the code may use lockA for access while another section of code can use lockB. Threads executing in these two code portions will create a data race, since each will assume it has exclusive access to the contested data.

Rule 8: Dare to Change the Algorithm for a Better Chance of Concurrency

For comparing performance of applications, both serial and concurrent, the bottom line is wall clock execution time. When choosing between two or more algorithms, programmers may rely on the asymptotic order of execution. This metric will almost always correlate with an application's relative performance to another. That is, with everything else held constant, an application that uses an $O(n \log n)$ algorithm (like Quicksort) will run faster than an $O(n^2)$ algorithm (such as selection sort) and will generate the same results.

In concurrent applications, algorithms with a better asymptotic order of execution will run faster, too. Nonetheless, there will be times when the best serial algorithm will not be amenable to parallelization. If you cannot easily turn a hotspot into threaded code (and you can't find a point higher in the call stack of the hotspot that can be made concurrent), you should consider using a suboptimal serial algorithm to transform, rather than the algorithm currently in the code.

For example, consider the linear algebra operation for the multiplication of two square matrixes. Strassen's Algorithm has one of the best asymptotic orders of execution, $O(n^{2.81})$. This is better than the $O(n^3)$ of the traditional triple-nested loop algorithm. Strassen's method divides up each of the matrixes into four chunks (or submatrixes) and uses seven recursive calls to multiply the n/2 × n/2 submatrixes. To parallelize these recursive calls, you could create a new thread to execute each of the seven independent submatrix multiplications. The number of threads will increase exponentially (much like the wives, sacks, cats, and kittens coming from St. Ives). As the submatrixes get smaller and smaller, the granularity of the assigned work given to a newly created thread will get finer and finer. When the submatrixes achieve a given size, switch to a serial algorithm.

A much easier means to parallelize matrix multiplication is to use the asymptotically inferior triple-nested loop algorithm. There are several ways to perform a data decomposition on the matrixes (divide by rows, divide by columns, or divide by blocks) and assign the necessary computations to threads. You can do this using OpenMP pragmas at one of the loop levels or by using explicit threads that implement the division of the loop indexes as needed. Less code modification is required for the simpler serial algorithm, and the structure of the code would likely be left more intact than it would be if you attempted to thread Strassen's Algorithm. Better yet, follow Simple Rule 4 and use a concurrent library function that performs the matrix-matrix multiplication.

Summary

I've given you eight simple rules that you should keep in mind when designing the threading that will transform a serial application into a concurrent version. By following the rules presented here, I've been able to more easily create concurrent solutions that are more robust, less likely to contain threading problems, and that move toward optimal performance with less development time. I'm sure you will, too.

CHAPTER FIVE

Threading Libraries

THIS CHAPTER WILL REVIEW SOME OF THE DETAILS OF THE THREADING LIBRARIES used in subsequent chapters to implement the algorithms. I am assuming that you are already familiar with at least one of these threading methods. I'm not expecting proficiency, but I hope you've at least tried some coding examples when you first looked at learning how to write threaded code.

If you are unfamiliar with any of the threading libraries I've used here, this chapter should provide you with enough details to understand the algorithms implemented with such a library and any library-specific features that are used. (If you want more details, find one of the fine reference texts or an online tutorial.) Otherwise, this should be a review. If you're chomping at the bit to get into the algorithm design parts of the book, you can skip over this chapter for now and come back when you might have a question about syntax or threading.

Implicit Threading

Implicit threading libraries take care of much of the minutiae needed to create, manage, and (to some extent) synchronize threads. All the little niggly details are hidden from programmers to make concurrent programming easier to implement and understand. Of course, by not allowing (forcing?) you to deal with these details, the expressiveness and flexibility of implicit threading libraries are not as great as you might find with explicit threading. However, a majority of algorithms that can be written concurrently can take advantage of the limited scope of features within the implicit libraries.

The two libraries that are covered in this section approach concurrent programming differently. OpenMP implements concurrency through special pragmas and directives inserted into your source code to indicate segments that are to be executed concurrently. These pragmas are recognized and processed by the compiler. Intel TBB uses defined parallel algorithms to execute methods within user-written classes that encapsulate the concurrent operations.

OpenMP

OpenMP is a set of compiler directives, library routines, and environment variables that specify shared-memory concurrency in FORTRAN, C, and C++ programs. The OpenMP Architecture Review Board (ARB), which oversees the specification of OpenMP, is made up of members from many different commercial and academic institutions. The rationale behind the development of OpenMP was to create a portable and unified standard of shared-memory parallelism. OpenMP was first introduced in November 1997 with a specification for FORTRAN, and in the following year, a specification for C/C++ was released. As of this writing, the current OpenMP specification is version 3.0, released in May 2008.

All major compilers support the OpenMP language. This includes the Microsoft Visual C/C++ .NET for Windows and the GNU GCC compiler for Linux. The Intel C/C++ compilers, for both Windows and Linux, also support OpenMP.

OpenMP directives demarcate code that can be executed in parallel (called *parallel regions*) and control how code is assigned to threads. The threads in an OpenMP code operate under the fork-join model. When the main thread encounters a parallel region while executing the application, a team of threads is forked off, and these threads begin executing the code within the parallel region. At the end of the parallel region, the threads within the team wait until all other threads in the team have finished before being "joined." The main thread resumes serial execution with the statement following the parallel region. The implicit barrier at the end of all parallel regions (and most other constructs defined by OpenMP) preserves sequential consistency.

> **NOTE**
>
> Due to the high overhead of creating and destroying threads, quality compilers will create the team of threads when the first parallel region is encountered and will then simply put the team to sleep at the join operation and wake the threads for subsequent forks.

For C/C++, OpenMP uses pragmas as directives. All OpenMP pragmas have the same prefix of `#pragma omp`. This is followed by an OpenMP construct and one or more optional clauses to modify the construct. To define a parallel region within an application, use the `parallel` construct:

```
#pragma omp parallel
```

This pragma will be followed by a single statement or block of code enclosed with curly braces. When the application encounters this statement during execution, it will fork a team of threads, execute all of the statements within the parallel region on each thread, and join the threads after the last statement in the region.

In many applications, a large number of independent operations are found in loops. Using the loop worksharing construct in OpenMP, you can split up these loop iterations and assign them to threads for concurrent execution. The `parallel for` construct will initiate a new parallel region around the single `for` loop following the pragma and divide the loop iterations among the threads of the team. Upon completion of the assigned iterations, threads sit at the implicit barrier at the end of the parallel region waiting to join with the other threads.

It is possible to split up the combined `parallel for` construct into two pragmas: a `parallel` construct and the `for` construct, which must be lexically contained within a parallel region. Use this separation when there is parallel work for the thread team other than the iterations of the loop. You can also attach a `schedule` clause to the loop worksharing construct to control how iterations are assigned to threads. The `static` schedule will divide iterations into blocks and distribute the blocks among threads before the loop iterations begin execution; round robin scheduling is used if there are more blocks than threads. The `dynamic` schedule will assign one block of iterations per thread in the team; as threads finish the previous set of iterations, a new block is assigned until all blocks have been distributed. There is an optional chunk argument for both `static` and `dynamic` scheduling that controls the number of iterations per block.

By default, almost all variables in an OpenMP threaded program are shared between threads. The exceptions to this shared access rule are: the loop index variable associated with a loop worksharing construct (each thread must have its own copy in order to correctly iterate through the assigned set of iterations); variables declared within a parallel region or declared within a function that is called from within a parallel region; and any other variable that is placed on the thread's stack (e.g., function parameters). If you use nested loops within a loop worksharing construct in C/C++, only the loop index variable immediately succeeding the construct will automatically be made private. If other variables must be local to threads, such as the loop index variables for nested loops, add a `private` clause to the relevant construct. A local copy of the variables in the list will be allocated for each thread. The initial value of variables that are listed within the `private` clause will be undefined, and you must assign value to them before they are read within the region of use. OpenMP has synchronization constructs that ensure mutual exclusion to your critical regions. Use these when variables must remain shared by all threads, but updates must be performed on those variables in parallel regions. The `critical` construct acts like a lock around a critical region. Only one thread may execute within a protected critical region at a time. Other threads wishing to have access to the critical region must wait until no thread is executing the critical region.

OpenMP also has an `atomic` construct to ensure that statements will be executed in an atomic, uninterruptible manner. There is a restriction on which types of statements you can use with the `atomic` construct, and you can only protect a single statement. The `single` and `master` constructs will control execution of statements within a parallel region so that only one thread will execute those statements (as opposed to allowing only one thread at a time). The former will use the first thread that encounters the construct, while the latter will allow only the master thread (the thread that executes outside of the parallel regions) to execute the protected code.

A common computation is to summarize or reduce a large collection of data to a single value. For example, this may include the sum of the data items or the maximum or minimum of the data set. The algorithm to do such computations has a dependence on the shared variable used to collect the partial and final answers. OpenMP provides a clause to handle the details of a concurrent reduction. The `reduction` clause requires associative and commutative operations for combining data, as well as a list of reduction variables. Each thread within the parallel team will receive a private copy of the reduction variables to use when executing the assigned computations. Unlike variables contained in a private clause, these private variables are initialized with a value that depends on the reduction operation. At the end of the region with a `reduction` clause, all local copies are combined using the operation noted in the clause, and the result is stored in the shared copy of the variable.

The code in Example 5-1 is almost the same code given in Example 2-2. The application computes an approximation of the value for pi using numerical integration and the midpoint rectangle rule. The code divides the integration range into num_rect intervals and computes the functional value of $4.0/(1+x^2)$ for the midpoint of each interval (rectangle). The functional values (height) are summed up and multiplied by the width of the intervals in order to approximate the area under the curve of the function.

EXAMPLE 5-1. Computing pi with numerical integration using OpenMP

```
static long num_rects = 1000000;

int main(int argc, char* argv[])
{
  double mid, height, width, sum=0.0;
  int i;
  double area;

  width = 1./(double)num_rects;

#pragma omp parallel for private(mid, height) reduction(+:sum)
  for (i=0; i<num_rects; i++) {
    mid = (i + 0.5)*width;
    height = 4.0/(1.+ mid*mid);
    sum += height;
  }

  area = width * sum;
  printf("The value of PI is %f\n",area);
  return 0;
}
```

The difference in the current example is that an OpenMP loop worksharing construct has been added. The OpenMP-compliant compiler will insert code to spawn a team of threads, give a private copy of the mid, height, and i variables to each thread; divide up the iterations of the loop between the threads; and finally, when the threads are done with the assigned computations, combine the values stored in the local copies of sum into the shared version. This shared copy of sum will be used to compute the pi approximation when multiplied by the width of the intervals.

A new feature in OpenMP 3.0 is task concurrency, enabled through the use of the task construct. The task construct must be within a parallel region, and creates an assignable task from the associated block of code. Upon encountering a task construct, a thread may execute the task immediately or defer execution. If the task execution is deferred, any thread within the team may execute the task. You can use task synchronization constructs to ensure that previously created tasks have completed.

The OpenMP specification includes a set of environment variables and API functions to give the programmer more control over how the application will execute. Perhaps the most useful environment variable is OMP_NUM_THREADS, which will set the number of threads to be used for the team in each parallel region. The corresponding API function to set the number of threads is omp_set_num_threads(). This function takes an integer parameter and will use that number of threads in the team for the next parallel region encountered. If neither of these methods is used to set the number of threads within a team, the default number will be used. This default is implementation-dependent, but will most likely be the number of cores available on the system at runtime.

The OpenMP specification contains many more directives, environment variables, and API. Consult the specification document for full details at *http://www.openmp.org*.

Intel Threading Building Blocks

Intel TBB is a C++ template-based library for loop-level parallelism that concentrates on defining tasks rather than explicit threads. The components of TBB include generic parallel algorithms, concurrent containers, low-level synchronization primitives, and a task scheduler. TBB is available in both commercial and open source versions. At the time of this writing, TBB 2.1 is the most recent version.

Programmers using TBB can parallelize the execution of loop iterations by treating chunks of iterations as tasks and allowing the TBB task scheduler to determine the task sizes, number of threads to use, assignment of tasks to those threads, and how those threads are scheduled for execution. The task scheduler will give precedence to tasks that have been most recently in a core with the idea of making best use of the cache that likely contains the task's data. The task scheduler utilizes a task-stealing mechanism to load balance the execution.

The `parallel_for` template parallelizes tasks that are contained within a `for` loop. The template requires two parameters: a range type over which to iterate and a body type that executes iterations over the range or a subrange. The range class must define a copy constructor and a destructor, the methods `is_empty()` (which returns TRUE if the range is empty) and `is_divisible()` (which returns TRUE if the range can be split), and a splitting constructor (to divide the range in half). A partitioner class object can be used to heuristically find the smallest number of iterations that should be assigned. The TBB library contains two predefined range types: `blocked_range` and `blocked_range2D`. These ranges are used for single- and two-dimensional ranges, respectively.

The body class must define a copy constructor and a destructor as well as the `operator()`. The `operator()` will contain a copy of the original serial loop that has been modified to run over a subrange of values that come from the range type.

The `parallel_reduce` template will iterate over a range and combine partial results computed by each task into a final (reduction) value. The range type for `parallel_reduce` has the same requirements as `parallel_for`. The body type needs a splitting constructor and a `join` method. The splitting constructor in the body copies read-only data required to run the loop body and to assign the identity element of the reduction operation that initializes the reduction variable. The `join` method combines partial results of tasks based on the reduction operation being used.

Other generic parallel algorithms included in the TBB library are:

- `parallel_do`, which executes independent loop iterations with unknown or dynamically changing bounds

- `parallel_scan`, which computes the parallel prefix of a data set
- `pipeline`, for data-flow pipeline patterns
- `parallel_sort`, an iterative version of Quicksort that has been parallelized

Intel TBB also defines concurrent containers for hash tables, vectors, and queues. The C++ STL containers are not thread-safe. The TBB containers are designed for safe use with multiple threads attempting concurrent access to the containers. Not only can you use these containers in conjunction with the TBB parallel algorithms, but you can also use them within concurrent codes implemented with other threading libraries.

Mutex objects, on which a thread can obtain a lock and enforce mutual exclusion on critical code regions, are available within TBB. There are several different types of mutexes. A `spin_mutex` object will put a thread requesting a lock on the mutex into a spin-wait loop until the mutex is available. A `queuing_mutex` object is scalable, which means it tends to take the same amount of time regardless of the number of threads. It is also fair, meaning that it will block a thread until the mutex is available (`spin_mutex` does not have these properties). There are also readers/writer lock versions of these two mutex types. The other type of synchronization that TBB supports is atomic operations. Besides a small set of simple operators, there are atomic methods `fetch_and_store` (update with given value and return original), `fetch_and_add` (increment by given value and return original), and `compare_and_swap` (if current value equals second value, update with first; always return original value).

The code in Example 5-2 is the TBB version of the midpoint rectangle rule for numerical integration. The computation of the heights and areas is encapsulated in the `MyPi` class and implemented in the `operator()`.

EXAMPLE 5-2. Computing pi with numerical integration using Intel TBB

```
#include <stdio.h>

#include "tbb/parallel_reduce.h"
#include "tbb/task_scheduler_init.h"
#include "tbb/blocked_range.h"
#include "tbb/partitioner.h"

using namespace std;
using namespace tbb;

static long num_rects = 100000;

class MyPi {
  double *const my_rects;

public:
  double partialHeight;

  MyPi(double *const width) : my_rects(width), partialHeight(0) {}

  MyPi(MyPi& x, split) : my_rects(x.my_rects), partialHeight(0) {}
```

```
    void operator()(const blocked_range<size_t>& r) {
      double rectangleWidth = *my_rects;
      double x;
      for (size_t i = r.begin(); i != r.end(); ++i) {
        x = (i + 0.5) * rectangleWidth;
        partialHeight += 4.0/(1.+ x*x);
      }
    }

    void join(const MyPi& y) {partialHeight += y.partialHeight;}
};

int main(int argc, char* argv[])
{
  double area;
  double width = 1./(double)num_rects;
  MyPi my_block((double *const)&width);
  task_scheduler_init init;

  parallel_reduce(blocked_range<size_t>(0,num_rects), my_block, auto_partitioner());
  area = my_block.partialHeight * width;

  printf("The value of PI is %f\n",area);
  return 0;
}
```

This example uses the parallel_reduce algorithm to launch threads and compute the numerical integration. The task scheduler breaks up the iteration range into smaller chunks. The chunk of loop iterations is considered a separate task that can be executed by a thread. Once the local partialHeight variables calculated within each task are added together through the join method, the final sum of heights is multiplied by the width and the computed approximation to pi is printed.

> **NOTE**
>
> Lambda functions in the planned C++0x standard make writing and using many TBB algorithms easier, since you don't need to write whole class definitions as in Example 5-2. Since the new C++ standard was not finalized at the time this book went to press and there was sparse support in compilers, the TBB examples in upcoming chapters will fall back on the "old" ways and define new classes to encapsulate code for tasks. If you have a compiler that supports lambda functions, you can try rewriting the examples given here with them.

Explicit Threading

Explicit threading libraries require the programmer to control all aspects of threads, including creating threads, associating threads to functions, and synchronizing and controlling the interactions between threads and shared resources. The two most prominent threading libraries in use today are POSIX threads (Pthreads) and Windows Threads by Microsoft. While the syntax is different between the two APIs, most of the functionality in one model can be found in the other. Each model can create and join threads, and each features synchronization objects to coordinate execution between threads and control the access to shared resources by multiple threads executing concurrently. Let's start with Pthreads for readers who use Linux.

Pthreads

Pthreads has a thread container data type of `pthread_t`. Objects of this type are used to reference the thread (borrowing terms from Windows Threads, I tend to call this object the *handle* of the created thread). To create a thread and associate it with a function for execution, use the `pthread_create()` function. A `pthread_t` handle is returned through the parameter list. When one thread needs to be sure that some other thread has terminated before proceeding with execution, it calls `pthread_join()`. The calling thread uses the handle of the thread to be waited on as a parameter to this function. If the thread of interest has terminated prior to the call, `pthread_join()` returns immediately with the threaded function's exit code (if any) from the terminated thread; otherwise, the calling thread is blocked until that currently executing thread has completed.

The two synchronization objects most commonly used with Pthreads are the mutex (`pthread_mutex_t`) and the condition variable (`pthread_cond_t`). You must first initialize instances of these objects before you can use them within a program. Besides providing functions to do this initialization, the Pthreads library includes defined constants that you can use for default static initialization when objects are declared. Only one thread at a time can hold a mutex object. Threads request the privilege of holding a mutex by calling `pthread_lock()`. Other threads attempting to gain control of the mutex will be blocked until the thread that is holding the lock calls `pthread_unlock()`.

Condition variables are associated (through programming logic) with an arbitrary conditional expression and signal threads when the status of the condition under consideration may have changed. Threads block and wait on a condition variable to be signaled when calling `pthread_cond_wait()` on a given condition variable. A mutex object is always coupled with a condition variable. This mutex protects the shared variables involved in the conditional expression associated with the condition variable. When `pthread_cond_wait()` is called, the mutex is unlocked and made available to another thread.

At some point in the execution, when the status of the condition may have changed, an executing thread calls `pthread_cond_signal()` on a condition variable to wake up a thread that has been blocked. A thread that receives the signal will return from the `pthread_cond_wait()` only after the thread has been given control of the related mutex. Upon that return, the thread should first check the state of the conditional expression and either return to waiting on the condition variable (condition is not met) or proceed with execution. Signals to condition variables do not persist. Thus, if there is no thread waiting on a condition variable when it is signaled, that signal is discarded. The pthread_cond_broadcast() function will wake all threads that are waiting on the condition variable.

The code in Example 5-3 is the Pthreads version of the midpoint rectangle rule for numerical integration. The computation of the heights and areas is encapsulated in the function threadFunction(). When created, each of the four threads (NUM_THREADS) begins execution on this function.

EXAMPLE 5-3. Computing pi with numerical integration using Pthreads

```c
#include <stdio.h>
#include <pthread.h>

#define NUM_RECTS 1000000
#define NUM_THREADS 4

double gArea = 0.0;
pthread_mutex_t gLock;

void *threadFunction(void *pArg)
{
  int myNum = *((int *)pArg);
  double partialHeight = 0.0, lWidth = 1.0 / NUM_RECTS, x;

  for (int i = myNum; i < NUM_RECTS; i += NUM_THREADS)
  {
    x = (i + 0.5f) / NUM_RECTS;
    partialHeight += 4.0f / (1.0f + x*x);
  }

  pthread_mutex_lock(&gLock);
   gArea += partialHeight * lWidth;
  pthread_mutex_unlock(&gLock);
}

void main()
{
  pthread_t tHandles[NUM_THREADS];
  int tNum[NUM_THREADS];

  pthread_mutex_init(&gLock, NULL);
  for (int i = 0; i < NUM_THREADS; i++ ) {
    tNum[i] = i;
    pthread_create(&tHandles[i], NULL, threadFunction,(void *)&tNum[i]);
  }

  for ( int j=0; j<NUM_THREADS; ++j ) {
    pthread_join(tHandles[j], NULL);
  }

  pthread_mutex_destroy(&gLock);
  printf("Computed value of Pi: %f\n", gArea);
}
```

The main() routine in this example spawns four threads to divide up the loop iterations of the area computation. A thread ID number is assigned to each thread through the single parameter to threadFunction(). This number determines which threads execute which iterations of the loop. Each thread has a private copy of partialHeights to store the results of assigned iterations. The shared variable, gArea, is updated within a critical region protected by the gLock mutex. Back in the main() routine, the process thread waits for all the worker threads to complete execution, calling pthread_join() with each handle, before printing the computed area held in gArea.

Windows Threads

Windows Threads uses the ubiquitous kernel object HANDLE type for the handle of a thread. The _beginthreadex() function is recommended for creating a thread, especially if the code will be using the C runtime library. The return value of this function will need to be cast to HANDLE. The alternate CreateThread() function returns the HANDLE of a spawned thread. These two functions have the exact same set of parameters, but the former is safer to use with regard to initialization of thread resources and more reliable in the reclamation of allocated resources at thread termination.

To make one thread wait for another thread to terminate, call WaitForSingleObject(). Since any kernel object in a program is referenced through a HANDLE, this function will block the calling thread until the HANDLE parameter is in the signaled state. If the HANDLE references a thread, the object will be signaled when the thread terminates. What it means for a HANDLE to be signaled is different for each type of kernel object. Windows also provides the function WaitForMultipleObjects(), which makes a thread wait until at least one or all of up to 64 HANDLEs are in the signaled state. Thus, with a single function call, a thread can join multiple threads.

Windows Threads provides two basic mutual exclusion synchronization objects: the mutex and the CRITICAL_SECTION (you may recall that this object name is why I prefer to use the term "critical region" to refer to those code segments that require a CRITICAL_SECTION for mutually exclusive access). A mutex is a kernel object accessed and managed through a HANDLE. The CreateMutex() function will initialize a mutex object. To lock the mutex, call the function WaitForSingleObject(); when the mutex handle is in the signaled state, the mutex is available and the wait function will return. When a thread is finished with the mutex, ReleaseMutex() unlocks the object to allow another thread to gain control. Windows mutexes, like other kernel objects, can be shared between different processes to create mutually exclusive access to shared resources.

Windows CRITICAL_SECTION objects function like mutexes, but since they are user space objects, they are only accessible within the processes in which they have been declared. These objects are initialized with the InitializeCriticalSection() function before use. When mutual exclusion is required to share resources, place EnterCriticalSection() and

LeaveCriticalSection() calls around the critical region of code with a reference to an appropriate CRITICAL_SECTION object as the parameter. Probably the more important advantage of using a CRITICAL_SECTION is that the overhead of using this method of mutual exclusion will be considerably smaller (faster) than that of using a mutex or other kernel objects.

Windows events send signals from one thread to another in order to coordinate execution. Events are kernel objects and are manipulated by use of a HANDLE. Threads use one of the wait functions to pause execution until the event is in the signaled state. The CreateEvent() function initializes an event and selects the type of event: manual-reset and auto-reset. The SetEvent() function will set either type of event to the signaled state. All threads waiting on a manual-reset event, once it has been signaled, will return from the wait function and proceed. Plus, any thread that calls a wait function on that event will be immediately released. No threads will be blocked waiting on a signaled manual-reset event until a call to ResetEvent() has been issued. In the case of auto-reset events, only one thread waiting, or the first thread to begin waiting for the event, will return from the wait function, and the event will be automatically reset to the nonsignaled state. Unlike condition variables in Pthreads, a signal to a Windows event will persist until either it is reset or the required number of threads have waited for the event and been released.

What Else Is Out There?

This is not all there is. There are many different options available for concurrent programming. Some are dependent on the language that you're using, whereas others are parallel programming languages in their own right. A few of the more recent entries that I've heard something about are Microsoft's Task Parallel Library and Concurrency Runtime, Cilk++, Haskell, Erlang, X10 (from IBM), Chapel (from Cray, Inc.), Fortress (from Sun Microsystems), F#, Co-array Fortran, and threads in Java and C#. Plus, all the languages like CUDA (from NVIDIA), Ct (from Intel), and OpenCL, are specifically designed for data parallel programming on graphics processing units (GPU). Some of the other notable languages I've tried in my career include occam, C*, and CM Fortran.

Lately it seems that every other university research professor is developing or has developed a different library/language/methodology for parallel programming. And that's a good thing. The more ideas that are put forward, the better the chances are that we'll end up with something that is powerful, yet easy to use—maybe not the best, but something that most folks will be able to get behind and support.

Domain-Specific Libraries

Simple Rule 4 recommends that we use threaded libraries whenever possible. Even though the libraries I'm discussing here don't allow you to directly implement threaded solutions, I stuck this section in since it is related more to concurrent programming than software tools for analyzing programs. Two examples of such libraries are the Intel Math Kernel Library (MKL) and Intel Integrated Performance Primitives (IPP). There are five distinct sections to the MKL: Basic Linear Algebra Subroutines (BLAS), Linear Algebra Package (LAPACK), Discrete Fourier Transforms (DFT), Vector Math Library (VML), and Vector Statistics Library (VSL). From these first two sections, the amount of computation versus thread management costs limits threading to the Level 3 BLAS routines along with select LAPACK and FFT routines. Other routines from the VML and VSL sections are also threaded depending on the routine and processor that will be used for execution. All threading within the MKL is done with OpenMP, and all routines within the library are designed and compiled for thread safety.

The Intel IPP library contains a broad range of functionality. These areas include image processing, audio and video coding, data compression, cryptography, speech coding and recognition, and signal processing. Due to the number of functions within the IPP, separate library linkable files support different processing areas. Dynamic libraries are threaded internally; static libraries are not threaded. Whether or not a library version is threaded, all functions within the IPP library are thread-safe.

Before you think I've been completely swayed by the dark side and have become just another mindless corporate tool, let me point out some other examples of parallel or threaded libraries. ScaLAPACK is a parallel and scalable version of LAPACK routines that relies on the Basic Linear Algebra Communication Subroutines (BLACS) functions for distribution and management of data as well as for communication. PLAPACK is a parallel linear algebra package from the University of Texas at Austin. Besides implementing the library routines to take advantage of parallel machines, this library can also be used from a higher level of abstraction without sacrificing performance. The Numerical Algorithms Group (NAG) SMP Library is a version of the NAG numerical libraries written for parallel execution on shared memory platforms.

Most of the scientific and technical libraries available for parallel computation that I've heard about or used in the last 10–15 years have been designed for distributed-memory platforms (e.g., PETsC, PINEAPL, ParMETIS). Threaded libraries are becoming more prevalent to take advantage of ubiquitous multicore processors.

CHAPTER SIX

Parallel Sum and Prefix Scan

Summing the elements of an array or finding all partial sums of the elements in an array are basic algorithmic problems. The solution to these problems is easy to describe in a single sentence or two. The concurrent versions of these algorithms, known as *parallel sum* and *prefix scan* (or *parallel scan*), are simple and easy to understand. Since they are so simple, these problems have been extensively analyzed and are used as bellwether algorithms within the parallel programming community. Description, design, analysis, and implementation of these two algorithms will get our feet wet for the rest of the algorithms contained in the text.

Study of these two concurrent algorithms is all well and good, but if you can't find a use for them, you might think that reading through this chapter could be a waste of time. I'm sure you can imagine cases in which you might need to find the sum of an array of items or figure out the largest item within an array. These are examples of parallel sum. Prefix scan is a bit more abstract and its use as part of another algorithm is less obvious. So, after going over the design and implementation of these two concurrent algorithms, I'll point out some other algorithms where prefix scan is used.

Parallel Sum

You may need to compute the sum of all values within a given array. Example 6-1 shows a serial code that will perform such a summation of the N elements within the integer array A. After execution of the code, the sum variable will have the total sum of all elements from the A array (assuming no overflow or other exception was encountered).

EXAMPLE 6-1. Serial summation of integer array

```
int sum = 0;
for (int i = 0; i < N; i++)
  sum += A[i];
```

The parallel sum operation can work with any associative and commutative combining operation. For example, the operations of multiplication, maximum, minimum, and some logical operations would all be appropriate. In a serial program, the commutative property of the operation is not important, since the order with which the serial execution combines the elements is the same each and every time. Nevertheless, to have any chance of performing the computation concurrently, we rely on this property of the operation, since concurrent execution does not impose a fixed schedule on the order of independent computations. Throughout this chapter, I'll talk about addition or the summing of elements as the combining operation. Be aware that you can replace this with another appropriate operation when needed.

Looking closer at the serial code, since the value of sum at any single iteration depends on all the previous additions to sum, this might look like a situation that cannot be made concurrent. Luckily, this is a special case of an induction variable where the purpose of the computation is to "reduce" a collection of data into a single value. I've already told you that such a reduction operation can be made concurrent, so let's see how you can do it.

PRAM Algorithm

Imagine a complete binary tree with the same number of leaf nodes as there are elements in the vector to be summed. If we assign a vector value to individual leaf nodes and make the internal nodes of the tree correspond to the addition of child nodes, we can find the sum of all the leaf node values by working up the tree and carrying out the addition operations. Figure 6-1 shows an inverted binary tree with eight leaf nodes (squares) and assigned values. The internal nodes (circles) hold the sums of the node's children, and the root will have the sum of all vector values.

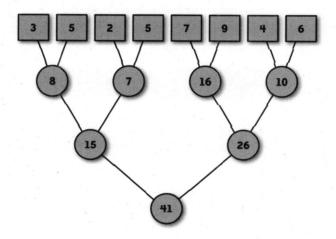

FIGURE 6-1. Binary tree illustration of parallel sum computation

Each addition within the same level of the tree is independent of all the other additions within that level. This is where the concurrency of the algorithm is to be found.

For a PRAM model, if you have a processor for each element of the array (leaf node), you can compute the parallel sum in a logarithmic number of steps. Example 6-2 shows the pseudocode for this computation adapted from the Daniel Hillis and Guy Steele paper, "Data Parallel Algorithms" (*Communications of the ACM*, 1986).

EXAMPLE 6-2. PRAM algorithm for parallel sum

```
for j := 1 to log_2(n) do
  for all k in parallel do
    if (((k + 1) mod 2^j) = 0) then
      X[k] := X[k - 2^(j-1)] + X[k]
    fi
```

od
od

The parallel sum is done in-place (within the confines of the same array). Figure 6-2 shows the progression of the code in Example 6-2 on an eight-element array X. The arrows for each value of j point to the array element that receives the (partial) sum at each iteration of the outer loop. The final sum will be in the highest indexed element, X[7].

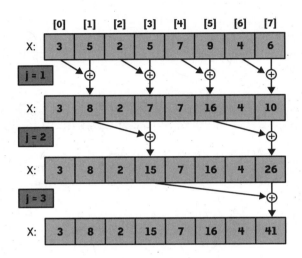

FIGURE 6-2. PRAM parallel sum algorithm example

A dash of reality

Can we use the PRAM algorithm for parallel sum (as given in Example 6-2) in a threaded code? Even overlooking the assumption of having a number of processors equal to the number of array elements available for any size array, a quick interleaving analysis of the algorithm with just two threads reveals a problem. If you divide up the inner loop between the threads, one of these can finish the assigned iterations and start up on the next set before the other thread has completed. Data races or the use of incorrect intermediate results can occur. Before you can compute any of the partial sums within a given iteration of the outer loop, you must be sure that all the previous inner loop iterations have been completed.

The pseudocode in Example 6-2 has no explicit indication of how to achieve this correctness property. The PRAM algorithm depends on having the execution of the body of the inner loop executed on separate processors all at the same time in lockstep synchronization. With the need for an unbounded number of processors and the reliance on lockstep execution, which is well nigh impossible without specialized hardware and operating system combinations, the PRAM algorithm isn't of much practical use.

A More Practical Algorithm

Parallel sum is a reduction algorithm. The concurrent algorithm for a reduction is based on data decomposition. To start, divide the data array into chunks equal to the number of threads to be used. Next, assign each thread a unique chunk and sum the values within the assigned subarray into a private variable. Finally, add these local partial sums to compute the total sum of the array elements.

OpenMP and Intel TBB have direct support for these operations built into each threading library. OpenMP includes a predetermined set of operations within the reduction clause that you can use to combine data. TBB allows more flexibility in that you must write your own code to sum items within chunks of data (inside the operator()) and how the results of those reduced chunk values are combined (through the join method). Example 6-3 has a summation code implemented with OpenMP.

EXAMPLE 6-3. Parallel sum using OpenMP reduction clause

```
int main(int argc, char* argv[])
{
  int sum = 0;
  int *X;
  int N;

  InitializeArry(X, &N);

#pragma omp parallel for reduction(+:sum)
  for (int i = 0; i < N; i++)
    sum = sum + X[i];

  printf("The sum of array elements is %d\n", sum);
  return 0;
}
```

After the initialization of the X array (InitializeArray(), not given), the loop worksharing construct divides the iterations of the loop into chunks and assigns those chunks to threads in the OpenMP team. The reduction clause ensures that each thread is allocated a properly initialized local copy of the sum variable. This local copy collects the partial sums of assigned iteration chunks. Once the threads have executed all the iterations, the reduction clause adds together (based on the + operator in the clause) and stores the sum of the partial sums into the global copy of the sum variable. The value within this global copy is then printed out.

The bulk of the work is done for you when using OpenMP or TBB for a reduction operation, especially when pulling together the partial sums into the final summation. Thus, citing Simple Rule 5, I recommend that you *use these to implement your parallel sum algorithms whenever possible*.

Should you find yourself in the position of writing your own reduction computation, you will need to divide the array elements and perform the final sums of partial sums explicitly. When there are a small number of threads, use a single thread to do the final summation in serial. This will require you to have the partial sums stored in globally accessible locations. Example 6-4 includes Pthreads code to implement the simple summation application. To keep things as uncomplicated as possible, I've set the number of threads to a fixed value (NUM_THREADS). Details about how the data is initialized (InitializeArray()) are left out of this code, too.

EXAMPLE 6-4. Parallel sum using POSIX threads and global partial sum storage

```c
#include <pthread.h>
#include <stdio.h>
#include <stdlib.h>

#define NUM_THREADS 4

int N;  // number of elements in array X
int *X;
int gSum[NUM_THREADS];  // global storage for partial results

void *Summation (void *pArg)
{
  int tNum = *((int *) pArg);
  int lSum = 0;
  int start, end;

  start = (N/NUM_THREADS) * tNum;
  end = (N/NUM_THREADS) * (tNum+1);
  if (tNum == (NUM_THREADS-1)) end = N;
  for (int i = start; i < end; i++)
    lSum += X[i];
  gSum[tNum] = lSum;
  free(pArg);
}

int main(int argc, char* argv[])
{
  int j, sum = 0;
  pthread_t tHandles[NUM_THREADS];

  InitializeArray(X, &N);  // get values into X array; not shown
  for (j = 0; j < NUM_THREADS; j++) {
    int *threadNum = new(int);
    *threadNum = j;
    pthread_create(&tHandles[j], NULL, Summation, (void *)threadNum);
  }
  for (j = 0; j < NUM_THREADS; j++) {
    pthread_join(tHandles[j], NULL);
    sum += gSum[j];
  }
  printf("The sum of array elements is %d\n", sum);
  return 0;
}
```

The main routine creates the threads that execute the Summation() function. Each thread first finds the boundaries of the X array chunk that it will be assigned. These boundaries are stored in local copies of start and end. The boundary computation requires that each thread be assigned a unique, consecutive integer ID number, starting with 0. The thread ID is passed to the thread via the single parameter allowed. The last thread (whose ID number is NUM_THREADS – 1) must be sure to pick up the final elements of the X array, since the code uses integer division. The if statement after the assignment of end will do this.

Once the boundaries are known, each thread loops over the chunk of X and sums those values into a local integer. After processing a chunk, each thread will copy the value of the locally computed partial sum into a unique global array element for the main thread to sum up into the final total.

As for the main thread, after initializing the X array, a number of threads are created (I've used the defined constant NUM_THREADS to set the number of threads in Example 6-4). Each thread's ID number is stored in a newly allocated integer and sent to the created thread through the single parameter. Before termination, threads must be sure to free the memory allocated for the thread ID to avoid a memory leak.

The main thread waits for each of the created threads to complete execution. Once a thread has terminated, the main thread will know that the associated partial sum for that thread is available in the global array and can be added to the overall sum variable. The total sum is printed after all partial sums have been combined.

Astute readers will realize that once the data has been reduced to a number of partial sums equal to the number of threads, you could use a concurrent algorithm, based on the PRAM algorithm. We'll take a look at another method for a reduction computation based more closely on the PRAM algorithm in Chapter 7.

Design Factor Scorecard

How efficient, simple, portable and scalable is the parallel sum code described earlier? Let's examine the algorithm with respect to each of these categories.

Efficiency

The addition of code to compute chunk boundaries is overhead to the concurrent execution. However, if the addition of two assignments and an if statement causes a noticeable degradation of performance, the data chunks may not be big enough to warrant concurrent execution. In this case, you need to increase the granularity of the chunks by reducing (or completely eliminating) the number of threads used.

You can completely eliminate the need for computing chunk boundaries by starting each thread at a different element of the array, based on thread ID, and accessing every fourth (or NUM_THREADS[th]) element. The code change for this scheme is given in Example 6-5.

```
for (int i = tNum; i < N; i += NUM_THREADS)
  lSum += A[i];
```

This change introduces a need to share cache lines between cores with threads accessing every fourth element (Example 6-4). However, since this will only involve read-access of the cache data, there should be no false sharing penalty. Still, this modification will make use of only a small set of items within a whole cache line. Thus, the time to read a full cache line will be practically wasted due to the fact that not all of the data in each line is used by a thread.

There will be some false sharing potential with multiple threads updating different elements of the gSum array. However, it is always better to have one possible false sharing incident per thread than to have one per data item if the threads are updating a single shared global variable for each addition (not to mention the multiple threads contending for the same synchronization object). As an alternative, you could offset each element in gSum used by the number of bytes in a cache line.

Simplicity

The two concurrent solutions here are very simple data decompositions of the original serial code. It is straightforward to compute partial sums of chunks from the array and then add those partial sums together into a final total.

While there appears to be a huge code explosion between the simple three-line serial version in Example 6-1 and the Pthreads version, the ratio in this case is a bit lopsided due to the very tiny amount of serial code that was used initially. Other algorithms that we will examine will start with more code, and, in my experience, the absolute number of added lines for implementing explicit threading will typically be close to the number of additional lines shown in Example 6-4.

Portability

The Pthreads algorithm translates pretty easily to other explicit threading models. There is nothing unique to Pthreads used here. The explicit threads algorithm uses the same idea as a distributed-memory algorithm. Processes are assigned a chunk of data, the data is summed locally, and the partial results are sent to a single process for final summation. If all processes require the answer, the final answer must be broadcast to all the other processes.

Scalability

With increases in the amount of data, the algorithm will scale well. If the data size remains fixed but the number of cores and threads increases, there will be a point (of diminishing returns) where dividing up the data into smaller chunks for more threads will begin to yield worse performance. TBB attempts to control the chunk size behind the scenes, while OpenMP has the schedule clause to give the programmer some control. For an explicitly threaded solution, you will need to determine the crossover point and build in limiting logic that controls either the number of threads that can be created or the minimum chunk size allowed in order to execute the parallel sum with multiple threads.

Prefix Scan

Prefix scan computes all partial sums of a vector of values. That is, the results of a prefix scan will be a vector—the same size as the original vector—where each element is the sum of the preceding elements in the original vector up to the corresponding position. Two uses of the results of this algorithm are to find the longest sequence of 1s in a binary array (sequence) and packing only the desired elements from an array (which I'll demonstrate later in this chapter). See *Principles of Parallel Programming* by Calvin Lin and Lawrence Snyder (Pearson Education, 2008) or Selim G. Akl's *Parallel Computation: Models and Methods* (Prentice Hall, 1997) for other uses of prefix scan.

Figure 6-3 shows an eight-element vector and the results of the prefix scan operation on that vector.

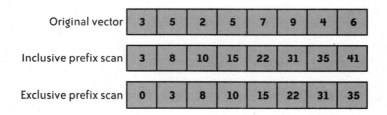

FIGURE 6-3. Prefix scan examples

There are two versions of prefix scan: *inclusive* and *exclusive*. For an inclusive scan, the result is the sum of all preceding values, as well as the value of the element in the position under consideration. To compute the inclusive prefix scan of the fifth position in the vector, you need to add 3 + 5 + 2 + 5 + 7 = 22. The exclusive version does not include the value of the vector element at the position of interest. Thus, the exclusive scan result for the fifth position is 3 + 5 + 2 + 5 = 15.

As with parallel sum, the prefix scan operation can work with any associative combining operation. Besides addition, you can also use the operations of multiplication, maximum, minimum, and such logical operations as AND, OR, and eXclusive OR (but I'll continue to make reference to prefix scan using the addition operation). Unlike parallel sum, the combining operation does not need to be commutative because of the fixed order used to combine elements. Example 6-6 shows serial code to implement the inclusive prefix scan of an array of N integers, storing the results in corresponding elements of the array prefixScan.

EXAMPLE 6-6. Serial prefix scan computation of integer array

```
prefixScan[0] = A[0];
for (int i = 1; i < N; i++)
  prefixScan[i] = prefixScan[i-1] + A[i];
```

The code first stores the A[0] value into the prefixScan[0] slot to initialize the results array. Subsequent iterations of the loop use the (i-1)th value of the results array added to the A[i] value to compute the value to be stored in the prefixScan[i] element.

NOTE

If you want to have an in-place version of the serial inclusive prefix scan, simply replace the prefixScan array with A. The exclusive version of the prefix scan is a bit more complicated, but I'll have a version of that later in the chapter.

Upon examination of the serial code in Example 6-6, you should recognize the use of induction variables in the body of the loop. Unlike the parallel sum code, which used a single induction variable throughout, this algorithm uses a different induction variable for each iteration, and the value of that induction variable relies on the values of all the previously computed induction variables. It certainly looks less likely that we'll be able to create a concurrent solution for prefix scan than we were for parallel sum.

If you're familiar with TBB, you will know that one of the parallel algorithms included in the library is parallel_scan. This algorithm can compute the prefix scan of an array of values with multiple threads. So, citing Simple Rule 4, if you can use TBB and need a prefix scan operation, then make use of the library functions already written and optimized (and skip to "Selection" on page 112—of course, you never know what dollop of knowledge or juicy tidbit I might drop over the next few pages, so you might want to keep reading).

PRAM Algorithm

For those of you still reading, let's first take a look at how you can implement the prefix scan operation on the PRAM model. In "Data Parallel Algorithms" (*Communications of the ACM*, 1986), Hillis and Steele recognized that in their parallel sum algorithm (Example 6-2), most of the processors would be idle for most of the time. In fact, half of the processors would never be used at all. Making good use of the idle processors enables machines to carry out the computation of all partial sums in the same execution time as the parallel sum algorithm.

To illustrate this better utilization of processors, Figure 6-4 shows how data will be accessed (arrows) and combined in-place for computing the prefix scan on an eight-element array. Rather than showing the data, the figure shows the range of indexes that have been summed (using bracket notation) within the array element.

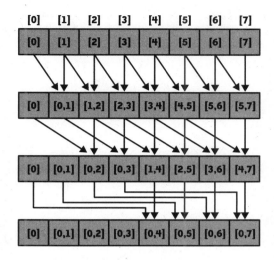

FIGURE 6-4. Example of PRAM computation for prefix scan

Before I give you the code for this operation, let's examine the operation of the PRAM algorithm by focusing on the slot of the array with index 5 and see how the prefix scan of the preceding elements is computed in that slot. The initial value is simply the data that is stored there (denoted by [5]). In the first step, the processor assigned to that position of the array will read the current contents of the index 4 element and will add that value to the contents of the index 5 slot, yielding the sum of the index 4 and 5 elements ([4,5]). The processor will then read the current contents of the index 3 element and will add that value (the sum of the original index 2 and 3 elements) to the contents of the index 5 slot. This will be the sum of the original elements from index 2 through and including index 5 ([2,5]). In the next step (the final step for eight elements), the processor will read the current contents of the index 1 slot and will add this value to the contents of the index 5 slot, which gives us the sum of all elements indexed from 0 through 5 ([0,5]). You can follow the arrows in the figure to see how each individual sum is computed from one step to the next.

We know that each step illustrated in Figure 6-4 is completed before the next step begins because the PRAM model works in lockstep execution. The algorithm assumes there is a separate processor assigned to compute each element within the array. All processors will take the same time to read the current contents of a lower-indexed slot, add the value found to the current contents of the assigned array element, and store the result back into the assigned array position. Thus, there is no need for explicit synchronization and we know there is no chance of data races in which one processor attempts to read a value at the same time the assigned processor is updating the contents of an array element.

The pseudocode for the PRAM inclusive prefix scan algorithm given in Example 6-7 is adapted from Hillis and Steele's "Data Parallel Algorithms." The only difference between this code and the code in Example 6-2 is the if test for determining which processors are active in the inner loop. This test uses the processor index (k) and determines whether looking back in the array a number of slots (2^{j-1}) is still within the lower bound of the array. If it is, the value in that lower indexed element is added to and stored in the current array element value.

EXAMPLE 6-7. PRAM algorithm for prefix scan

```
for j := 1 to log_2(n) do
  for all k in parallel do
    if (k ≥ 2^(j-1)) then
      X[k] := X[k - 2^(j-1)] + X[k]
    fi
  od
od
```

A less heavy dash of reality

Some interleaving analysis reveals that the practical problems we saw with the PRAM algorithm for parallel sum will also be problems when trying to directly implement the prefix scan algorithm from Example 6-7. We could simulate the PRAM algorithm after dividing the array into chunks for a finite number of threads. However, we'd still need to synchronize access to be sure data in lower indexed slots was read before it was updated. Also, we would need to make sure all computation for each iteration of the outer loop was complete before threads proceeded to the next outer loop iteration. This latter coordination task is further complicated as the number of array slots requiring computation shrinks for each iteration of the outer loop. In the last iteration, only half of the array elements are updated.

Looking back even further, the serial algorithm (Example 6-6) has far too many dependences and can't be directly adapted to a concurrent solution. If this is going to work concurrently, we'll need to invoke Simple Rule 8 and devise an equivalent algorithm that is more amenable to concurrency.

A More Practical Algorithm

Taking a cue from the parallel sum implementation, we can also approach prefix scan as a data decomposition design (there is no TBB version showing how to use the parallel_scan algorithm here; you'll have to look that one up yourself or wait until you get to the "Selection" section of this chapter). We can divide the array into a number of (roughly) equal-sized chunks, one per thread, and have each thread execute a serial prefix scan on the assigned chunk. Now we've got a set of "partial" prefix scans, one per chunk. How does that help? To compute the final answer for any one chunk, we need the sum of all the preceding chunks.

Luckily, the final element of an inclusive prefix scan is the total of all the elements in the array. If we run an exclusive prefix scan over just those final elements (maybe after copying them into an array), we will have the sums of all preceding chunks in the array location corresponding to a chunk (thread). We can then simply have each thread add this sum of preceding totals to all elements in the assigned chunk and compute the final prefix scan values. Figure 6-5 gives a pictorial example of this three-step algorithm on 16 elements using 4 threads.

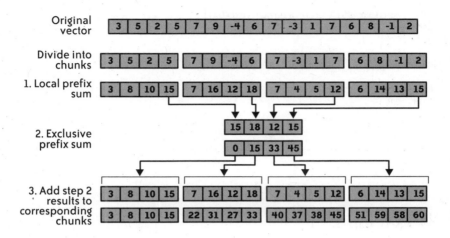

FIGURE 6-5. Prefix scan algorithm example

The first step (local prefix scan) and third step (adding the preceding chunk's sum to local chunk) can be done independently. The second step requires a prefix scan computation with a number of elements equal to the number of threads. We could implement an adaptation of the PRAM algorithm for this situation or take a hint from the parallel sum implementation and do this second step in serial.

If we do the second step in serial, we don't want to terminate the threads after completion of the first step, since we would need to recreate them for the third step. Starting and stopping threads is too much overhead and should be avoided if at all possible. Still, the serial thread executing the second step needs to know when all the chunk totals have been computed before it can start the prefix scan of the chunk totals. And, on that same side of the coin, the computational threads must wait until the serial prefix scan of chunk totals is complete before starting on the third step. Thus, we need some way to signal the completion of these two events.

Example 6-8 shows threaded code using Windows Threads and event synchronization objects to implement an inclusive prefix scan. As before, to keep things simple, I've written code that handles integers as the data on which to find the prefix scans, and set the number of threads to a fixed value (NUM_THREADS). Details about how the data is initialized (InitializeArray()) are omitted.

EXAMPLE 6-8. Prefix scan using Windows Threads

```
#include <windows.h>
#include <process.h>
#include <stdio.h>
```

```
#define NUM_THREADS 4

int N, *A;
int inTotals[NUM_THREADS], outTotals[NUM_THREADS];
HANDLE doneStep1[NUM_THREADS];
HANDLE doneStep2;

unsigned __stdcall prefixScan(LPVOID pArg)
{
  int tNum = *((int *) pArg);
  int start, end, i;
  int lPrefixTotal;

  free(pArg);
  start = (N / NUM_THREADS) * tNum;
  end = (N / NUM_THREADS) * (tNum + 1);
  if (tNum == (NUM_THREADS-1)) end = N;

// Step 1
  for (i = start+1; i < end; i++)
   A[i] = A[i-1] + A[i];

  inTotals[tNum] = A[end-1];
  SetEvent(doneStep1[tNum]); //signal completion of Step 1

// wait for completion of Step 2
  WaitForSingleObject(doneStep2, INFINITE);

// Step 3
  lPrefixTotal = outTotals[tNum];
  for (i = start; i < end; i++)
    A[i] = lPrefixTotal + A[i];

  return 0;
}

int main(int argc, char* argv[])
{
  int i, j;
  HANDLE tH[NUM_THREADS];

  InitializeArray(A,&N);  // get values into A array; not shown
// Create manual reset events initially unsignaled
  for (i = 0; i < NUM_THREADS; i++)
   doneStep1[i] = CreateEvent(NULL, TRUE, FALSE, NULL);
  doneStep2 = CreateEvent(NULL, TRUE, FALSE, NULL);

  for (i = 0; i < NUM_THREADS; i++) {
    int *tnum = new int;
    *tnum = i;
    tHandles[i] = (HANDLE) _beginthreadex(NULL, 0, prefixScan, (LPVOID) tnum, 0, NULL);
  }
// wait for Step 1 completion
  WaitForMultipleObjects(NUM_THREADS, doneStep1, TRUE, INFINITE);
```

```
// Step 2
  outTotals[0] = 0;
  for (j = 1; j < NUM_THREADS; j++)
    outTotals[j] = outTotals[j-1] + inTotals[j-1];

  SetEvent(doneStep2);  //signal completion of Step 2

// wait for completion of Step 3
  WaitForMultipleObjects(NUM_THREADS, tHandles, TRUE, INFINITE);

  return 0;
}
```

What the main thread does

The main thread creates an array of event objects (doneStep1) for the computation threads to use in signaling when they have completed the work in step 1. Also, a single event object (doneStep2) is set up for the main thread to signal that it has completed the exclusive prefix scan computation of the chunk totals. After the events are set up, the computation threads are created and the process thread waits for all of the doneStep1 events to be in the signaled state.

The exclusive prefix scan computation for step 2 uses two arrays: one to hold the original data, and one to hold the scan results. This makes the implementation simple, since it only requires one line of code. This one line of code works because we preserve the original data even when the corresponding result element is updated (I've included an in-place variation of this exclusive prefix scan in Example 6-9).

Once the exclusive serial prefix scan is complete, the main thread signals the computational threads that it is safe to begin step 3. The only thing left for the main thread to do is wait for the termination of the computational threads; this indicates that the scan of the original array is complete.

What the spawned threads are doing

Each computational thread first figures out which chunk is assigned to it using the thread ID number sent as a parameter to the prefixScan() function and stored locally as tNum. This is done in the same manner as the parallel sum code in Example 6-4. The threads compute the prefix scan on the chunk of assigned data. The value from the final chunk element (the total of all array elements within the chunk) is copied to the shared inTotals[tNum] slot. Since this completes processing for step 1, the thread sets the event object doneStep1[tNum] and waits for the signal that the main thread has completed step 2.

After receiving the doneStep2 signal, each computational thread copies the value from the outTotals[tNum] slot and stores this value in the local lPrefixTotal variable. Each of the partial prefix scan values from step 1 in the assigned chunk is updated with the addition of lPrefixTotal to compute the final scan results. Termination of all threads clues in the main thread to the fact that the computation is complete and that it can use the results as needed.

NOTE

If you think back to the beginning of the prefix scan discussion, I stated that the combining operation must be associative but does not have to be commutative. This is due to the unambiguous order in which the results are combined. In "Data Parallel Algorithms," Hillis and Steele make note of this and point out that the code that does the combination within their PRAM pseudocode is written in a specific order, namely:

```
X[k] := X[k - 2^(j-1)] + X[k]
```

where the values and previous results that occur in lower indexed elements always appear on the left of the combining operator within the righthand side of the assignment statement. Faithfulness to this format will preserve the correctness of the algorithm if you ever find yourself using a noncommutative operator in place of the addition operation shown.

I've adhered to this ordering in all of the code presented in this chapter rather than using the shortcut operator +=.

Design Factor Scorecard

How efficient, simple, portable, and scalable is the prefix scan code described earlier? Let's examine the implementation with respect to each of these categories.

Efficiency

As with the parallel sum implementation, the code to compute chunk boundaries is overhead. The same analysis of chunk size applies here. Unlike the parallel sum implementation, the loop code modification to assign alternate iterations to threads shown in Example 6-5 cannot be used since the prefix scan algorithm relies on having contiguous chunks of data elements.

With multiple threads updating different elements of the inTotals array during the last part of step 1, there is a chance for false sharing. Concurrent access to the outTotals is read-only, so there should be no detriment from false sharing on that array in preparation for step 3.

If memory is tight and an additional totals array (outTotals) may be too much, you can use an in-place serial version of exclusive prefix scan. Code for this algorithm is given in Example 6-9.

EXAMPLE 6-9. In-place exclusive prefix scan in serial

```
int nexT = Totals[0], curr;
for (j = 1; j < NUM_THREADS; j++) {
  curr = Totals[j];
  Totals[j] = nexT;
  nexT = nexT + curr;
}
Totals[0] = 0;
```

Only two extra variables (rather than an entire array) are needed to keep track of the next prefix scan value (nexT) to be stored in the Totals array and to hold the current data value from the array (curr) before that value is overwritten. The final step of the code sets the first element in the array to 0.

Simplicity

Like parallel sum before, the concurrent solution in Example 6-8 is a data decomposition. This is not a straightforward decomposition of the serial code, since there are three steps, with one of those steps actually being a prefix scan computation across threads. Implementing something closer in structure to the PRAM algorithm for step 2 might be possible, but, due to the required synchronization to keep execution order, the code wouldn't be as simple as the serial version.

Even so, I think once you understand the three steps of the concurrent algorithm and what they accomplish, the code is easy to understand and to modify for some other operation besides addition. Lin and Snyder, in *Principles of Parallel Programming*, give an implementation for an abstract parallel prefix scan method (as well as one for reduction). Their algorithm isolates the combining operation of the scan and would allow you to easily reuse the code with a different combining operation.

Portability

The Windows Threads algorithm translates pretty easily to other explicit threading models. There is nothing uniquely Windows used here. You could implement this algorithm in a distributed-memory environment, too, with some message-passing between steps to gather data for the exclusive prefix scan of totals. The results of the exclusive scan are then scattered back out to processes for local processing.

You could also use this algorithm under OpenMP. The API finds the number of threads (thread ID number are required) and carries out the serial prefix scan of the Totals array under the single pragma. In my opinion, if you have to go to the OpenMP API functions and use those values to divide the data array into chunks, you have gone outside the realm of how best to use OpenMP. If you're going to go to that trouble, why not just write the code with an explicit threading library? If you've got other parts of your application in OpenMP and want to keep the entire application in OpenMP, then I'm OK with writing a small part of the code using OpenMP as if it were explicit threads. (You're free to do what you want, of course, I just ask that you don't tell me about it.)

Scalability

The prefix scan code given here is going to have the same scaling characteristics as the parallel sum. With an explicit threads implementation, you'll need to find where too little data in each chunk causes the implementation performance to degrade below acceptable bounds.

Selection

Studying parallel sum and prefix scan is instructive in its own right, but there are actually larger algorithms that incorporate these operations. Selecting the kth-largest element from an unsorted list is a good example. In this section I'll describe serial and concurrent solutions for this example algorithm and show how you can apply the parallel sum and prefix scan operations.

One obvious solution is to first sort the elements of the list and then pick out the item in the kth position. If you need to pull out different k^th items multiple times, it might be worthwhile to do the sorting. If, however, you only need to do this once, or if the list is updated between selections, you can use an algorithm with a better asymptotic complexity than sorting, namely *O(n)*.

The Serial Algorithm

When I was first shown this algorithm, early in my computer science academic years, I remember being flabbergasted at the simplicity of the idea and the insight it took to think of this problem in the way that led to this solution. The crux of the algorithm is in finding the median of a list. You will recall that the median of a data set is the item in the middle of the set; half the data is smaller than the median element, and half the data is greater than the median value. For a data set of *n* items, this median would be in the

$$k = \left\lceil \frac{n}{2} \right\rceil$$

position if the data were sorted.

The serial algorithm for selection is recursive and can be described with five algorithmic steps:

1. If the size of the data set to be used is less than some constant size, *Q,* sort the data and return the kth element; otherwise, subdivide the data set into chunks of size *Q* and whatever is left over.

2. Sort each chunk and find the median of each.

3. Recursively call the selection routine to find the median of the medians found in the previous step.

4. Partition the data set into three subsequences: those whose elements are less than the median of medians, those that are equal to the median of medians, and those that are greater than the median of medians.

5. Determine which subsequence contains the kth element, from the sizes of the three subsequences, and recursively call the selection routine on that subsequence. If the kth element is not in the subsequence of smaller or larger items, it must be in the subsequence equal to the median of medians, so just return the median of medians value.

The code given in Example 6-10 implements the algorithm just described as the
SequentialSelect() function. The code for two of the required support functions,
CountAndMark() and ArrayPack(), are given later in Example 6-11. From the analysis of Selim G.
Akl in *The Design and Analysis of Parallel Algorithms* (Prentice Hall, 1989), the value of Q can
be any integer greater than or equal to 5. I've chosen to define Q as 5 for my implementation.

EXAMPLE 6-10. Serial code to implement the selection algorithm

```
int SequentialSelect(int *S, int num, int k)
{
  if (num <= Q) return SortLessThanQ(S, num, k);

  int cNum = num/Q + 1;
  int *Medians = new int[cNum];
  int i = 0;
  for (int j = 0; j < num/Q; j++) {
    Medians[j] = SortSelect5(&S[i], 3);  // find medians of subsequences
    i += Q;
  }
  int lastNum = num - (Q * (num / Q));
  if (lastNum) {
    int lastQ = Q * (num / Q);
    Medians[cNum-1] = SortLessThanQ(&S[lastQ], lastNum, (lastNum+1)/2);
  }
  else cNum--;

  int M = SequentialSelect(Medians, cNum, (cNum+1)/2);

  int leg[3] = {0,0,0};
  int *markS = new int[num];
  CountAndMark(S, markS, num, M, leg);

  if (leg[0] >= k) {
    int *sPack = new int[leg[0]];
    ArrayPack(S, sPack, num, markS, 0);
    return SequentialSelect(sPack, leg[0], k);
  }
  else if ((leg[0] + leg[1]) >= k) return M;
  else {
    int *sPack = new int[leg[2]];
    ArrayPack(S, sPack, num, markS, 2);
    return SequentialSelect(sPack, leg[2], k-(leg[0]+leg[1]));
  }
}
```

The parameters to the SequentialSelect() routine are the array of data to be selected from (S),
the number of elements in the array (num), and the selection index (k). For simplicity, I've made
S an array of integers. The first step is to determine whether there are more than Q items to be
searched. If not, the code calls SortLessThanQ() (not shown), which simply contains a switch
statement to select the handcoded sort routine for the specific values less than or equal to Q. If
the number of elements in the list is larger than Q, the number of Q-sized chunks is computed

(cNum) and an array to hold the median of each chunk is allocated (Medians). The SortSelect5() routine (not shown) sorts each chunk and returns the median of the sorted data (in *The Art of Computer Programming, Volume 3: Sorting and Searching*, Second Edition [Addison-Wesley, 1998], Donald Knuth describes an algorithm that will sort five items with only seven comparisons). If there is a leftover chunk of less than Q elements (lastNum), the median of this chunk is found by calling SortLessThanQ().

Once all the medians of the chunks have been returned, the SequentialSelect() routine is called recursively on the Medians array to find the median (M) of this sublist. To partition the original list, the CountAndMark() routine (see Example 6-11) counts the number of elements that are less than, equal to, and greater than M. These counts are stored in the leg array (named for less than, **e**qual to, and **g**reater than). Besides counting, the markS array is filled with a value to denote into which partition the corresponding elements in the S array would fall.

Since we have the counts of each partition, it is easy enough to figure out which of the three partitions the kth element will be found. We don't have to actually divide the original list into the three partitions and incur a movement cost from all elements: it will be enough to gather the elements of the partition holding the item of interest into a new array (sPack). You will only have to do this data packing if the element is in the "less than" or "greater than" partition. The ArrayPack() function (see Example 6-11) moves the appropriate elements based on the markS array contents. The packed array is then sent to the SequentialSelect() routine to find the item being selected in the smaller data set.

Example 6-11 contains the code for the CountAndMark() and ArrayPack() support functions.

EXAMPLE 6-11. Support functions for serial selection algorithm

```
void CountAndMark(int S[], int Marks[], int num, int median, int leg[3])
{
  for (int i = 0; i < num; i++) {
    if (S[i] < median) {Marks[i] = 0; leg[0]++;} //less than
    else if (S[i] > median) {Marks[i] = 2; leg[2]++;} // greater than
    else {Marks[i] = 1; leg[1]++;} // equal to
  }
}

void ArrayPack(int S[], int sPack[], int num, int Marks[], int scanSym)
{
  int j = 0;
  for (int i = 0; i < num; i++)
    if (Marks[i] == scanSym) sPack[j++] = S[i];
}
```

The CountAndMark() function takes an array of data to be partitioned (S), the array that will hold a notation of which partition the corresponding element from S would be assigned (Marks), the number of elements in the first two parameter arrays (num), the value of the median that determines the three partitions (median), and the leg array to hold the counts of the number of elements that are less than, equal to, or greater than median. For each element of S, this function notes that element's relation to the `median` in the `Marks` array and increments the appropriate element of the `leg` array. Notice that the function computes three sums based on the contents of an array.

The `ArrayPack()` function takes a list of elements (`S`) and an array of items, noting which partition the elements from `S` should be assigned (`Marks`). Everywhere the `Marks` element and the `scanSym` match, the corresponding element from `S` is packed into `sPack`. While it may not be obvious, you can do this operation with a prefix scan of the `Marks` array. I'll show you how that's done in the next section.

I hope you can see that this algorithm works by using the median of medians to partition the data into three groups and then identifying the partition in which the kth element would be found. To prove that the algorithm runs in linear time, we need to demonstrate that at least 30% of the data will be in the partition that does not contain the item of interest. This is illustrated in Figure 6-6.

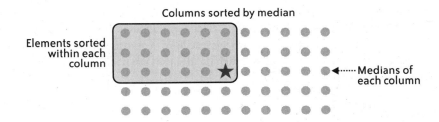

FIGURE 6-6. Selection diagram

Figure 6-6 contains 11 subsequences of 5 elements each. The 5 elements in each subsequence have been sorted. For the sake of the figure, assume that I've arranged these subsequences in sorted order by their median value. We can quickly identify which element would be the median of medians (shown as a star in the figure). The circled collection of elements is the set of items known to be less than or equal to the median of medians. Thus, if the element being sought through selection is greater than the median of medians, we are guaranteed to be able to eliminate at least 3/5 of half (or 30%) of the data for each recursive call in the final step of the algorithm. We can make the same claim if the item is smaller than the median of medians by shifting the gray box to surround the items in the lower-right corner of the elements.

If you're interested in the details of a more rigorous proof of runtime for this serial algorithm, see Akl's *The Design and Analysis of Parallel Algorithms* or *Fundamentals of Algorithmics* (Prentice Hall, 1996) by Gilles Brassard and Paul Bratley.

The Concurrent Algorithm

Three points within the serial algorithm contain independent operations: the determination of the medians from each of the *Q*-length subsequences, the counting and marking of elements according to the partitions defined by the median of medians, and the use of the prefix scan operation to pack the sPack array with the items from the partition containing the kth element. I'll discuss each of these in turn and show you how to transform the serial code to a concurrent equivalent using TBB.

I've chosen to use TBB because it contains the parallel_scan algorithm, which makes it easier to implement the array packing. Also, the points of concurrency are separated by some serial code. Thus, using TBB allows us to construct the concurrency at those points that can be made concurrent and to ensure concurrent operations are completed before proceeding to the next step of the algorithm. OpenMP would give us the same synchronization of threads between parallel regions, but without a prefix scan operation, we'd have had to write one by hand. An explicit threads solution would require us to incorporate the logic to do the execution order synchronization. I'm going to wait until Chapter 7 before giving details and an example that illustrates what can be done with explicit threads that need to coordinate execution order of tasks within threads.

Before we examine each of the changes for concurrency in depth, let's look at the changes to the overall selection function, ParallelSelect(). This code segment is shown in Example 6-12. I've left out the required TBB include lines. You can use this as an exercise to determine whether you can identify all the include files that are needed when you implement concurrent codes with TBB.

EXAMPLE 6-12. ParallelSelect() code

```
int ParallelSelect(int *S, int num, int k)
{
  if (num <= Q) return SortLessThanQ(S, num, k);

  int cNum = num/Q + 1;
  int *Medians = new int[cNum];

  parallel_for(blocked_range<int>(0, num/Q), FindMedians(S, Medians), auto_partitioner());

  int lastNum = num - (Q * (num / Q));
  if (lastNum) {
    int lastQ = Q * (num / Q);
    Medians[cNum-1] = SortLessThanQ(&S[lastQ], lastNum, (lastNum+1)/2);
  }
  else cNum--;

  int M = ParallelSelect(Medians, cNum, (cNum+1)/2);

  int *markS = new int[num];
  CountAndMark camBody(S, markS, M);
  parallel_reduce(blocked_range<size_t>(0,num), camBody, auto_partitioner());

  int numLessEqual = camBody.leg.less + camBody.leg.equal;
  if (camBody.leg.less >= k) {
    int *sPack = new int[camBody.leg.less];
    ArrayPack(S, sPack, num, markS, 0);
```

```
    return ParallelSelect(sPack, camBody.leg.less, k);

  }
  else if ((numLessEqual) >= k) return M;
  else {
    int *sPack = new int[camBody.leg.greater];
    ArrayPack(S, sPack, num, markS, 2);
    return ParallelSelect(sPack, camBody.leg.greater, k-(numLessEqual));
  }
}
```

The basic structure of the concurrent code is the same as the serial version from Example 6-10. The for loop that finds the set of medians of the subsequences has been replaced by calling the parallel_for algorithm on the FindMedians class (defined in Example 6-13). After the median of medians (M) is determined, a parallel_reduce algorithm on the CountAndMark class (defined later in Example 6-14) counts the number of elements in the three partitions (in relation to the value of M) and marks which partition each element belongs to in the markS array. The partition of interest is packed into the sPack array by calling the ArrayPack() function (defined later in Example 6-15). This function will use the parallel_scan algorithm to identify the elements that need to be gathered into the sPack array, and a parallel_for call will pack the relevant items into the array. If the kth item is equal to the median of medians, this value is immediately returned instead.

Finding the medians of subsequences

The code for the FindMedians class is shown in Example 6-13. The class includes the required methods for TBB to divide up the tasks and assign them to threads through the parallel_for algorithm.

EXAMPLE 6-13. FindMedians class definition

```
class FindMedians {
  int *S;
  int *M;

public:
  void operator()(const blocked_range<int>& r) const {
    int i, j;
    for (j = r.begin(); j < r.end(); j++) {
      i = j * Q;
      M[j] = SortSelect5(&S[i], 3);  // find medians of subsequences
    }
  }

  FindMedians(int *_S, int *_Medians): S(_S), M(_Medians){}

  FindMedians(FindMedians& x, split): S(x.S), M(x.M) {}
};
```

This is all pretty straightforward. The body of the loop simply calls the serial SortSelect5() function to sort the five (from Q) elements of the subsequence. If the final chunk has fewer than Q elements, the median selection of that last chunk is done in the ParallelSelect() routine immediately following parallel_for.

One difference between this loop and the corresponding loop from the serial code is that the serial code loop uses i as an induction variable (incremented by Q each iteration). For the concurrent version, I reconfigured the code to compute the value of i based on the value of j in each iteration, which eliminated the induction dependence. Did you notice the range given to the parallel_for of this step in Example 6-12 was (0, num/Q)? This makes an iteration independent of the other iterations and allows TBB to divide them up into independent tasks.

Counting and marking elements for partitions

The LEG and CountAndMark classes are shown in Example 6-14. The LEG class, used in place of the three-element leg array from the serial code, holds the number of elements that are less than, equal to, and greater than the median value. The CountAndMark class defines the methods to find the number of elements within the three partitions and to determine the partition of each element. The TBB parallel_reduce algorithm is used on the CountAndMark class.

EXAMPLE 6-14. LEG and CountAndMark classes

```
class LEG {

public:
  int less, equal, greater;

  LEG(): less(0), equal(0), greater(0) {}
};
class CountAndMark {
  int *S;
  int *Marks;
  int median;

public:
  LEG leg;

  void operator()(const blocked_range<size_t>& r) {
    for (size_t i = r.begin(); i != r.end(); ++i) {
      if (S[i] < median) {Marks[i] = 0; leg.less++;}
      else if (S[i] == median) {Marks[i] = 1; leg.equal++;}
      else {Marks[i] = 2; leg.greater++;}
    }
  }

  void join (const CountAndMark& y) {
    leg.less += y.leg.less;
    leg.equal += y.leg.equal;
    leg.greater += y.leg.greater;
  }
```

```
CountAndMark(int *_S, int *_Marks, int _median):
  S(_S), Marks(_Marks), median(_median) {}

CountAndMark(CountAndMark& x, split):
  S(x.S), Marks(x.Marks), median(x.median) {}
};
```

Not one, not two, but three separate parallel sums are computed with the CountAndMark class. These sums are kept in the three fields of the LEG object. You can see that the join method in Example 6-14 adds the less, equal, and greater partial sums together after threads have gone through all elements in assigned chunks.

The operator() computes the partial sums for each of the three partition choices. The if-then-else tests determine which partial sum is incremented in each loop iteration. In addition, the corresponding Marks array elements are assigned a notation value to indicate in which partition the element under scrutiny belongs. The Marks array's actual parameter will be used in the ArrayPack() function to identify which elements from the original array are in the desired partition.

The ArrayPack() function

From the point of view of the ParallelSelect() function, the ArrayPack() function does nothing different than it did in the serial version. The concurrent version of ArrayPack() is shown in Example 6-15. The support classes, PackingScan and PackingMove, are shown later in Examples 6-16 and 6-17, respectively.

EXAMPLE 6-15. ArrayPack() function

```
void ArrayPack(int S[], int sPack[], int num, int Marks[], int scanSym)
{
  int *scanIdx = new int[num];
  PackingScan body(scanIdx, Marks, scanSym);

  parallel_scan(blocked_range<int>(0,num), body, auto_partitioner());

  if (scanIdx[0]) sPack[0] = S[0];  // move if first element is marked
  parallel_for(blocked_range<int>(1,num), PackingMove(scanIdx,sPack,S),
               auto_partitioner());
}
```

The Marks and scanSym parameters identify the elements that are to be moved from the S array to the sPack array. A prefix scan recognizes the elements to be moved and computes the index where they are to be relocated within sPack. I've used the TBB parallel_scan algorithm to accomplish this. The actual movement is done concurrently through a parallel_for after the first element if checked and moved, if needed. See the sidebar "Array Packing with Prefix Scan" for information on using prefix scan to pack arrays.

ARRAY PACKING WITH PREFIX SCAN

Given an array of data elements and a corresponding "mark" array that indicates some elements as being of interest (assuming 1 indicates interest in the data element and 0 indicates no interest), the task is to gather all the marked elements into a contiguous range of elements within an array. A prefix scan of the binary array of marks is first computed. From the results of this computation, the set of originally marked elements can be identified by the change in value of a mark element and the immediate prior element (i.e., the value in the [i] position is one greater than the value in the [i-1] position). The value of the scanned mark array—for each marked element—directly determines the index within the packed array to which the marked element will be copied. Figure 6-7 shows an example of the computation.

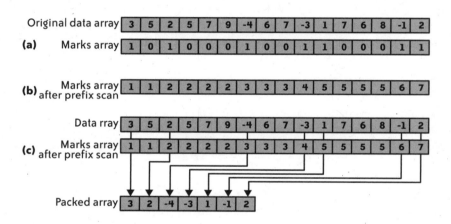

FIGURE 6-7: Prefix scan to pack an array

Figure 6-7 (a) shows an array of 16 integers (labeled "Original data array") and an array of "Marks" identifying those elements whose value is less than five (1) and greater than or equal to five (0). Figure 6-7 (b) is the Marks array after an inclusive prefix scan has been run on the binary values. You can see from Figure 6-7 (c) that the elements from the original array that are less than five in value are copied into contiguous elements of the Packed array via the results of the prefix scan. If the first element of the Marks array is 1, the first element (3 in this example) was an originally marked item and needs to be moved into the Packed array. For every other element of the Marks array, if the value is different from the value in the element to the immediate left, the corresponding item from the Data array is moved into the Packed array (shown via the arrows in the figure). The index of the slot in the Packed array to receive a data item is the value of the Marks array (minus 1 for 0-based array indexing).

If you need to pack the marked elements and unmarked elements in-place, you can use the following steps after running the prefix scan of the Marks array:

1. Allocate a separate integer array that is equal in size to the number of data elements, initialized to 1 (I am assuming the size of the data elements is large enough that this allocation is relatively small). This array will hold the destinations for each data element. The first element from the Marks array that corresponds to the lowest indexed nonmarked data element is assigned a value that is one greater than the number of marked elements.

2. Copy the negative of the destination indexes for all marked elements from the scanned array into the destination array.

3. Run a prefix scan of only the positive elements (the lowest-indexed nonmarked element's value and all the initial 1 values) within the destination array. That is, treat the negative values as 0, but don't change them.

4. Use the absolute values of destination array elements to move each element from its current location to the index location in the array given in the corresponding element of the destination array. Be careful, though; this mass movement of data is easy to do concurrently using a PRAM with a number of processors equal to the number of items, but will be much trickier with a finite number of threads and cores.

If you can get away with a serial scan, you can just use the original Marks array, but you will need to identify the unmarked data elements and treat these as if the value 1 were stored there in order to compute destination index values.

Once you know the destination indexes, you can move data elements from the original array to the packed array concurrently. Copying data from one memory location to another doesn't rely on any other copy operation, unless there is a potential for conflict at the receiving locations. The indexes for receiving a data item are precomputed, and you can see that they are all going to be unique, thus, no data races.

The PackingScan class in Example 6-16 sets up the TBB class requirements to compute the prefix scan on the Marks array. The PackingMove class shown later in Example 6-17 gives the class declarations to pack the data items concurrently from the selected partition.

EXAMPLE 6-16. PackingScan class

```
class PackingScan {
  int sum;
  int* const y;
  const int* const x;
  const int symbol;

public:

  template<typename Tag>
```

```
void operator()(const blocked_range<int>& r, Tag) {
  int temp = sum;
  for (int i = r.begin(); i < r.end(); ++i) {
    if (x[i] == symbol) temp++;
    if(Tag::is_final_scan())
      y[i] = temp;
  }
  sum = temp;
}

PackingScan(int y_[], const int x_[], const int sym_) :
          sum(0), x(x_), y(y_), symbol(sym_) {}

PackingScan(PackingScan& b, split) :
          sum(0), x(b.x), y(b.y), symbol(b.symbol) {}

void reverse_join(PackingScan& a) {sum = a.sum + sum;}

void assign(PackingScan& b) {sum = b.sum;}
};
```

The PackingScan class is based directly on the parallel_scan example found in the Intel TBB example codes. The only change, besides the logical parameter list, is that a test for whether or not the symbol in the x array (Marks in Example 6-15) is equal to the symbol identifying the desired partition. This test is in the operator() definition. Since the x array contains three different values, we need to use this as a logical binary array. That is, if the value in the x array matches the symbol being examined, the value is to be treated as if it were a 1; otherwise, if the symbol doesn't match the contents of the array being scanned, that element is treated as a 0. When there is a match, the temp value is incremented (as if adding 1 to the running scan total). If there is not a match, the temp value is left unchanged (as if adding 0 to the running total). During the final scan phase, which is denoted by the value of Tag, this running sum value is stored in the scan's output array (y).

EXAMPLE 6-17. PackingMove class

```
class PackingMove {
  const int *scanIdx;
  int *sPack;
  const int *S;

public:
  void operator()(const blocked_range<int>& r) const {
    for (int i = r.begin(); i < r.end(); i++) {
      if (scanIdx[i-1] != scanIdx[i])
        sPack[scanIdx[i]-1] = S[i];
    }
  }
  PackingMove(const int sIdx_[], int sPack_[], const int *S_) :
            scanIdx(sIdx_), sPack(sPack_), S(S_) {}
  PackingMove(const int sIdx_[], int sPack_[], const int *S_, split) :
            scanIdx(sIdx_), sPack(sPack_), S(S_) {}
};
```

Finally, you can use the `PackingMove` class with the `parallel_for` algorithm call from within the `ArrayPack()` function (Example 6-15). You can use the results of the prefix scan to identify which elements are to be moved and where to copy the items into the packed array. In the `operator()` code in Example 6-17, the value of each element in the scanned array (`scanIdx`) is compared to the value of the preceding element. If these two elements are different, the value of the element minus 1 is used to index the packed array (`sPack`) slot that will receive the value being copied (from `S`). We know that each destination is given to only one element from the `S` array, so there are no conflicts or data races.

Once the elements from the appropriate partition are packed, the `ArrayPack()` function returns and a recursive call to `ParallelSelect()` with this new partition and the value of k, adjusted as needed, is executed.

Some Design Notes

Rather than breaking down the Selection code in terms of efficiency, simplicity, portability, and scalability, I just want to conclude with some general design comments. All that I've said so far about these topics in reference to the parallel sum and prefix scan algorithms will apply to the use of those algorithms within the examples.

The simple algorithms for parallel sum and prefix scan are merely the basis for the steps needed in the selection algorithm. Rather than a single sum, the `CountAndMark` class ran three separate sums simultaneously. Also, the scan operation needed to interpret the data values and compute with logical binary equivalents based upon the value of each element. This sort of algorithm transmogrification is nothing new. Programmers routinely take the concept of an algorithm and reshape it to fit the current needs of the application they are working on. The trick, of course, is being able to determine which base algorithm is the best to modify.

> **NOTE**
>
> *Transmogrification* is the act of changing into a different form or appearance. I've liked this word ever since seeing the misadventures caused by writing "Transmogrifier" on a cardboard box in the "Calvin and Hobbes" comic strip.

A Final Thought

I don't mean to use PRAM algorithms as the basis for all future algorithms in this book. I'm trying to present you with information that is more practical than theoretical. The parallel sum and prefix scan algorithms are quite easy to implement on a PRAM, though. I wanted to give you a taste of what you might face if you pick up another parallel algorithms book that uses PRAM implementations of the algorithms. Assuming you're not a computer science graduate, this exposure will better equip you as far as how to interpret those algorithms and what steps you may need to go through to adapt them into practical code. While it should be possible to simulate the unbounded number of processors of a PRAM algorithm with a finite number of threads and cores, you must be aware of the assumptions that are built into the PRAM model and be ready to deal with them. Chapter 7 includes a more concrete example of issues that you might face when adapting PRAM algorithms.

CHAPTER SEVEN

MapReduce

MAPREDUCE IS AN ALGORITHMIC FRAMEWORK, LIKE DIVIDE-AND-CONQUER or backtracking, rather than a specific algorithm. The pair of operations, *map* and *reduce*, is found in LISP and other functional languages. MapReduce has been getting a lot of buzz as an algorithmic framework that can be executed concurrently. Google has made its fortune on the application of MapReduce within a distributed network of thousands of servers (see "MapReduce: Simplified Data Processing on Large Clusters" in *Communications of the ACM* [2008] by Jeffrey Dean and Sanjay Ghemawat), which has only served to heighten awareness and exploration of this method.

The idea behind *map* is to take a collection of data items and associate a value with each item in the collection. That is, to match up the elements of the input data with some relevant value to produce a collection of key-value pairs. The number of results from a map operation should be equal to the number of input data items within the original collection. In terms of concurrency, the operation of pairing up keys and values should be completely independent for each element in the collection.

The *reduce* operation takes all the pairs resulting from the map operation and does a reduction computation on the collection. As I've said before, the purpose of a reduction is to take in a collection of data items and return a value derived from those items. Parallel sum (from Chapter 6) is an example of a reduction computation. In more general terms, we can allow the reduce operation to return with zero, one, or any number of results. This will all depend on what the reduction operation is computing and the input data from the map operation.

Before looking at the implementation and other details, let's look at an example of MapReduce in action. Consider the task of counting the number of vowels and consonants in the following sentence:

> The quick brown fox jumps over the lazy dog.

In my head, I run through the sentence, character by character, once to count the consonants and then again to count the vowels. The results would then be two integers: the number of vowels (12) and the number of consonants (23). Did you only count 11 vowels? Since "lazy" has two syllables, which requires two vowel sounds, there must be at least two vowels. Thus, "y" is doing duty as a vowel in this sentence. Example 7-1 has pseudocode of the MapReduce operation that would compute these values. For this example, S is the string of characters (array) holding the sentence.

EXAMPLE 7-1. MapReduce pseudocode example

```
// Map
  for i = 1 to length(S) {
    if (S[i] is a consonant)
      generate_pair(key[i]=S[i], value[i]=1);
    else
      generate_pair(key[i]=S[i], value[i]=-1);
  }
```

```
// Reduce
  cCount = 0; vCount = 0;
  for i = 1 to length(S) {
    if (value[i] > 0) cCount += value[i];
    else              vCount += abs(value[i]);
  }
```

For the given data set, S, the MapReduce solution first maps a value to each letter in order to create 35 key-value (letter-integer) pairs. The choice of values depends on whether the letter is a consonant (1) or a vowel (-1). The reduction operation will take each key-value pair and add the value into one of two counters based on the type of letter contained in the key.

> **NOTE**
> We will need some way to identify "y" as a vowel. This identification will need to influence the key-value pair created in the map phase so that the reduce computation can add the associated value to the correct counter.

If we wrote code for this letter-counting operation in serial, we could have simply examined each letter in turn and incremented the proper counter. In the (serial) MapReduce variation (Example 7-1), we're required by the framework to use the values associated with the keys in the reduction computation. While it may seem to be more work, this difference creates the situation where the data is divorced from the algorithm and makes the reduction computations more independent.

Map As a Concurrent Operation

Look back at the pseudocode of the vowel/consonant counting algorithm in Example 7-1. Can you see that the creation of each key-value pair in the map phase would be independent of every other pair creation? Simply divide the letters among threads and create key-value pairs for each letter. One goal I would urge you to keep in mind when using MapReduce is to make the reduction computation as simple as possible. This is why the algorithm in Example 7-1 decided the category of each letter in the map phase.

An alternate mapping would assign a value of 1 to each key (character) and let the reduce phase decide whether the key is a vowel or consonant. The context of the keys that exists in the map phase may not be available when the reduction computation is executed. Or, if not unavailable, it may require extra data to preserve the context and correctly process values in the reduction. Determining whether to label "y" as a consonant or a vowel requires the context of the word itself. If the map and reduce operations were in different functions and we used the alternate mapping of 1 for all keys, we would need to send the reduce function the context (the sentence) in order to classify the "y" properly.

Just to hammer one more nail into this idea, consider the classic MapReduce example of finding pages from a document (or set of documents) that contain a key phrase or word of interest. Since we might not be able to find the exact phrase on any pages that we want to search, we can devise a search-rating scheme that could rank pages that might have some subset of words in our phrase. For example, pages containing the exact phrase will be given the highest rating, pages that contain a subphrase (subset of words from the original phrase in the same order and next to each other) will be given slightly lower ratings, and pages that have disjointed words from the phrase will be given even lower ratings. For the final results of this example, we could specify the output as a list of the 20 pages with the highest scores.

The mapping computation should create key-value pairs with a pointer to one page of the document(s) as the key and the search rating of that page as the value. The rating of each page with regard to the search phrase is completely independent of rating any other page. The reduce phase now simply selects the 20 pages with the highest scores.

Implementing a Concurrent Map

How do you implement the map phase for concurrent execution? I'm sorry to say that I can't tell you, because each application that uses MapReduce will likely be different. So, the details are going to be up to you and will be based on the computational needs of the code. However, I can give you some general guidelines.

Whenever you find MapReduce applicable, the mapping operation will always be a data decomposition algorithm. You will have to turn a collection of data into key-value pairs. The items from the collection of data may require some "massaging" to determine the consequent key value. Or the map might simply attach a key to the value, or vice versa if the data is to be used as a key.

Whatever processing needs to be done in the map phase, you must design it with the reduce phase in mind. By doing more work in the map phase, you lessen the amount of work needed in the reduction operation and make it easier overall to write and maintain the MapReduce algorithm. The best reduce is going to be a single operation that you can apply to both individual elements and partial reduction results (if the reduce algorithm uses them). Writing a two-stage reduction (e.g., deciding on the type of a letter and adding a value to the right counter) can needlessly complicate your concurrent implementation.

Since the mapping operation on individual elements is independent of the computation on any other data item (Simple Rule 1), there won't be any data races or other conflicts. Of course, there will always be the exception that will prove me wrong on this. If you find that synchronization is necessary to avoid a data race, reexamine the mapping computation to see whether you should handle that data race in the reduce phase. Also, you may find that MapReduce is not the best algorithm for the problem you are trying to parallelize.

Finally, be aware of load balancing issues in the map computations. If you have something as simple as attaching a count value to a data item key (e.g., the letter counting example), then all of the individual map operations will take about the same amount of time, and you can easily divide them up with a static schedule. If you have a case where the computation time on individual elements will vary (e.g., finding key words and phrases within documents of different sizes), a more dynamic schedule of work to threads will be best.

Reduce As a Concurrent Operation

As I recommended in the previous chapter, if you have the chance, use either OpenMP or Intel TBB to do reduction computations. All of the grunt work and coordination of threads and partial values goes on "behind the scenes." Why would you want to do any heavy lifting if you don't have to? Plus, making use of code that is already written and debugged will give you more of a warm fuzzy feeling about your concurrent application.

If you don't have the option of using the reduction algorithms built into TBB or OpenMP, you will need an explicit threads solution. Example 6-4 includes a handcoded reduction for summing up all the items within an integer array. You can use this as a model for implementing reduce when there are few threads.

For this chapter, though, I want to present an alternative that doesn't use the serial processing at the final step to combine the partial results from the previous independent computations. Let's again take the summing of all elements from an array as the specific problem to be solved. As with the code in Example 6-4, we'll use Pthreads as the explicit threading library for implementation.

Handcoded Reduction

To get started, each thread working on the reduction is assigned a nonoverlapping chunk of the overall data set. Any of the previously discussed methods that ensures all of the data are assigned will work. A static division of data is best. Next, each thread calculates the sum of all the items assigned. This will yield a number of partial sums equal to the number of threads. At this point, we can use the PRAM version of the parallel sum algorithm presented in Example 6-2 (one thread per data item to be summed). However, since we probably don't have lockstep execution of threads built into the hardware, we will need to coordinate the threads' executions on the data and with each other.

As in Example 6-4, we will store the partial sums in separate elements of a global array. Threads use the assigned ID for the index into the global array gSum. We will compute the final sum concurrently using the global array data. The first element within the gSum array (index 0) will hold the computed total for the elements of the original array. Figure 7-1 shows a representation of the concurrent computations that we will need to take the partial sums and add them together for the final answer.

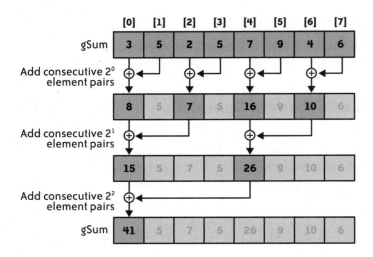

FIGURE 7-1. Reduction computation

Each array displayed in Figure 7-1 represents the contents of the gSum array after a round of computation. The arrows indicate where data is read from and where the results are stored in each round. The plus sign (+) within the circle is the combining operation (addition for this example) used in the reduction. The grayed numbers simply indicate that the data within that element of the array is no longer needed in further rounds of computation. For brevity, I've limited the example to eight threads. I think that once you've seen how two or three rounds are computed, you'll easily be able to extrapolate this algorithm to any number of threads.

In the first round (Add consecutive 2^0 element pairs), each thread whose ID is a multiple of 2 (2^1) reads the value stored in the element indexed by [thread ID] + 1 (2^0)—if such an element is part of the array—and adds this value to the value stored in the element indexed with the thread's ID. In the second round (Add consecutive 2^1 element pairs), each thread whose ID is a multiple of 4 (2^2) reads the value stored in the element indexed by [thread ID] + 2 (2^1)—if such an element is part of the array—and adds this value to the value stored in the element indexed with the thread's ID. In the third round (Add consecutive 2^2 element pairs), each thread whose ID is a multiple of 8 (2^3) reads the value stored in the element indexed by [thread ID] + 4 (2^2)—if such an element is part of the array—and adds this value to the value stored in the element indexed with the thread's ID, *und so veiter* (or "and so on" for my English readers). The pattern for each successive round simply repeats with the indexes involved growing by a factor of two.

The code to implement a reduction summation on an array of integers is given in Example 7-2. This code is modified from the code given in Example 6-4 with the differences highlighted in bold text.

EXAMPLE 7-2. Reduction code to sum elements of an array

```c
#include <pthread.h>
#include <stdio.h>
#include "pth_barrier.h"

#define NUM_THREADS 128

int N;   // number of elements in array A
int *A;
int gSum[NUM_THREADS];   // global storage for partial results
pth_barrier_t B;

void *SumByReduction (void *pArg)
{
  int tNum = *((int *) pArg);
  int lSum = 0;
  int start, end, i;

  start = ((float)N/NUM_THREADS) * tNum;
  end =   ((float)N/NUM_THREADS) *(tNum+1);
  if (tNum == (NUM_THREADS-1)) end = N;
  for (i = start; i < end; i++)
    lSum += A[i];
  gSum[tNum] = lSum;

  pth_barrier(&B);
  int p2 = 2;
  for (i = 1; i <= NUM_THREADS; i *= 2) {
    if ((tNum % p2) == 0)
      if (tNum+i < NUM_THREADS) gSum[tNum] += gSum[tNum+i];
    p2 *= 2;
    pth_barrier(&B);
  }
  free(pArg);
}

int main(int argc, char* argv[])
{
  int j, sum = 0;
  pthread_t tHandles[NUM_THREADS];

  InitializeArray(A,&N);   // get values into A array; not shown
  pth_barrier_init(&B, NUM_THREADS);
  for (j = 0; j < NUM_THREADS; j++) {
    int *threadNum = new(int);
    *threadNum = j;
    pthread_create(&tHandles[j], NULL, SumByReduction, (void *)threadNum);
  }
// just wait for thread  with id=0 to terminate; others will follow
  pthread_join(&tHandles[0], NULL);
  printf("The sum of array elements is %d\n", gSum[0]);
  return 0;
}
```

The first thing to notice about the code in this example is the inclusion of another header file, pth_barrier.h, and a barrier object globally declared by pth_barrier_t B. A *barrier* is a synchronization that will pause threads at the barrier point in the code until all threads working in the computation have reached that same point. Once all threads have arrived, the barrier releases the threads to begin execution of the succeeding code. This is like a starting line at a race that doesn't allow the competitors to start until all racers have reached the start line; once all the racers are ready, they are allowed to begin the event. See "A Barrier Object Implementation" on page 134 for details about implementing such a barrier object with the POSIX threads library.

If you look at the main() function, you will see the initialization of the array, the initialization of the barrier object, and the creation of threads to execute the SumByReduction() function. The main thread then waits for only the first thread created. This thread will have an ID (threadNum) of 0, and the pthread_t value returned from pthread_create() is stored in the index 0 element of the tHandles array. Since the final result will be in the gSum[0] location, and this "0" thread computes that final value and stores it in the location, once the 0 thread has terminated, the final sum has been stored and is ready to be used.

The first half of the SumByReduction() function code is taken verbatim from the corresponding function found in Example 6-4. The second half (in the bold text) is the reduction of the partial sums generated by the threads into a single summation value. Before reduction of the partial sums can begin, all of the partial sums must be computed. Even though we could assume that an equal distribution of chunks of data array will be assigned to each thread, we cannot assume (Simple Rule 6) that all threads will finish at the exact same time to store the partial sum result in the proper gSum slot. While there could be more than enough resources to assign one thread to a core exclusively, there are myriads of other factors within the operating system or the processor hardware that can slow down or inhibit the computation of one or more threads. Thus, we need to place a barrier after the assignment of each thread's partial sum into the gSum array. After the last thread has reached the barrier, we know that all the partial sums have been stored and the computation can safely proceed to the reduction. The whole key to the reduction algorithm working correctly (and being able to prove that this is a correct algorithm) is the barrier synchronization.

The reduction computation mimics the combining of data in Figure 7-1. The for loop counts off the rounds, with the i variable serving as the offset into the gSum array from which a thread will read data during the current round. The loop variable is multiplied by 2 in each iteration.

The p2 variable will be powers of 2 that are used to determine which threads need to read data from the gSum array and add that value to the value found in that thread's assigned gSum element. The outer if-then statement in the body of the loop makes this determination by dividing a thread's ID number by p2 and allowing those threads that are evenly divisible by the current

p2 to proceed to the inner `if-then` statement. The inner conditional expression (`tNum+i <`
`NUM_THREADS`) will ensure that the proposed element of the gSum array to be read actually exists
within the array bounds and, if so, increments the value of the thread's gSum slot with the value
accessed.

Regardless of whether or not a thread was allowed to participate in the addition operation,
every thread multiplies the local copy of p2 by 2 and then waits at a barrier until all threads
have completed whatever computation was allowed within the current round of the reduction.
All threads will execute something within each round of the reduction, even though half as
many are doing useful work in a given round than in the previous round. This may seem like
a waste of resources. However, since all threads must meet up at the barrier, we keep each
thread running and doing a minimal amount of work (doubling the value of p2 in each round)
to keep in sync with those threads that are still doing constructive work.

NOTE

While I've never written one or seen an implementation of one, creating a barrier that could
work with a different number of threads each time it was used sounds like such a complex
and daunting task. I'm afraid that the execution of such a beast would have massive amounts
of overhead—certainly much more than keeping some threads alive for a few microseconds
past the time they are doing anything practical.

Once you've had a chance to digest the code in Example 7-2 and probably traced the concurrent
execution of the code using the example given in Figure 7-1, you may be asking yourself if
this will work with a number of threads that is not a power of 2. All the instructions seem to
be predicated on powers of 2, but there may come a time when you can only use 14 or 57
threads for a reduction operation. Rest assured, the code does work for a number of threads
that is not a power of 2.

To prove this to yourself, try tracing the algorithm with nine threads (`#define NUM_THREADS 9`).
The gSum array will be indexed from [0] to [8] (visualize another element attached to the right
of the gSum array shown in Figure 7-1). There will be four rounds to the reduction algorithm,
where i will be assigned values 1, 2, 4, and 8. The first eight elements of the gSum array will be
processed as shown in Figure 7-1 during the first three rounds of the algorithm. The ninth
element (index [8]) will be unchanged, since all potential elements of gSum that would be read
and used to add into the contents of that slot are not within the bounds of the array. At the
fourth round, the 0 thread will read the contents of gSum[8] (0 + i = 8) and add that value to
the contents of gSum[0]. You can reproduce this idea to any number of threads between 9 and
16 (or any other nonpower of 2) where the upper slots of gSum will be summed (via reduction)
into the index [8] element during the first three rounds, and the fourth will bring the final
total into gSum[0].

Speaking of odd numbers of threads, did you notice the use of the (`float`) cast in the
computation of start and end in Example 7-2? Rather than hoping for a number of iterations

that will be evenly divisible by the number of threads, you can use this method to divide iterations more evenly than integer division. For example, suppose that you have a loop with 122,429 iterations to be divided among 16 threads. If you use integer division and an assignment statement for the last thread to use 122,429 for its end value, each thread would be assigned 7,651 iterations, except the last one, which would get 7,664 (if you don't have a calculator handy, just trust me on the arithmetic). When using floating-point division that truncates fractional parts when recast back to (int), 13 of the threads will be assigned 7,652 iterations and the other 3 get 7,651. If the time to compute one iteration is short, 13 extra iterations assigned to the last thread might not have much impact. If an iteration takes 30 seconds to compute, waiting six and a half minutes for one thread to finish is a serious load balance issue. Regardless of the time per iteration, for static scheduling of loop iterations, using (float) when computing the start and end bounds will always generate a better load balance between threads.

A Barrier Object Implementation

A barrier object can synchronize thread execution at a specific point within the code. Threads are blocked at a barrier until all threads have reached the barrier point, and then all threads are released. With this description, we can develop the code to implement a barrier object to be used in Pthreads codes.

A Pthreads condition variable will hold threads until they can be released. So, we need a condition variable and the associated mutex object. In addition, the barrier must know the total number of threads that are participating in the barrier and how many threads have arrived at the barrier. When the final thread has come to the barrier, use that thread to release all the other waiting threads and to reset the counters of the barrier for the next use.

In my initial implementations of the barrier object, since I was using the count of threads that have arrived as the condition to keep threads waiting, I had thought to have the last thread exiting the barrier do the reset of all the counters. By keeping the count of threads at the barrier equal to 0 until the last thread was ready to exit, I didn't take into account the chance of another thread reentering the barrier, acquiring the mutex, checking the conditional expression, and passing over the pthread_cond_wait(). When a thread external to the while loop usurps the mutex and isn't forced to wait as it should be, it is known as an *intercepted wait*. In this case, the intercepted wait of an external thread entering the barrier before all threads previously waiting on the barrier had left can lead to a deadlock.

Thus, I need a conditional expression for the condition variable that doesn't rely on the count of threads at the barrier. I've chosen to "color" each use of a barrier in a cyclic fashion. When threads enter a barrier, they must wait for all threads to enter the barrier while the barrier is the same color. When the final thread shows up, the color of the (future) barrier changes and the counter resets (for the next use). Threads that are signaled to wake up check the barrier color. If it is not the same color that they found when they entered, they know that the final thread has arrived and they can now exit the barrier. The structure for the `pth_barrier_t` type is given here:

```
typedef struct {
  pthread_mutex_t m;
  pthread_cond_t c;
  int count, color, numThreads;
} pth_barrier_t:
```

Following the convention of other Pthreads synchronization objects, I have written an initializing function to set up a barrier. This function simply calls the initialization functions for the condition variable and mutex. The total number of threads that will always participate in each use of the barrier is sent as a parameter to the initialization function. This value sets the two integer counters within the object. The `count` is decremented as threads come into the barrier and will reach 0 when the final thread has arrived. The `color` will actually toggle between "0" and "not 0," but I've added a definition of RED to be used in the initialization, for some extra flair. The initialization code is given here:

```
#define RED 0

pth_barrier_init (pth_barrier_t *b, int numT)
{
  pthread_mutex_init(&b->m, NULL);
  pthread_cond_init(&b->c, NULL);
  b->count = b->numThreads = numT;
  b->color = RED;
}
```

Upon entering the `pth_barrier()` function, a thread first gains control of the object's mutex and notes the current color of the barrier. The color is held in a variable (`kolor`) local to each thread entering the barrier function (since `kolor` is declared in a function called by a thread). The thread then determines whether it is the last to arrive. If not, it blocks itself on the condition variable (and releases the mutex). If the thread is the last to arrive, which it will know from the barrier's `count` being decremented to 0, it will reset the `color` of the barrier, set the `count`, and wake up all threads that have been waiting. The code for the `pth_barrier()` function is given here:

```
void pth_barrier (pth_barrier_t *b)
{
  pthread_mutex_lock(&b->m);
  int kolor = b->color;
  if (--(b->count)) {
    while (kolor == b->color) pthread_cond_wait(&b->c, &b->m);
  }
  else {  // last thread
    pthread_cond_broadcast(&b->c);
    b->count = b->numThreads;
    b->color = !b->color;
  }
  pthread_mutex_unlock(&b->m);
}
```

Could we still have a disastrous intercepted wait? Consider two threads running and needing to wait at the barrier. If T0 is already waiting, T1 will enter and realize it is the final thread. While still holding the mutex, T1 changes the color of the barrier (to BLUE, say), sets the count, and broadcasts the wake-up signal before releasing the mutex. If T1 races through the code following the barrier and encounters the barrier again (perhaps in a loop), it will see that it is not the last to arrive at a BLUE barrier. T1 decrements the barrier count and will call pthread_cond_wait(). From the fairness property of the interleaving abstraction, we know that T0 will eventually acquire the mutex. Upon return from waiting, it evaluates the while conditional expression. Since T0 was waiting at a RED (kolor) barrier, the expression is false (the current barrier color is BLUE) and the thread will exit the barrier. After running through the code following the barrier, the next instance of the same barrier encountered by T0 will be BLUE.

Threads under Windows Vista have added a CONDITION_VARIABLE object that works much like the Pthreads equivalent. A CRITICAL_SECTION object is associated and released when the thread waits by calling SleepConditionVariableCS(). Like many other Windows Threads functions that block threads, this function allows you to set a time limit. To wake threads sleeping on a CONDITION_VARIABLE, use a call to WakeConditionVariable().

I can't take too much credit for the barrier implementation here. I had tried using two decrementing counters, the second of which counted threads leaving the barrier so that the final thread could reset all the counts. When this method kept deadlocking, I turned to *Programming with POSIX® Threads* (Addison-Wesley Professional, 1997) by David R. Butenhof and got the color inspiration. The barrier implementation given here is a simplification of the barrier code in Butenhof's book. Of course, his implementation is much more detailed and portable than the one I've cobbled together. I urge you to go over his codes and consider using his full implementation if you need to use barriers in more complex situations.

Design Factor Scorecard

How efficient, simple, portable, and scalable is the reduce code described earlier? Let's examine the algorithm with respect to each of these categories.

Efficiency

The code declares a local sum variable for each thread (lSum) to hold the ongoing computation of the local partial sum. Even though each thread will update a unique element from the gSum array, using the local sum variable avoids all the false sharing conflicts that could arise for each and every item within an assigned chunk of data. By updating a gSum slot once per thread, you can limit the number of false sharing conflicts to the number of threads, not the number of items in the original data array.

The barrier implementation will be an efficiency concern for the reduction algorithm. Besides getting a thread to wait on a condition variable in Pthreads or in Windows Threads, there is the overhead that comes from the extra code needed to decide whether a thread entering the barrier is the final thread and, if so, releasing all other waiting threads. The attendant bookkeeping that goes along with all of this is just more computation to be synchronized for correctness and more time spent not actually doing productive work.

Simplicity

With the help of Figure 7-1, the code is pretty simple and straightforward. The use of i and p2 to determine which threads are allowed to proceed and from where data is gathered would be the most confusing parts to someone unfamiliar with the algorithm. (While I chose to handle them separately for the example, the i and p2 variables could be combined into the for loop.)

Portability

OpenMP has an explicit barrier for threads within an OpenMP team. There are also implicit barriers at the end of OpenMP worksharing constructs that you can use (or turn off with the nowait clause, if not needed). Instead of using the reduction clause in OpenMP, you could write the explicit algorithm in OpenMP by attaching thread ID numbers to each thread in the team and using the explicit barrier. Normally, knowing someone was even contemplating such a use of OpenMP would elicit howls of derisive laughter, Bruce. But, if I can replace all the code from "A Barrier Object Implementation" on page 134 with the single line #pragma omp barrier, I would be willing to swallow my prejudices and take the simpler path.

In a message-passing system, you can write an algorithmic construction for reduction, similar to the one discussed previously. In this case, each process has a chunk of the data, the reduction computation on that portion of the data is computed locally, and the process ID numbers are used to coordinate messages between processes to pass the local partial results to other processes. There is no need for explicit barrier synchronizations, since the act of passing messages can guarantee the correct order of data is sent and sent only when it is ready. Receiving processes need to block until the data is received. These processes can easily compute from where the data will be sent. Within the MPI message-passing library, there is a reduction function that will, more often than not, give better performance than a handcoded reduction algorithm.

Scalability

Is this algorithm, with the barrier and all, the best way to do a reduction when there are a large number of threads involved? The implementation of the barrier object will be the principal limit to scalability of this reduction algorithm. The synchronization objects used within the implementation of a user-coded barrier object can be a bottleneck as the number of threads increases.

In cases where a large number of threads are used and are available for the reduction computation, an alternative implementation would be to divide the elements of the global array holding the partial results generated by each thread among four or eight threads. These threads would divide up the partial sum elements, compute a reduction on the assigned chunk, and then allow one thread to do the final reduction on these results in serial. The code for this suggested algorithm isn't as simple as the one using barriers, but it could be more efficient.

Applying MapReduce

I want to give you an idea about how to determine when MapReduce might be a potential solution to a concurrent programming problem. The task we're going to carry out here is finding all pairs of natural numbers that are mutually *friendly* within the range of positive integers provided to the program at the start of execution (this computation was part of the problem posed during the Intel Threading Challenge contest in July 2008). Two numbers are mutually friendly if the ratio of the sum of all divisors of the number and the number itself is equal to the corresponding ratio of the other number. This ratio is known as the *abundancy* of a number. For example, 30 and 140 are friendly, since the abundancy for these two numbers is equal (see Figure 7-2).

$$\frac{1+2+3+5+6+10+15+30}{30} = \frac{72}{30} = \frac{12}{5}$$

$$\frac{1+2+4+5+7+10+14+20+28+35+70+140}{140} = \frac{336}{140} = \frac{12}{5}$$

FIGURE 7-2. Friendly numbers

The serial algorithm for solving this problem is readily evident from the calculations shown in Figure 7-2. For each (positive) integer in the range, find all the divisors of the number, add them together, and then find the irreducible fractional representation of the ratio of this sum and the original number. After computing all the ratios, compare all pairs of ratios and print out a message of the friendly property found between any two numbers with matching ratios.

To decide whether this problem will fit into the MapReduce mold, you can ask yourself a few questions about the algorithm. Does the algorithm break down into two separate phases? Will the first phase have a data decomposition computation? Are those first phase computations independent of each other? Is there some "mapping" of data to keys involved? Can you "reduce" the results of the first phase to compute the final answer(s)?

This is a two-part computation. We can think of the first phase as a data decomposition of the range of numbers to be investigated, and there is a natural mapping of each number to its abundancy ratio. Factoring a number to compute the divisors of that number is independent of the factorization of any other number within the range. Thus, this first phase looks like a good candidate for a map operation.

As for the reduce phase, each number-abundancy pair generated in the map phase is compared with all other pairs to find those with matching abundancy values. If a match is found within the input range of numbers, that match will be noted with an output message. There may be no matches, there may be only one match, or there may be multiple matches found. While this computation doesn't conform to the typical reduction operations where a large number of values are summarized by a single result, we can still classify this as a reduction operation. It takes a large collection of data and "reduces" the set by pulling out those elements that conform to a given property (e.g., the earlier document search application that finds the smaller set of pages containing keywords or phrases).

Thus, the serial algorithm for identifying mutually friendly pairs of integers within a given range can be converted to a concurrent solution through a MapReduce transformation. The code for an OpenMP implementation of this concurrent solution is given in Example 7-3.

EXAMPLE 7-3. MapReduce solution to finding friendly numbers

```
int gcd(int u, int v)
{
  if (v == 0) return u;
  return gcd(v, u % v);
}

void FriendlyNumbers (int start, int end)
{
  int last = end-start+1;
  int *the_num = new int[last];
  int *num = new int[last];
  int *den = new int[last];

#pragma omp parallel
  {int i, j, factor, ii, sum, done, n;
//   -- MAP --
#pragma omp for schedule (dynamic, 16)
  for (i = start; i <= end; i++) {
    ii = i - start;
    sum = 1 + i;
    the_num[ii] = i;
    done = i;
    factor = 2;
    while (factor < done) {
      if ((i % factor) == 0) {
        sum += (factor + (i/factor));
        if ((done = i/factor) == factor) sum -= factor;
      }
      factor++;
    }
    num[ii] = sum; den[ii] = i;
    n = gcd(num[ii], den[ii]);
    num[ii] /= n;
```

```
      den[ii] /= n;
   }  // end for

//  -- REDUCE --
#pragma omp for schedule (static, 8)
   for (i = 0; i < last; i++) {
     for (j = i+1; j < last; j++) {
       if ((num[i] == num[j]) && (den[i] == den[j]))
         printf ("%d and %d are FRIENDLY \n", the_num[i], the_num[j]);
     }
   }
 } // end parallel region
}
```

Ignore the OpenMP pragmas for the moment while I describe the underlying serial code. The FriendlyNumbers() function takes two integers that define the range to be searched: start and end. We can assume that error checking before calling this function ensures that start is less than end and that both are positive numbers. The code first computes the length of the range (last) and allocates memory to hold the numbers within the range (the_num). It also allocates memory space for the numerator (num) and denominator (den) of the abundancy ratio for each number. (We don't want to use the floating point value of the abundancy since we can't guarantee that two ratios, such as 72.0/30.0 and 336.0/140.0, will yield the exact same float value.)

The first for loop iterates over the numbers in the range of interest. In each iteration, the code computes the offset into the allocated arrays (ii), saves the number to be factored, and finds the divisors of that number and adds them together (sum). The internal while loop finds the divisors of the number by a brute force method. Whenever it finds a factor, it adds that factor (factor) and the associated multiplicand (i/factor) to the running sum. The conditional test makes sure that the integral square root factor is not added in twice. The done variable is the largest value that potential divisors (factor) can be. This value is set to i/factor whenever a factor is found, since there can be no other divisors greater than the one associated with the factor value in factor.

After summing all the divisors of a number, the code stores sum in the appropriate numerator slot (num), and stores the number itself in the corresponding denominator slot (den). The gcd() function computes the greatest common divisor (GCD) for these two numbers (via the recursive Euclidean algorithm) and divides each by the GCD (stored in n) to put the ratio of the two into lowest terms. As noted in the comments, the factoring and ratio computations will be the map phase.

The nested for loops that follow compare the numerators and denominators between unique pairs of numbers within the original range. To ensure only unique pairs of ratios are compared, the inner j loop accesses the numerator and denominator arrays from the i+1 position to the last.

If the [i] indexed numerator and denominator values match the [j] indexed numerator and denominator values, a friendly pair is identified and the two numbers stored in the_num[i] and the_num[j] are printed with a message about their relationship. This is the reduce phase.

The code in Example 7-3 uses OpenMP pragmas to implement concurrency. The code includes a parallel region around both the map and reduce portions. Within this region are the declarations of the local variables i, j, factor, ii, sum, done, and n.

The for loop of the map phase is located within an OpenMP loop worksharing construct to divide iterations of the loop among the threads. Notice that I've added a schedule clause to the pragma. I've specified a dynamic schedule, since the amount of computation needed to find divisors of numbers will vary widely, depending on the number itself. Within the inner while loop, the number of factors that must be considered will be smaller for a composite number than a prime of similar magnitude (e.g., 30 and 31). Also, larger numbers will take more time than smaller numbers, since there will be more factors to test and, likely, there will be more divisors of the larger number (e.g., 30 and 140). Hence, to balance the load assigned to threads, I've elected to use a dynamic schedule with a chunk size. Threads that are assigned subrange chunks that can be computed quickly will be able to request a new chunk to work on, while threads needing more time to continue with the assigned subrange chunk will continue factoring.

For the reduce phase implementation, another loop worksharing construct is placed on the outer for loop (Simple Rule 2). As with the worksharing construct in the mapping code, a schedule clause has been added to yield a more load balanced execution. In this case, I've used a static schedule. You should realize that the number of inner loop iterations is different for every iteration of the outer loop. However, unlike the inner loop (while) within the map phase, the amount of work per outer loop iteration is monotonically decreasing and predictable. The typical default for an OpenMP worksharing construct without the schedule clause is to divide the iterations into a number of similar-sized chunks equal to the number of threads within the OpenMP team. In this case, such a schedule would assign much more work to the first chunk than to subsequent chunks.

I visualize such a default static division of iterations like the triangle shown in Figure 7-3, where the vertical axis is the outer loop iterations, the horizontal axis is the inner loop, and the width of the triangle represents the number of inner loop iterations executed. The area of the triangle associated with a thread is in direct proportion to the amount of work that the thread is assigned. The four different shades of gray represent a different thread to which the chunk of work has been assigned.

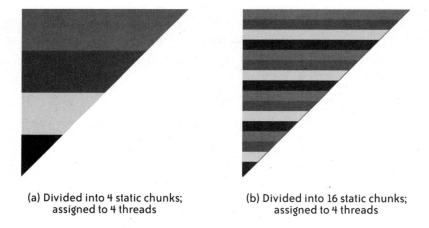

(a) Divided into 4 static chunks;
assigned to 4 threads

(b) Divided into 16 static chunks;
assigned to 4 threads

FIGURE 7-3. Two static distributions of monotonically decreasing amounts of work among four threads

The more equitable division of area (i.e., work) among threads is shown in Figure 7-3 (b), which includes smaller and more numerous chunks. Those chunks are assigned to each thread in a round-robin fashion. The sum of the areas is then much more equal between threads and, thus, the load will be better balanced. You can accomplish the division of work shown in Figure 7-3 (b) by using the schedule (static, 8) clause given in Example 7-3. While a dynamic schedule may give a tighter overall load balance, the overhead associated with distributing chunks of iterations to threads might be more adverse than simply using the "good enough" static schedule.

There is no magic reason for using the chunk sizes that we used here. When using an OpenMP schedule clause (or implementing such behavior using an explicit threading library), test several different values to see whether there are significant performance differences. Choose the one that gives the better performance in the majority of potential input data set cases. Keep in mind the size of a cache line and choose a chunk size that will allow full cache lines to be used by a single thread whenever possible, especially when updates are required.

Friendly Numbers Example Summary

In this section, I've shown how you can apply the MapReduce framework to a serial code in order to find a concurrent equivalent. While the reduce phase of the friendly numbers problem might seem atypical, you need to be prepared to see past the standard many-to-one reduction case in order to be better equipped to translate serial codes to a MapReduce solution.

MapReduce As Generic Concurrency

I think the biggest reason that the MapReduce framework has gotten such a large amount of notoriety is that it can be handled in such a way that the programmer need not know much about concurrent programming. You can write a MapReduce "engine" to execute concurrently when it is given the specifications on how the mapping operation is applied to individual elements, how the reduction operation is applied to individual elements, and how the reduction operation handles pairs of elements. For the programmer, these are simply serial functions (dealing with one or two objects). The engine would take care of dividing up the computations among concurrent threads. The TBB parallel_reduce algorithm is an example of this, where the operator() code would contain the map phase computation over a subrange of items and the join method would implement the reduce phase.

This is the reason that I recommend structuring your map and reduce phases in such a way that you can apply the reduction computations to individual items and partial results of previous reductions. For example, in finding the maximum value from a data set, the definition of the reduction operation is to simply compare two items and return the value of the largest. Such code would work whether it was being applied to pairs of elements from the original collection or from partial results that had used this code to whittle down the original set into fewer partial results. If the MapReduce engine only has to deal with the details of dividing up the data and recombining partial results, the programmer simply supplies the comparison function to the engine. The limitations of a generic MapReduce engine might preclude the use of such a system if the reduction computation were more complex, such as the reduction computation used in the friendly numbers problem.

I predict that providing generic concurrency engines and algorithms that allow programmers to write only serial code or require a minimum of concurrency knowledge will become popular in the coming years. This will allow programmers who do not have the training or skills in concurrent programming to take advantage of multicore and manycore processors now and in the future. Of course, until we get to the point where we can program by describing our problem or algorithm in English (like in countless episodes of *Star Trek*), someone has to understand concurrent programming to build such engines, which could be you.

CHAPTER EIGHT

Sorting

THIS CHAPTER EXAMINES THE OPERATION OF CONCURRENT SORTING. At times, sorting has been estimated to account for over 80% of all processing cycles. Presenting the results from database queries, compiling a list of business investments with associated risk-reward measures, and figuring the company payroll are all operations that require sorting. Even with the large amounts of processing time spent on graphical interfaces, visualization processing, and video games, sorting remains a vital part of computation. Every time you get a list of URLs from a search engine, the results have been sorted, typically by some measure of relevance to your original query.

In this chapter I will first consider compare-exchange sorts. These are sorting algorithms that use the results from comparing two keys to determine the relative order of the elements with those keys. Movement of data items will be based on those results and will be the exchange of the positions of the two items under consideration. The final algorithm considered is radix sort, which compares bits within keys to determine movement of data. Example codes presented in this chapter will use arrays of integers, but you can apply these techniques to structures with a key field to distinguish between elements.

Bubblesort

Bubblesort was the first sorting algorithm I ever learned. It is easy to code and simple to understand. A serial version of the algorithm appears in Example 8-1.

EXAMPLE 8-1. Serial Bubblesort

```
void BubbleSort(int *A, int N)
{
  int i, j;
  int temp;
  for (i = N-1; i > 0; i--) {
    for (j = 0; j < i; j++) {
      if (A[j] > A[j+1]) {
        temp = A[j]; A[j] = A[j+1]; A[j+1] = temp;
      }
    }
  }
}
```

Through each iteration of the outer loop, some elements that have not reached their final position within the array will move at least one step closer to that final sorted position, plus the element with the largest key value that is not at its final position will "bubble up" to its final sorted position. Thus, the inner loop will pass through a decreasing set of elements from the array until there are only two elements left to consider. After these are verified to be in the proper order, the sort will be complete. This "brute force" version can be accentuated with a test for exchanges. If no exchanges are found in any iteration of the outer loop, the array is sorted and there is no need for additional passes. Figure 8-1 shows the comparisons that are made in the first two passes through an array of 10 integer keys. The results of data movement are reflected in successive arrays shown.

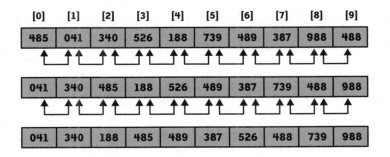

FIGURE 8-1. Comparisons made in Bubblesort

If we have a large collection of things to be sorted, typically in an array, the first concurrent design that comes to mind is a data decomposition approach. So, we can think about dividing up the array of elements to be sorted into nonoverlapping chunks that can be assigned to threads. Because of the overlapping nature of compare-exchange operations within the inner loop, we can foresee both an execution order dependence and a data dependence. The serial algorithm inherently contains the execution order of compare-exchange operations that is needed to propagate an element through the array. An item traversing the array from the low-index end to somewhere in the high-index end must go through all intervening array slots. Dividing up the array into chunks for threads puts boundaries between chunks that elements will need to cross at some point in the sorting process. Synchronizing threads to cooperate at these border crossings can be a bigger nightmare than it was to get from East to West Berlin through Checkpoint Charlie. All of this overhead will likely defeat any parallel performance that results from threading the algorithm.

If we approach Bubblesort as a task decomposition where a task is one full and complete pass through the data (i.e., a single iteration of the outer loop), we can resolve both of the dependence problems. By executing one full pass through the array in a single thread, we don't have any boundaries between chunks that need synchronization for data movement. How can iterations of the outer loop be independent if the data being accessed still overlaps? This will require some synchronization between threads as to when they are allowed to start execution of the iteration. Obviously, the iterations must be executed in the same order as they would be for the serial algorithm, but the start of each iteration will be delayed. The thread assigned to some iteration is allowed to start only after the previous thread has progressed some number of elements into the array. Using this delayed start method of launching threads, we can preserve the execution order of the serial algorithm and attempt to prevent data races.

The general algorithmic structure I've just described is known as a *wavefront* approach. Like waves washing onto a beach, the threads sweep through the data one after the other. As long as one wave doesn't catch up to another, you can avoid data races. Threads can execute with varying speeds depending on the amount of time a thread is given within a processor core. Even if all threads were given the same number of cycles or each thread had exclusive access to a core, different amounts of computation can propel a thread further along than another thread executing the same algorithm. This is why I said that we could "attempt to prevent" data races at the end of the previous paragraph. Without guarantees in the algorithm, there is still the chance of one thread catching up to another. For example, if the leading thread were always doing an exchange of elements and the trailing thread did few or no exchanges, the trailing thread could eventually be accessing the same array elements as the leading thread.

What's the worst that could happen in this case? We can construct an interleaving of two threads where thread T1, started after thread T0, evaluates the same pair of elements as T0. Furthermore, T0 and T1 can both decide that they need to swap the data elements. If T0 makes the swap before T1, the data items are left in the same unsorted order after T1 makes the swap. If T1 found no other exchanges, two more phases would be needed to complete the sort: one to swap those last two elements, and one to find no exchanges.

Two extra runs through the data? Is that the worst? Unfortunately, the two threads that execute those extra phases, T2 and T3, could meet at the same adjacent elements and achieve the same result that T0 and T1 did. We can perpetuate these bad interleavings indefinitely. This scenario describes a *livelock* situation. Threads are doing some computation (sweeping through the data array looking for out-of-order elements), but they are unable to proceed due to the actions of some other thread (the duplicate swap of data from the same two array slots). Contrast this to *deadlock*, where a thread is blocked, waiting for something to happen.

One mechanism for starting threads could simply be to have a thread send a signal to the next scheduled thread when the leading thread has reached a point that is "safe" and we know that the trailing thread will not overlap its predecessor in all situations. That is, thread T0 starts off down the array comparing and swapping items. After processing a number of items, say 10, thread T1 is given the signal to start. When T1 reaches the 10th item, it will signal T2 to begin, and so on.

Where is that "safe" point? The most obvious point is after the leading thread has gone through all the elements of the array. This is the serial algorithm executing with the overhead of threads and their synchronization. If we have only a single point within the processing of the array that is safe for a new thread to begin, we have set a limit on the scalability of the algorithm, since we would have no more than two or three threads executing at any time.

A refinement that will better maximize the number of threads is to divide the data into a number of nonoverlapping zones at least equal to the number of threads. Threads are not allowed to enter a zone until the preceding thread has completed the computations within that zone. These zones are like critical regions. We can use an appropriate synchronization mechanism for critical regions of code to control access to the data zones. The size of the zones can be dynamically shrunk as the number of unsorted elements decreases in each pass.

How much additional overhead does this modification add to the Bubblesort algorithm? We would need to check after each compare-exchange to determine when the end of a zone had been reached. At the end of each zone, a thread would exit the critical region (yield the lock) and attempt to enter the succeeding zone. The more zones we install for scalability, the more overhead there will be of exiting and entering critical regions. Example 8-2 is an implementation of the BubbleSort() function based on these ideas using Windows Threads. Notice that the simple code shown in Example 8-1 has bloated to at least five times the size, and that is without counting all the support code outside of this function needed to prepare the set of locks for the critical regions.

EXAMPLE 8-2. Threaded version of Bubblesort

```
unsigned __stdcall BubbleSort(LPVOID pArg)
{
  int i, j, k, releasePoint, temp, rpInc;
  BOOL exch;

  rpInc = N/NUM_LOCKS;
  rpInc++;

  while (!Done) {
    k = 0;
    exch = FALSE;
    EnterCriticalSection(&BLock[k]);
      i = iCounter--;
      releasePoint = rpInc;
      if (i <= 0) {
        Done = TRUE;
        LeaveCriticalSection(&BLock[k]);
        break;
      }

      for (j = 0; j < i; j++) {
        if (A[j] > A[j+1]) {
          temp = A[j]; A[j] = A[j+1]; A[j+1] = temp;
          exch = TRUE;
        }
        if (j == releasePoint) {
          LeaveCriticalSection(&BLock[k++]);
          EnterCriticalSection(&BLock[k]);
          releasePoint += rpInc;
        }
      }
    LeaveCriticalSection(&BLock[k]);
    if (!exch) Done = TRUE;
  }
  return 0;
}
```

This example uses a while loop to keep threads executing passes as long as there is still a chance that some data remains to be sorted. For each pass through the data, the maximum number of unsorted elements (iCounter) is accessed (protected by the CRITICAL_SECTION object BLock[0]) and stored locally in i. If the number of potential unsorted items is less than or equal to zero, the sorting is done and the Done flag is set. When other threads complete their current pass, the while conditional test will terminate them. Before this determination is made, the index of the last slot in the first data zone is stored in releasePoint.

The j loop passes through the array element by element, compares the values of A[j] with A[j+1], and swaps them if they are out of order. If the thread has reached the end of the current data zone, it releases the CRITICAL_SECTION object on that zone and waits for the thread in the next zone to release that lock before proceeding. Once the end of the array has been reached, the thread in that zone releases the last CRITICAL_SECTION object used. If no exchanges were made during the just completed pass, the thread sets the Done flag.

Will It Work?

Looking at the code in Example 8-2 should get your Concurrency Sense tingling. In the midst of execution of the for loop, if j is at the last element of a data zone (j == releasePoint), won't the thread be accessing (and maybe updating) an item from within the next zone (A[j+1])? Is there a chance that this data race could cause a problem? Or, can we prove that it doesn't? Three cases must be addressed: T0 will swap, but T1 does not; T1 will swap, but T0 does not; and both threads must swap. These are illustrated in Figure 8-2. For concreteness, we'll examine the first two data zones on the array, though we could use any two adjacent zones and any contiguous indexes. The end of the first data zone is the element at index position [4], which is distinguished by the darker gray shade and lighter key value.

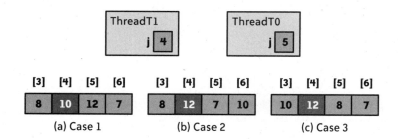

FIGURE 8-2. BubbleSort() interleaving cases

In all three cases, thread T0 has gone through the first data zone, released the lock and acquired the lock for the next zone, and is ready to start execution with the local j=5. Thread T1 acquires the lock to the first zone (after the release by T0) and reaches the last comparison within that first zone (j=4) before T0 is allowed to proceed with the first comparison in the second zone. Thus, both threads are poised to execute the if test at the start of the for loop body. The overlapping element is in the A[5] slot (A[j+1] for T1), and it is for this element that we need to show there is no data race.

In Case 1, shown in Figure 8-2 (a), T0 will determine that the A[5] and A[6] elements must be swapped and T1 will not need to swap A[4] and A[5]. Thus, there is no data race on A[5]. T1, after finding no need to swap, will wait for T0 to relinquish the lock for the second zone before it will touch A[5] again.

In Case 2, shown in Figure 8-2 (b), T0 will not need to swap A[5] and A[6], while T1 will swap A[4] and A[5]. Again, there is no data race on A[5].

In Case 3, shown in Figure 8-2 (c), where both T0 and T1 will be swapping their respective pairs of elements, things get a lot more interesting. Figure 8-3 gives an example of one potential interleaving of the swap instructions after each thread has executed the if test and found that a swap is required. Figure 8-3 also shows the resulting state of the array portion for each step of the interleaving.

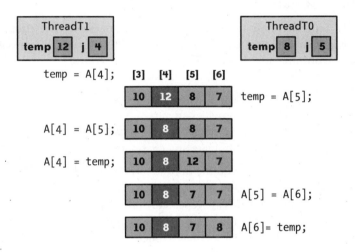

FIGURE 8-3. BubbleSort() Case 3 interleaving

By Grabthar's Hammer! Anytime you can "lose" a data item from a concurrent algorithm, you've got a big problem. The interleaving shown in Figure 8-3 looks like a disastrous data race that could scuttle use of the code in Example 8-2. What if, just before the last comparison in a zone, we required the thread to acquire the lock on the next zone? For that last element where the overlap occurs, a thread would need to be holding two locks. This solves our problem, but the already complicated code would just get more convoluted. Plus, the additional overhead wouldn't help performance and the number of threads that can be executing within the array at the same time would be restricted even further (lowering the scalability of the code). It's looking grim.

Take heart—there is a silver lining to this gray cloud. If you do some algorithmic analysis, you will find that Case 3 is impossible. In fact, Case 2 can never occur in practice either. After a thread has gone through a zone, the first element just beyond the boundary item will be greater than all the items in the previous zone. In each pass, Bubblesort pushes items with larger key values into higher indexed slots. In the cases given in Figure 8-2, consider what would happen if 12 were the largest key value in the first zone, Thread T0 would swap this value into A[5] before relinquishing the lock on the first zone to T1. If 12 were not the largest key value in the first zone, A[5] would contain that largest value (or a value larger than the largest in the first zone). Thus, the only valid case we need to consider for interleaving analysis is Case 1, and that case has no data race.

When trying to prove or disprove the correctness of your concurrent algorithms, don't rely solely on an interleaving analysis. You must also consider the properties of the serial algorithm and how those may or may not be changed by the transformation of the serial code.

Design Factor Scorecard

Bubblesort is a difficult algorithm to parallelize and may not be worth the effort. Even so, how efficient, simple, portable, and scalable is the concurrent Bubblesort code described earlier? Let's review the algorithm with respect to each of these categories.

Efficiency

The linear access of array elements provides an almost foolproof way to predict which cache line of data will be needed next. If you can define the data sizes of zones on cache line boundaries, you should be able to eliminate any chance of false sharing.

The linear access of array elements and the need to pass over all potentially unsorted items doesn't allow for the reuse of cache. Sure, this "property" is inherent in the nature of the serial algorithm, but when multiple threads are repeatedly bringing array elements into cache, looking at them twice, and then not needing them until the next iteration of the while loop, you can quickly choke the memory bus with too much data. This is going to directly affect the scalability of this algorithm.

Simplicity

It sucks. I mean, just look at the difference between the serial code (Example 8-1) and the threaded code (Example 8-2). There's nothing simple about the zone implementation to keep threads out of the way of each other.

Fortunately, not all sorting algorithms are this difficult to transform. Later sections cover concurrent versions of other compare-exchange based sorting algorithms that will prove to be easier to understand and be much simpler to parallelize.

Portability

Not so good. You could do a translation of Example 8-2 into Pthreads. However, since this is a task decomposition, I'm not too sure how easy it would be to use an implicit threading library. And while you could use the explicit task facilities under OpenMP or Intel TBB, the problem of coordinating threads to not overlap each other would still remain.

A distributed-memory implementation would, by necessity, need to be an algorithm based on data decomposition. The movement of data between assigned blocks would require a message to be sent and received. The amount of such data traffic, even in the average case, would be prohibitive.

Scalability

This sucks, too. There will be a tradeoff between the number of threads you can use, based on the number of zones, and the amount of synchronization overhead and time spent waiting at locks. The more zones within the data, the more threads you can use; the more zones, the more locks will have to be acquired and released, and the more opportunity there will be for threads to sit idle waiting for access into the next data zone.

I suppose you could set up twice as many zones as threads to alleviate the contention on locks. You could delay threads starting so that there is a "free" zone between each thread as it passes through the array. There would be less chance for idle threads, but using twice as many locks would increase the overhead by a factor of two.

None of the above even takes into account the fact that after each pass, the number of potentially unsorted elements decreases. When the algorithm progresses to the point where there are fewer zones than threads, you can't help but have idle threads.

Odd-Even Transposition Sort

The *odd-even transposition sort* compares adjacent pairs of items in an array to be sorted and exchanges them if they are found to be out of order relative to each other. Unlike Bubblesort, which also compares adjacent elements, the odd-even transposition sort compares disjointed pairs by using alternating odd and even index values during different phases of the sort. That is, on one pass through the data, it compares an odd index [i] and the adjacent even index [i+1] element; in the succeeding phase, it compares an even index [i] and the adjacent odd index [i+1] element. The odd and even phases are repeated until no exchanges of data are required. Two phases of the odd-even transposition sort are shown in Figure 8-4.

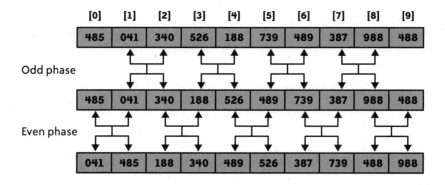

FIGURE 8-4. Odd-even transposition sort

From Figure 8-4 you should be able to see that each comparison within a given phase of the sorting algorithm can be done concurrently. Example 8-3 gives the serial code for odd-even transposition sort. The while loop continues to make passes through the data, comparing adjacent items, until a complete pass generates no exchange of items. We have to be sure to run through one odd phase and one even phase to ensure that the first and last items have had a chance to be compared. This is the purpose of using the start variable in the while conditional expression. The comparisons in the for loop start on alternating odd and even element indexes, and there is no overlap of elements compared within the for loop body.

EXAMPLE 8-3. Odd-even transposition sort serial code

```
void OddEvenSort(int *A, int N)
{
  int exch = 1, start = 0, i;
  int temp;

  while (exch || start) {
    exch = 0;
    for (i = start; i < N-1; i += 2) {
      if (A[i] > A[i+1]) {
        temp = A[i]; A[i] = A[i+1]; A[i+1] = temp;
        exch = 1;
      }
    }
    if (start == 0) start = 1;
    else start = 0;
  }
}
```

A Concurrent Code for Odd-Even Transposition Sort

We can use a data decomposition design on the odd-even transposition sort algorithm. Dividing the array into chunks will keep all comparisons and data movement resulting from those comparisons within the chunk. And for those comparisons that might be on the edge of a chunk in one phase and split between chunks in the other (e.g., the [4] and [5] elements in Figure 8-4), we can simply let the thread assigned to the chunk containing the lower indexed element do the comparison. There will be no possibility of contention from the thread assigned the adjacent chunk, since any item used within a comparison in either the odd or the even phases will only be touched once.

The iterations of the inner for loop can be divided to form independent data chunks for threads. OpenMP can easily parallelize this for loop, as shown in Example 8-4. We can use the implicit barrier at the end of the parallel region to ensure that all the comparisons and data movement within a phase have completed before the next phase is launched.

EXAMPLE 8-4. Concurrent version of odd-even transposition sort with OpenMP

```
void OddEvenSort(int *A, int N)
{
  int exch = 1, start = 0, i;
  int temp;

  while (exch || start) {
    exch = 0;

#pragma omp parallel for private(temp) shared(start, exch)
    for (i = start; i < N-1; i += 2) {
      if (A[i] > A[i+1]) {
        temp = A[i]; A[i] = A[i+1]; A[i+1] = temp;
        exch = 1;
      }
    }

    if (start == 0) start = 1;
    else start = 0;
  }
}
```

The temp variable is a work variable, and each thread requires a separate copy, thus I've added a private clause to the pragma. I've added the shared clause more for documentation than necessity. The code updates the exch variable within the loop and then reads the value outside of the parallel region. Since it is only read within the parallel region and updated outside of the region, start does not need any protection.

If you further consider the update of exch, you may wonder whether any protection is required, since each thread is updating exch with the same value. In fact, whenever the same thread detects multiple swaps within the data chunk assigned by the OpenMP loop worksharing construct, it will reassign the same value. This is known as a *benign data race*. Because multiple threads may be updating the value concurrently, it is considered a data race, but it does no harm to leave off the protection of this variable, since it is the same value being assigned each time. Besides, the atomic pragma doesn't work on a simple assignment of a value. On the other hand, if the algorithm needed to keep count of the number of exchanges—rather than just using exch as a signal—the data race would no longer be benign, and we would be required to protect the increment operation.

Trying to Push the Concurrency Higher

The implementation in Example 8-4 does an adequate job of parallelizing the odd-even transposition sort algorithm. However, since the parallel region is within the body of the while loop, each iteration will cost the execution some overhead from starting and stopping threads. Can we move the parallelism to a "higher" level within the code (Simple Rule 2) and at least prevent the repeated waking and sleeping of OpenMP threads? Even though the while loop iterations can't be executed concurrently, we can place a while loop within a parallel region as long as we're careful to be sure each thread executing the loop will execute the same number of iterations. Otherwise, we can end up in deadlock with some threads at the end of the parallel region and others at some implicit barrier in the body of the while loop. Example 8-5 moves the parallel region to encompass the while loop and include the interchange of values in the start variable.

EXAMPLE 8-5. Second concurrent version of odd-even transposition sort with OpenMP

```
void OddEvenSort(int *A, int N)
{
  int exch = 1, start = 0, i;
#pragma omp parallel
  {
   int temp;
   while (exch || start) {
     exch = 0;
#pragma omp for
     for (i = start; i < N; i += 2){
       if (A[i] > A[i+1]) {
         temp = A[i]; A[i] = A[i+1]; A[i+1] = temp;
         exch = 1;
       }
     }
#pragma omp single
     if (start == 0) start = 1;
     else start = 0;
   }
  }
}
```

As before, temp is required within each thread and we make it private by moving the declaration into the parallel region. The for loop reads the start variable within the loop worksharing construct, and the succeeding single construct updates start once the loop has completed. Placing the update of start into a critical region would be a mistake. With a critical region, each thread in the team will be given access, in turn, to update start. The value of start will ping-pong back and forth between 0 and 1. For example, if start holds the value 0, the first thread into the critical region would change start to 1. The next thread into the critical region would find start holding a 1 and would change it to 0. If there were an odd number of threads, the final value assigned in the critical region would be correct. I'm not aware of any powers or multiples of 2, which seems to be the basis for the number of cores available on multicore processors, that are odd.

Instead of allowing one thread at a time to have access to update start, we need one thread alone to update this variable. For this, we use a single construct. There is the added bonus of an implicit barrier at the end of the single construct to ensure that no threads will go onto the next set of for loop iterations with the old value of start.

There is no easy way to protect the reading of the exch value as the conditional expression of the while loop. Does the reading of exch need to be protected? Isn't this also a benign data race because each thread will be reading the same value from the variable in order to test whether or not to proceed into the while loop? Unfortunately, this whole solution isn't as benign as we might have hoped.

The implicit barrier of the single construct assures us that there will be no data races on the comparing and swapping of data between odd and even passes. However, we can still run into a catastrophic data race at the point where threads enter the while loop, even the initial entry. Consider the initial entry into the parallel region. The shared value of exch is 1, and all threads should enter the while loop. What is the first thing that a thread does when it enters the while loop? That thread resets the value of exch to 0. If any threads within the OpenMP team don't access the value of exch in the conditional expression before some thread has changed it, those threads will be convinced that the sorting has completed and will proceed to the end of the parallel region to wait for the other threads to realize that the sorting has finished. In the worst case, all but one thread (the thread that was lucky enough to perform the original reset of exch) will be sidelined. We'll have a deadlock situation because any thread that gets into the sorting code will be waiting at the barrier of the loop worksharing construct while all others are waiting at the implicit barrier of the parallel region.

Can we fix this? The binary nature of exch is tripping us up. Simply protecting the reset of exch with some form of synchronization won't get around this. We need to set up exch to allow N threads to pass into the while loop if any of the threads have performed an exchange in the previous phase. What if, rather than setting exch to 1 when an exchange is executed, we assigned the number of threads in the team to exch? With that change, the reset of exch within the while loop would be a (protected) decrement, and exch would not be 0 until every thread had entered the while loop. The changes needed to implement this method within the while loop conditional expression and body are shown in Example 8-6.

EXAMPLE 8-6. While-loop changes to odd-even transposition sort code

```
#pargma omp parallel
 {int temp;
  while (1) {
    if (exch == 0 && start == 0) break;
```

```
#pragma omp critical
    exch--;
#pragma omp for
    for (i = start; i < N; i += 2) {
        if (A[i] > A[i+1]) {
            temp = A[i]; A[i] = A[i+1]; A[i+1] = temp;
#pragma omp critical
            exch = omp_num_threads();   // Assign with the number of threads
        }
    }
#pragma omp single
    if (start == 0) start = 1;
    else start = 0;
    }
}
```

The first thing to note is that we've turned this into an infinite loop that will break when there have been no exchanges in the previous phase (and the minimum number of phases have been processed). This change is necessitated by the fact that we cannot protect the read access in the while loop conditional. Pulling that reference out of the expression and restructuring the loop as shown is necessary to make sure that all required accesses to exch are protected.

The initial access of exch within the if condition is not in a critical region. If we had placed that line of code within the critical region protecting the decrement of exch, we would have two exits from a block of code (within a critical region): the normal exit point for the case that exch is not 0, and the execution of the break. Even if such bad coding practice were allowed, consider the consequences of the case where the initial if statement has been put in an OpenMP critical region. Whenever there were no exchanges of items from the previous phase, the first thread into the region would acquire the synchronization object that OpenMP uses for a critical, execute the break, fall to the implicit barrier at the end of the parallel region, and remain holding the critical sync object. This would deadlock the rest of the threads, since the next thread and all other threads would sit waiting at the entry to the critical region. Not good.

What about the unsafe state of not protecting the access of exch in the initial if test access? Could the protected decrement of the exch variable interfere with this to cause problems? If the value of exch is 0, there is no problem, since all threads will execute the break and exit the parallel region. If the value of exch is the number of threads executing the sort (either set in the declaration outside the parallel region or set from an exchange of items in the previous phase) as each thread enters that first critical region to decrement exch, we know that only the last thread to perform the decrement will bring the value down to 0. Thus, no thread will fail to enter the loop worksharing region from an interaction of threads checking for the end of sorting and executing the decrement of exch.

What about the other update of exch within the loop worksharing region? The same OpenMP critical region protects it, so no two threads can be decrementing exch and resetting it to the number of threads at the same time. Still, there is a subtle bug that exists within the code of

Example 8-6. Can you see it? Consider what will happen if some threads enter the loop worksharing portion of the while loop when others are still waiting to get through the critical region for decrementing exch. When a swap of items is detected, the value of exch is set to the number of threads; those threads that haven't passed through the critical region will then decrement this value to a number that is not 0 and is less than the number of threads. Any swap after all threads have passed the initial critical region will set the value of exch correctly and there will be no problem for the next phase. But, can you guarantee that there will be another swap?

Doing interleaving analysis on your concurrent algorithms, you may also have to specify the data set that can trigger bad behavior among threads. To show off this subtle bug in the implementation, imagine the worst-case data set for odd-even transposition sort: a sorted list, but with the final element at the head of the list. During any phase, there will be a single swap until the final element reaches its sorted position. With only a single swap in a single thread, if there are threads that haven't passed through the decrement critical region, there is no chance to correct the problem of having the wrong value in exch for the next time through the while loop.

Let me illustrate why, with a concrete interleaving, having the wrong value in exch will lead to catastrophe. Assume we have eight threads running the code shown in Example 8-6. After three of these threads pass through the critical region and decrement exch, one of the three identifies two elements that must be swapped and enters the critical region within the loop worksharing region. Even if there is a queue to order access to the critical synchronization object, this interleaving example will have the other five threads still preparing to check whether exch is equal to 0. The thread that found the one exchange to be done during this phase of the sort will set exch to 8. After the final five threads pass through the decrementing critical region, the value of exch will be 3. Once the threads meet at the implicit barrier at the end of the single region, they will all start back into the body of the while loop. However, after the first three threads have executed the decrement, any of the other five threads that haven't already been able to perform the first check of (exch == 0) will break out of the while loop and wait at the end of the parallel region. We will have some threads at the barrier at the end of the parallel region and the rest at the barrier at the end of the loop worksharing construct. None of these threads can be released until all threads have met at the same barrier. Since that will never happen, the code is in deadlock.

NOTE

Even using the interlocked intrinsics of Windows Threads will not eliminate this problem. We can use the intrinsics for every access of exch, but the interaction between threads can still set exch to the number of threads before all threads have started the sorting phase.

Can we fix this? An explicit barrier after the critical region to decrement exch should do the trick. However, our original goal was to remove the overhead of continually starting and stopping the team of threads for each phase of the sort. The code in Example 8-6 now has two critical regions, an additional implicit barrier (from the `single` construct), and, if we want to fix this latest problem, an explicit barrier. I think we can be happy that the code in Example 8-4 works. There is minimal synchronization overhead required, and the overhead of repeatedly entering and exiting a parallel region looks to be mitigated by not needing all of the additional synchronization that would be necessary to drive the concurrency higher in the code.

Keeping threads awake longer without caffeine

If we can't efficiently minimize thread sleeping and waking overhead without adding a bunch of other overheads, we can cut down on the number of times we need to start and stop threads within the odd-even transposition sort implementation. Inside each parallel region, rather than doing either an odd phase or an even phase, we can do one of each. Code for this variation of the sort algorithm is given in Example 8-7.

EXAMPLE 8-7. Concurrent double-phase implementation

```
void OddEvenSort(int *A, int N)
{
  int exch0, exch1 = 1, trips = 0, i;

  while (exch1) {
    exch0 = 0;
    exch1 = 0;

#pragma omp parallel
    {int temp;

#pragma omp  for
      for (i = 0; i < N-1; i += 2) {
        if (A[i] > A[i+1]) {
          temp = A[i]; A[i] = A[i+1]; A[i+1] = temp;
          exch0 = 1;
        }
      }
      if (exch0 || !trips) {
#pragma omp  for
        for (i = 1; i < N-1; i += 2) {
          if (A[i] > A[i+1]) {
            temp = A[i]; A[i] = A[i+1]; A[i+1] = temp;
            exch1 = 1;
          }
        }
      } // if exch0
    } // end parallel
    trips = 1;
  }
}
```

The *double-phase* algorithm uses two exchange flags: exch0 and exch1. Execution of the while loop body is predicated on the exch1 variable. The two flags are reset and the thread enters the parallel region. The first loop worksharing construct divides up the data array, and if any thread performs an exchange, it sets exch0. After being released from the implicit barrier of the first worksharing construct, each thread tests exch0. If the variable has been set (or the trips counter has not been set after the first pair of phases), the thread enters the second loop worksharing construct. If any thread performs an exchange in the second loop, exch1 is set. After threads are released from the end of the parallel region barrier, the conditional expression of the while loop is evaluated. If there was an exchange (exch1), the threads reset the flags and enter the parallel region.

The double-phase variation cuts the number of entries and exits from the parallel region in half. The start index on each of the for loops is hardcoded into the algorithm, which eliminates the need for the single region to flip the start variable. The reduction of thread synchronization from unrolling iterations of the original while loop should prove to be well worth the extra coding.

Design Factor Scorecard

How efficient, simple, portable, and scalable are the first concurrent version and the double-phase version of the odd-even transposition sort code? Let's review these algorithms with respect to each of these categories.

Efficiency

Cache use for the odd-even transposition sort (Example 8-4) is very good. Items from the array are accessed in linear order. Once a thread has a starting point within the array, it will be easy to predict the next cache line needed to be brought in from memory. Thus, we should assign large blocks of the array to each thread. With OpenMP, the schedule (static) clause ensures that the data is divided into a number of chunks equal to the number of threads (if this is not already the default for loop worksharing). Explicit threading models can divide the inner for loop to assign data in the same way.

If the data sets are large enough that you must perform cache evictions before a pass through the data is complete, you can tweak the double-phase implementation (Example 8-7) to alternate the choice of incrementing or decrementing the loop iterator. That is, for the first for loop phase, increment the iterations controlling the index of array items, and during the second for loop phase, decrement the iterations from the upper end of the array. After the first phase, the cache will contain the highest indexed elements from the array chunk, and the second phase would start the compare-exchange operations and access items in reverse order from the first phase. The succeeding first phase will then have the lowest indexed array elements stored in cache on which to work.

Simplicity

From the previous discussions, you should be able to see that the simplest implementation of a concurrent odd-even transposition sort is given in Example 8-4. The original serial code is well preserved and recognizable. In fact, even the addition of a second for loop and loop worksharing construct (Example 8-7) yields code that is easy to understand. The code from Example 8-6, with an added explicit barrier, would not be so simple.

Portability

Using an explicit threading model, a concurrent odd-even transposition sort will require dividing the for loop iterations among threads. This is easy, but we must preserve the barrier at the end of the for loop to ensure that all of the compare-exchange operations have completed in one phase before threads move on to the next phase. If not, there is a potential data race on the last indexes compared by one thread during phase k and the first indexes touched by the thread assigned to the adjacent array chunk in phase $k+1$. For example, the last comparison done by thread T0 in phase k could be elements with indexes [53] and [54]. If thread T1 has started onto phase $k+1$ at the same time, it will compare elements with indexes [54] and [55]. That shared, even indexed element ([54]) is the potential data race. Thus, some form of barrier synchronization between phases is needed.

A distributed-memory version of odd-even transposition sort takes the linear order of the ranks of processes and executes a compare-split operation between alternating neighbor processes. After sorting the local data in each process, the sorting takes place in alternating phases. In the odd phase, odd-ranked processes exchange a copy of their data with a copy of the data held by the even-ranked processes whose rank is one less. Even-ranked processes exchange data with the odd-ranked processes whose rank is one greater. All processes perform a mergesort of the data sets, with the odd-ranked processes keeping the upper half of the data and the even-ranked processes keeping the lower half. In the even phase, even-ranked processes exchange with odd-ranked processes whose rank is one greater and keep the upper half of the merged data; odd-ranked processes exchange with even-ranked processes and keep the lower half of the merged data. After a number of phases equal to the number of processes—half odd phases and half even phases—the data is sorted along the linear order of processes.

Scalability

The odd-even transposition sort is very scalable. The amount of data to be compared and exchanged per thread remains constant throughout the execution of the algorithm.

Shellsort

Before we look at Shellsort, let's review insertion sort, since the two are related. I won't give a concurrent algorithm or implementation of insertion sort, though I will describe an algorithmic idea that you could use. You should imagine me waving my hands and operating sock puppets as you read that part.

Quick Review of Insertion Sort

Insertion sort is such a simple algorithm to remember and code that I've always used it as my "go to" sort whenever I needed a quick and dirty algorithm. For me, the definitive example of the algorithm is to imagine being dealt and holding a hand of bridge. Every bridge player I know keeps cards of the same suit together and ranks the cards by face value within each suit. In the player's mind, at least, there is a total order to the 52 cards of a deck of standard playing cards. For each new card that is dealt, a player picks up the new card and scans the current cards in her hand from one side to the other until she finds the place that the new card fits into the sequence.

Implementation of insertion sort starts with an unsorted list of items. This is typically an array, but you can also use it with a linked list of items. At any time during the sort, the list of items is separated into two parts: the sorted portion and the remaining unsorted items. To insert a new item, the next unsorted item is chosen, and the sorted list is scanned from the biggest index down to the smallest. Items larger than the item to be inserted are moved down one place in the array. When the first item from the sorted portion smaller than the item to be inserted is located, the position of the inserted item (within the current set of sorted items) has been found and the item is stored in the array. Example 8-8 has the code for sorting an array of integers with the insertion sort algorithm.

EXAMPLE 8-8. Insertion sort algorithm

```
void InsertionSort(int *A, int N)
{
  int i, j, v;
  for (i = 1; i < N; i++) {
    v = A[i];
    j = i;
    while (A[j-1] > v) {
      A[j] = A[j-1];
      j--;
      if (j <= 0) break;
    }
    A[j] = v;
  }
}
```

Figure 8-5 shows the state of an array of 10 integer keys at the end of each of three iterations of the outer for loop on 10 integer keys. The shaded elements of the array show the sorted portion.

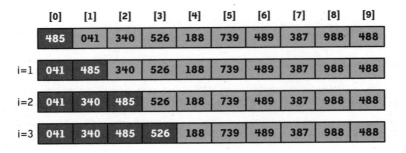

FIGURE 8-5. Insertion sort

Insertion sort is an inherently serial algorithm. Items are inserted one at a time. For a concurrent version of insertion sort, you might imagine starting in the middle and working out, giving two fronts that could each be handled by a different thread. One unsorted area contains the lower indexed slots and the other contains the higher indexed slots. Looking at the original data list in Example 8-8, imagine the sorted portion to be the [4] and [5] indexed items. What happens when one thread attempts to insert 489 and the other thread tries to place the 526 item? Each thread's search for insertion points crosses the search of the other thread. What protections of the shared array would we need to do this correctly? How complex does the code become when dealing with a shifting end boundary to terminate the insertion of the "largest" or "smallest" seen item? Even if all of these questions can be answered satisfactorily, the algorithm is restricted to using two threads and is not very scalable.

Serial Shellsort

Shellsort is a version of insertion sort that does an *h-sort* across the whole array (see Example 8-9). That is, the algorithm is working an insertion sort in *h* separate, interleaved partitions at the same time. After each pass with a given *h*, the value of *h* is reduced and another pass over the list is done to *h*-sort the list. When the value of *h* reaches 1, a simple insertion sort of the whole list is performed.

EXAMPLE 8-9. Serial Shellsort algorithm

```
void Shellsort(int *A, int N)
{
  int i, j, h, v;
  h = 1; while (h < N) h = 3*h + 1;
  h /= 3;
  while (h != 1) {
    for (i = h; i < N; i++) {
      v = A[i]; j = i;
      while (A[j-h] > v) {
        A[j] = A[j-h];
        j -= h;
        if (j <= h) break;
```

```
      }
      A[j] = v;
    }
    h /= 3;
  }
  InsertionSort(A, N);  // clean up
}
```

Figure 8-6 shows an array of 10 integer keys before and after Shellsort with h=3. With such an *h* value, the array contains three sorted lists interleaved. The three lists are identified in the figure with squares, circles, and triangles over the index values on the second array.

FIGURE 8-6. Shellsort with h=3

If you focus on just the items indexed with multiples of 3 from the original array (485, 526, 489, 488), the second array has sorted this list in the slots identified by squares in the second array. The other two sublists (marked with circles and triangles) have been similarly sorted.

The advantage of Shellsort over insertion sort is that items are moved closer to their final position with fewer exchanges of items. While insertion sort exchanges adjacent items, Shellsort exchanges "adjacent" items that are actually *h* items apart. If the item destined to be first, within an array of N items, is located at the opposite end of the array, it will take (at most) N/*h* exchanges to place this element within the first *h* locations in the array.

Concurrent Shellsort

For a given value of *h*, the Shellsort algorithm interleaves *h* independent insertion sorts. In the code in Example 8-9, the *h*-sorted partitions each contain one element (before the i loop starts). Within the body of the for loop, the code inserts an unsorted item into each of the *h* partitions before adding another unsorted item to each. This is like playing a card game by yourself, dealing out one card and inserting that card into a hand before dealing out the next card to the next hand and inserting into that hand.

As written, the code in Example 8-9 doesn't expose the data decomposition opportunities of each independent *h*-partition. For concurrent design and implementation purposes, it would be better for the serial algorithm to sort an entire *h*-partition of data before going to the next *h*-partition. This scheme would be like dealing out all of the cards to each hand, then sorting all the cards in a hand before moving on to another hand. That way, it is easier to invite other players into the game and have each hand sorted concurrently. Example 8-10 shows the modified Shellsort code to add an outer loop to sort a single *h*-partition before going on to the next *h*-partition.

EXAMPLE 8-10. Modified serial Shellsort to sort an h-partition all at once

```
void Shellsort(int *A, int N)
{
  int i, j, k, h, v;
  h = 1; while (h < N) h = 3*h + 1;
  h /= 3;
  while (h != 1) {
    for (k = 0; k < h; k++) {
      for (i = k; i < N; i += h)  {
        v = A[i]; j = i;
        while (A[j-h] > v) {
          A[j] = A[j-h];
          j -= h;
          if (j <= h) break;
        }
        A[j] = v;
      }
    } // for k
    h /= 3;
  }
  InsertionSort(A, N);  // clean up
}
```

This modification of the serial algorithm is an application of Simple Rule 8. With this formulation of Shellsort, we can easily parallelize the code. On the outer k-loop, a loop parallel solution such as OpenMP or Intel TBB will work. Example 8-11 shows the OpenMP version of the code from Example 8-10. It declares the i, j, and v variables within the scope of the k-loop to make them private. The firstprivate clause on the parallel pragma creates a private copy of the variable h and will initialize it with the value of the shared copy prior to entering the parallel region.

EXAMPLE 8-11. OpenMP version of Shellsort

```
void ParallelShellsort(int *A, int N)
{
  int k, h;
  h = 1; while (h < N) h = 3*h + 1;
  h /= 3;
#pragma omp parallel firstprivate(h)
  {
  while (h != 1) {
#pragma omp for
    for (k = 0; k < h; k++) {
      int i, j, v;
      for (i = k; i < N; i += h)  {
        v = A[i]; j = i;
        while (A[j-h] > v) {
```

```
        A[j] = A[j-h];
        j -= h;
        if (j <= h) break;
      }
      A[j] = v;
    }
  } // for k
  h /= 3;
  } // end while
  } // end parallel region
  InsertionSort(A, N);
}
```

The code in Example 8-11 illustrates placing a while loop into a parallel region for each thread to execute as I discussed at the end of "Odd-Even Transposition Sort" on page 153. The reason that the parallelization of the while loop is easy in Shellsort but nearly impossible in odd-even transposition sort is the fact that the while loop test is independent of the computations performed in Shellsort. The firstprivate clause gives each thread in the team a copy of h that has been initialized from the value assigned to the shared copy prior to entering the parallel region. Within the parallel region, iterations of the k loop are divided among the threads and the implicit barrier holds threads until all the partitions have been sorted. After release from the barrier, each thread updates the local copy of h. Since each thread will hold the same value of h, the number of iterations of the while loop executed will be the same for each thread, and threads will terminate execution of the parallel region at the same time.

Design Factor Scorecard

How efficient, simple, portable, and scalable is the concurrent Shellsort code described earlier? Let's review the algorithm with respect to each of these categories.

Efficiency

The computational complexity of Shellsort is not well understood and relies heavily on the sequence of decreasing values for h. It does seem to perform better than some other sorts, such as insertion and selection sorts, which both have asymptotic complexity of $O(n^2)$.

> **NOTE**
>
> In *Algorithms* (Addison-Wesley, 1983), Robert Sedgewick notes that the sequence ..., 1093, 364, 121, 40, 13, 4, 1 has been shown to provide good speed. This sequence is built into all code examples used in this section.

The algorithm's strength of fewer exchanges done over long distances to quickly place items closer to their final position is the concurrent algorithm's weakness when it comes to efficiency. In the serial version of the algorithm (Example 8-9), the long-distance moves of data can take advantage of some cache reuse. At the start of execution, two different cache lines would be used to hold items that are h units apart in the array. Consecutive iterations of the i loop would use the next consecutive item from a cache line already in memory. As the algorithm progresses and the length of the sorted h-partitions grows, more cache lines are needed, but the next insertion is done one array item down from the previously accessed item. Thus, it uses a nice and orderly progression of cache lines that an automatic prefetch mechanism should be able to recognize.

With the code modifications in Example 8-10, we have even better cache reuse for each iteration of the i loop. In fact, by working through the entire h-partition all at once, subsequent processing of h-partitions will likely find many, if not all, of the necessary cache lines already loaded.

Assigning consecutive h-partitions to different threads will lead to false sharing problems. These two h-partitions will share almost all of the same cache lines. The concurrent algorithm is constantly reading (for comparison of the item to be inserted) and writing (moving items down to make an insertion point) elements from the cache lines for each iteration of the while loop within the i loop.

A scheduling clause on the OpenMP pragma in Example 8-11 might yield better cache reuse behavior. If we know how many items to be sorted will fit into a cache line, we can set the schedule for the i loop iterations to ensure that each thread will handle chunks of consecutive h-partitions and reuse the same cache lines. For example, in the sorting of integers (4 bytes), with a 128-byte cache line and the data aligned on cache boundaries, you can use the clause schedule(static, 32).

Unfortunately, the schedule clause may only ensure that the first cache line touched by a thread would be touched exclusively by only one thread. Unless the h values used were powers of 2, the code would still be prone to some false sharing. Looking over the list of h values endorsed by Sedgewick, you may notice that two of the six values are prime (1,093 and 13) and none of them, except 1, is a power of 2. After the first cache line, the cache line holding an array item that is h elements away will be found on a cache line shared by another thread.

On top of all of this, there may be a problem with cache eviction, too, if cores have shared caches. Depending on the size of the data and the number of cores and threads sharing a cache, as lines are loaded in, there is the chance that an early line (used as the algorithm moves items to find the proper insertion point) will be removed to make room. As the algorithm progresses and the value of h decreases, the number of elements within a partition and the number of cache lines needed to hold an entire partition will increase. In the extreme case, each time a new item is to be inserted, all of the cache lines may need to be reloaded.

Simplicity

The addition of the k loop and the changes to the body of this loop (the previous i loop and body) were very minor and easy to understand. The addition of the two OpenMP pragmas is also a minor change to the serial code that keeps the basic algorithm intact.

Portability

The OpenMP solution is portable. Using TBB for this algorithm would take a similar tack. Some form of barrier synchronization is required to make sure threads don't proceed to the next iteration of the while loop before all the h-partitions have been sorted with the previous value of h. OpenMP gives us this synchronization automatically at the end of the loop worksharing construct.

The native threads solution simply needs to divide up the k loop iterations. The explicit barrier that TBB would need is a requirement for native threads, too.

A distributed-memory version is tricky, since there is the movement of data from one part of the array to another and those two parts may be assigned to different processors. In *Introduction to Parallel Computing: Design and Analysis of Parallel Algorithms* (Benjamin Cummings, 1994), Vipin Kumar et al. describe an algorithm on a hypercube network where the gray code numbering of nodes used to form a ring also defines the order of nodes for the sorted data. The basic algorithm is in two phases. The first phase has d steps, one for each bit position in the binary representation of node labels in the d-dimension cube. Each step has each node sort the data assigned and then do a compare-split operation between pairs of nodes whose label differs at the current bit position. The compare-split operation exchanges the upper half of the data in the node with a 0 in the bit position with the lower half of the data in the node having a 1 in the relevant position. After the d steps of the first phase, taking each bit position in turn, the data to be sorted is moved to a position closer to its final location. The second phase is an odd-even transposition sort across the nodes, which should proceed with fewer moves of data items.

Scalability

The scalability of concurrent Shellsort starts out good. At any time during the sorting, there will be h different independent partitions that will differ in size by one item at most. However, while load balance between partitions remains good, the number of partitions steadily decreases as the algorithm proceeds, but the granularity of sorting each partition increases (which sounds like good news, bad news, good news). Eventually, there will be a single partition of data to be sorted. Regardless of the data size, the scalability of this concurrent algorithm gets worse as the computation proceeds.

Quicksort

The serial Quicksort algorithm is implemented recursively. You choose an element from the unsorted array as the "pivot" element, and then partition the array contents such that the pivot item ends up at the point that divides the array into elements that are less than or equal to the pivot item and elements that are greater than the pivot item. The Quicksort routine can then sort each "half" of the data.

Data sets that are sorted or nearly sorted present performance problems for the Quicksort algorithm. In these cases, one of the partitions will dwarf the other partition in size. The best performance will be from data sets that are equal in length after partitioning. Example 8-12 gives code for the Partition() function and the recursive QuickSort() function.

EXAMPLE 8-12. Serial Quicksort algorithm

```
int Partition (int p, int r)
{
  int x = A[p];
  int k = p;
  int l = r+1;
  int t;

  do k++; while ((A[k] <= x) && (k < r));
  do l--; while (A[l] > x);

  while (k < l) {
    t = A[k];  A[k] = A[l];  A[l] = t;
    do k++; while (A[k] <= x);
    do l--; while (A[l] > x);
  }
  t = A[p];  A[p] = A[l];  A[l] = t;
  return l;
}

void QuickSort(int p, int r)
{
  if (p < r) {
    int q = Partition(p, r);
    QuickSort (p, q-1);
    QuickSort (q+1, r);
  }
}
```

The code assumes that a global array, A, holds the data to be sorted and the QuickSort() function needs to have only the start and end index values (p and r, respectively) of the subportion of the array to be sorted. The q variable holds the index of the pivot element after the partitioning around this item has completed. Two calls to the QuickSort() function complete the algorithm. The first call to QuickSort() works on the lower partition up to, but not including, the pivot element (from p to q-1); the second call deals with the upper partition from the element just after the pivot to the end of the array (from q+1 to r). If the number of elements in the array is zero (p < r), that recursive call is halted and the empty subarray has been sorted.

Figure 8-7 shows three views of an array of 10 integer keys. The first line shows the original data, the second displays the data after the array has been partitioned, and the third shows how each of the two partitions from the second line would be partitioned. The boxes encapsulate the portions of the array that need to be sorted.

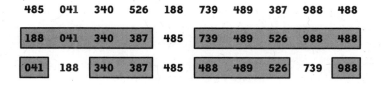

FIGURE 8-7. QuickSort partitioning

NOTE

Due to the expense of recursion, Quicksort is often implemented with a "short-circuit" sort routine (e.g., Bubblesort, insertion sort) that sorts the current subarray when the size of the array to be sorted is less than some threshold.

The Partition() function chooses a pivot element from the data to be sorted and then moves elements to either side of the pivot item depending on the element's relation to the pivot value. In the example code, I simply chose the first element within the array to act as the pivot. You can minimize the data movement by stepping through the elements from both ends of the array, and when an element is found to be in the wrong partition, it is swapped with the other "wrong" element from the other partition. When the two index pointers meet, the last swap places the pivot element into its sorted position. The function returns the index of the pivot element.

Concurrency Within Recursion

Since there is no overlap in elements, each of the two partitions created from a call to Partition() can be sorted independently. But can we thread the recursion of the algorithm?

One method that immediately springs to my mind is to create a new thread in place of each recursive QuickSort() call. Each spawned thread would sort a partition. Example 8-13 shows the changes that you can make to QuickSort() using Windows Threads.

EXAMPLE 8-13. Create a new thread for each QuickSort() recursive call

```
unsigned __stdcall QuickSort(qSortIndex *m)
{
   int p = m->lo;
   int r = m->hi;
   if (p < r)
   {
     qSortIndex s, t;
     HANDLE tH[2];
     int q = Partition(p, r);
     s.lo = p; s.hi = q-1;
     tH[0] = (HANDLE)_beginthreadex (NULL, 0, QuickSort, &s, 0, NULL);
     t.lo = q+1; t.hi = r;
```

```
    tH[1] = (HANDLE)_beginthreadex (NULL, 0, QuickSort, &t, 0, NULL);
    WaitForMultipleObjects(2, tH, INFINITE);
  }
  return 0;
}
```

The struct type qSortIndex contains two integers, lo and hi, to hold the low and high index values of a partition to be sorted. Once the partitioning is complete, the two index bounds for the lower partition are stored in one of the locally declared qSortIndex objects and a new thread is created to sort that partition. The index values for the remaining partition are loaded into the other qSortIndex object and a thread is created to sort that partition. Once the two sorting threads have been launched, the spawning thread blocks, waiting for the two new threads to complete their sorting missions.

This is a horrible way to parallelize this algorithm (I'm the first to admit that some of my initial ideas aren't really all that great). Yes, it works. Yes, it will provide the correct sorted order. Nonetheless, it uses an excessive amount of resources. This algorithm will create at least one thread for each element in the array to be sorted. The overhead this causes will not allow this implementation to achieve any speedup. If there is a limit to the number of threads that an application can spawn, the code may run into this limit before all the work has been divided. Although this solution may be simple to code and keeps the form of the original algorithm, you should not use it.

NOTE

To reduce the number of threads, rather than creating two threads, the QuickSort() function could spawn one thread to sort one partition and simply call itself recursively on the other. This would not only reduce the thread creation overhead (and reduce the amount of system resources spent on short-lived threads), but having just run through the array portions, it is likely that the data for at least part of one of the partitions would be held within the cache of the processor. Upon the return of each recursive call, there is still the need to wait on the created thread to finish the assigned sorting task.

Concurrency Within an Iterative Version

You can simulate recursion in an iterative fashion by mimicking the execution stack of a process with a stack data structure and an appropriate loop that will perform the computations and place computation states (recursive calls) into the stack. We can perform this algorithmic transmogrification on the Quicksort algorithm to devise a version that you can parallelize almost as easily as the recursive version, but with much less overhead.

Iterative Quicksort

Example 8-14 shows the QuickSort() function after rewriting the recursion as an iterative equivalent.

EXAMPLE 8-14. *Iterative version of QuickSort() function*

```
void QuickSort(LPVOID pArg)
{
  int p, r, q;
  qSortIndex *d = NULL, *d1, *d2;

  while (notEmpty(Q)) {
    dequeue(Q, d);  //pull out next index pair
    p = d->lo;
    r = d->hi;
    free(d);

    if (p < r) { // if there is one or more things to sort...
      q = Partition(p, r);

// encapsulate the indices for the lower portion of the partition and enqueue
      d1 = new qSortIndex;
      d1->lo = p;
      d1->hi = q-1;
      enqueue(Q, d1);

// encapsulate the indices for the upper portion of the partition and enqueue
      d2 = new qSortIndex;
      d2->lo = q+1;
      d2->hi = r;
      enqueue(Q, d2);
    }
  }
}
```

This example assumes that we have defined some queue data structure with at least the following methods defined on it:

notEmpty(Q)

Returns TRUE if there is at least one item on the structure, Q; otherwise, it returns FALSE.

dequeue(Q, &item)

Removes one element from the structure, Q, and returns a pointer to this element through item.

enqueue(Q, &item)

Adds the element item to the structure Q.

If items are placed into the structure in a FIFO (first in, first out) manner, the structure is a *queue*; if the items are placed into the structure in a LIFO (last in, first out) manner, the structure is a *stack*. It won't matter which configuration you use. The only difference in the algorithm will be the order in which parts of the array are sorted relative to each other. Since I've already used "Q" to reference this structure, I'll call it a "queue" for the rest of the discussion. The items that are stored within the queue will be qSortIndex objects.

The iterative code enters the `while` loop, which continues to iterate until the queue is empty. This requires that you store the initial array index values into a `qSortIndex` object and place that object on the queue before initially calling `QuickSort()`. Each iteration of the `while` loop removes an index pair from the queue, partitions the shared array between those index values, and then places the indexes of the two resulting partitions back into the queue. If the index pair taken from the queue describes a partition that is one element or less, there is no need to call the `Partition()` function and no index pair will be placed back on the queue.

NOTE
Breshears's Fundamental Law of Sorting states that one item, by itself, is in sorted order.

We can assure ourselves that since the size of the partitions decreases after each call to `Partition()`, the loop will eventually find the queue to be empty during an evaluation of the `while` conditional expression. At this point, the `QuickSort()` function will return and the elements in the array are sorted.

Concurrent iterative version

Data or task decomposition? Since the serial algorithm carves out chunks (partitions) of data and sorts them, a data decomposition sounds like the way to go for Quicksort. Whether or not it proves to be the *best* method, there must be some kind of static chunking method in an algorithm to make us think about trying data decomposition. There is no static decomposition within Quicksort. The partitioning of the array into two chunks depends on the choice of pivot item.

Looking at the iterative algorithm implemented in Example 8-14, we can see that each of the index pairs defines an independent task ("Sort the array within the index range [lo..hi]"). No one task relies on the sorting of any other partition that resides in the queue at the same time. Any available thread can do that sorting. Thus, we can parallelize this version of Quicksort by using a *thread pool*. A thread pool is a set of threads to which you can assign computations. Thread pools are nothing new; OpenMP uses thread pools but calls them *teams* of threads.

When implementing a thread pool as part of a concurrent solution, we must define and implement three properties for the proper use of the pool:

- Signaling the threads when all computations have been accomplished
- Distributing work to the threads
- Terminating threads at the end of the computation

Over the next few pages, I will address each of these issues within the specific example of implementing a concurrent version of the iterative Quicksort algorithm. It may not seem the most natural order in which to address these properties, but the order will allow us to deal with them from easiest to hardest.

Letting threads know the work is done. How do we know when the data has been sorted and threads no longer need to look for more partitions? The serial code in Example 8-14 uses the fact that the queue eventually becomes empty. This won't work in the concurrent version. Consider the case that uses only two threads for sorting. Before threads are allowed to start accessing the shared queue, the "pump needs to be primed" with an index pair that sets the entire array as the initial partition. Typically, some external thread, like the main thread, will be responsible for doing this. The first sorting thread pulls out this first task (partition). While the first thread is calling Partition(), the second thread will encounter an empty queue and terminate. At this point, a single thread ends up sorting the entire array. Imagine any number of threads greater than two, and there is an easy interleaving that will always end up with one thread doing all the work.

Instead of starting with an index pair for the entire array, what if the external thread first calls Partition() and then loads index pairs for each of the two partitions? This will likely solve the case when we have only two threads. However, for a scalable solution, we need to consider cases when there are 4, 8, 16, or more threads. It would not be a prudent use of resources to delay the concurrent execution of multiple threads so that the external thread can call Partition() often enough to set up an initial index pair for each available thread.

Plus, at the other end of the computation, you can probably imagine cases where threads have exhausted the queue of new partitions to be sorted, but one other thread is processing a large partition that will yield more work. If threads terminate because they assume that an empty queue means that all the work has been done, the work from the still-working thread will have to be executed by that remaining thread. We need some other way to determine the difference between when the sorting is complete and when threads are seeing a temporary absence of work to be done.

Recall that each execution of Partition() places one element into its sorted position within the array. Also, whenever a partition has only a single element (p == r-1), that element is known to be in its sorted position. Since each of these two events are easily detected within the QuickSort() function, by keeping track of how many elements are placed in their final sorted location, we can tell when the sorting process is complete. We can use an atomically incremented, shared counter to monitor the progress of the sorting. Threads will know all array elements have reached their final positions when they notice that the counter has reached the target value. We will need to restructure the code to use an infinite while loop in place of the conditional expression testing for an empty queue. You can terminate threads within the pool by simply executing a break from the infinite while loop.

> NOTE
>
> If the threads within the pool are to be used for some other tasks, you do not have to terminate them. The threads could just return from the QuickSort() function to await the next set of tasks to be computed.

Finding work for threads. For the Quicksort implementation, I've already addressed this property of thread pools by using a shared queue structure. Of course, since multiple threads will share this, we need to make certain the queue implementation is thread-safe. A user-defined queue needs some form of synchronization to ensure that elements are inserted (enqueue()) and removed (dequeue()) correctly when using multiple threads.

Even if the execution of enqueue() and dequeue() are thread-safe, we must be sure that a dequeue() operation will not attempt to pull something out when the queue is empty. Example 8-15 shows a method for blocking a thread on an empty queue.

EXAMPLE 8-15. Blocking on an empty queue

```
while (notEmpty(Q)) {} // busy wait until Q has some item
dequeue(Q, d);
```

While the code in Example 8-15 uses a spin-wait, we would hope that the wait would be brief and that no other threads would need to be scheduled on the core held by the thread executing the spin-wait. Even if our hopes are answered, a problem still remains.

Assume that the queue contains one item. Thread T0 begins executing the code in Example 8-15 and finds that the queue is not empty. T0 immediately falls out of the while loop. At this point in the interleaving, T0 is taken out of the core in favor of thread T1 (or T1 is running in parallel on another core). If T1 starts execution of this same code, it will also find that the queue is not empty and will remove the one item in the queue. Once T0 has been put back into a core, it will be under the mistaken impression that there is at least one item in the queue. We can't know what data T0 will get out of the empty queue, but it will most certainly lead to disastrous consequences. We need a more atomic method of ensuring that threads finding a nonempty queue will be guaranteed to pull out a valid item. The TBB concurrent_queue container blocks a thread if the queue is empty (if you are going to always use the TBB container, you can skip to the text following Example 8-16).

If you are using a hand-rolled version of a thread-safe queue, you could attempt to implement this blocking behavior, but you will still have a problem if there is a point in the code where it is possible to interrupt a thread between testing the queue for being empty and pulling an element from the queue.

> **NOTE**
>
> If your home-grown thread-safe queue has a fixed capacity, there will be a reflexive problem when checking to see whether the queue is full before inserting a new element.

Rather than relying on our luck in timing between checking for a nonempty queue and pulling out something from the queue, we can use a semaphore object to keep track of the number of items remaining in the queue. There is a twofold advantage to the use of a semaphore in this fashion. First, threads will be automatically blocked if there are no items currently on the queue (semaphore count is zero). Second, once a thread has passed through the semaphore, it will have an irrevocable reservation on one item from the queue, even if the thread were removed from the core before calling the dequeue() function.

To illustrate this second advantage, again assume that there is only one item on the queue and, consequently, the count of the semaphore is one. T0 calls the wait operation on the semaphore and finds that the count is nonzero. Before returning from the wait call, the count of the semaphore is decremented to zero (and both the count checking and decrementing are an atomic operation). If T0 is now blocked and removed from the core, any other thread attempting to get something from the queue will be blocked at the wait operation on the semaphore. Once T0 is allowed to resume, it will call dequeue() with confidence that there is (at least) one item on the queue to be retrieved. In fact, no matter how many other items might be added and removed from the queue during the time that T0 is blocked, when it resumes, there will always be some item for it to take out of the queue.

Example 8-16 shows the code fragment in Example 8-15 with the spin-wait loop replaced by a Windows Threads semaphore to protect access to the shared queue. The semaphore, hSem, is initialized with a value of zero (the number of items in the initially empty queue). Each time an enqueue() operation completes, the thread that has just added to the queue increments the semaphore by calling ReleaseSemaphore(hSem, 1, NULL).

EXAMPLE 8-16. Using a semaphore to assure items are in the queue to be removed

```
WaitForSingleObject(hSem, INFINITE);
dequeue(Q, d);
```

The TBB concurrent container, concurrent_queue, is thread-safe, and you can use it in place of the handcoded queue that we've been using for the Quicksort code. However, when the sorting of the array is complete, we've got to be able to get the attention of all the computation threads to finish their work and either terminate or go to sleep until the next time the pool is needed. With both the TBB and semaphore methods, threads are not able to break out if they are waiting on an empty queue. The next section, dealing with the third thread pool property, details some of these problems and a solution for getting threads to quit when the work is done.

Giving threads their pink slips. I have now covered how to determine when the sorting process is complete (number of items placed in their sorted positions reaches the total number of elements to be sorted) and how to distribute work safely to each thread (semaphore-protected queue). The last thing to discuss with regard to implementing a thread pool solution is how to terminate the threads in the pool running the QuickSort() function. Regardless of what happens to the sorting threads, there is probably at least one external thread waiting for the completion of the sort. We can set up the system so that when a pool thread notices the sorting has finished, it will send a signal to any thread that may be waiting for the sorted results.

With regard to terminating the sorting threads, one extreme option is to use one of the threads waiting on the sort completion signal to actually terminate (with extreme prejudice) the threads in the pool. If we do not need the pool threads after `QuickSort()` has completed, keeping them around will be a drain on system resources, even if they are not taking processing cycles. If I could, I would put the first two sentences of the next paragraph in a flashing box with a grating, mechanical voice repeating "Warning! Danger! Pay Attention!" as you read it. Since I can't, please imagine red lights and sirens going off around you.

Since threads may be in the process of updating shared data or holding a synchronization object, it is generally not a good idea to terminate threads from an external thread. If you are not careful about which algorithmic state threads are executing when they receive the termination signal, data corruption and deadlock are both real potential outcomes. In the case of the concurrent implementation of Quicksort, once all processing has completed, there will be no chance that the threads in the pool will be in the middle of updating array elements. Also, the only synchronization object that may be adversely affected is the semaphore. In fact, it is most likely that a majority of pool threads, if not all, will be blocked on the semaphore and waiting for the queue to hold another partition to be sorted. Thus, termination by an external thread will not cause any problems from a computation thread holding a synchronization object.

If you prefer a less gory demise to your threads, we can set up a means for the threads to terminate from natural causes (i.e., returning from the threaded function). If you intend to reuse the pool threads later in the computation for some other task, it is possible to get the threads to a point outside of the `QuickSort()` function (see the discussion of helper functions in Chapter 9). The semaphore again comes to our rescue. Once an external thread has received the signal that the sorting is complete, it sets a pool termination flag variable and increments the semaphore count by the number of threads in the pool. Within the code of the pool threads, place a test to determine the state of the pool termination flag between the two lines of code in Example 8-16. If the flag is not set, threads continue sorting; if the flag is set, threads break out of the infinite `while` loop to either terminate gracefully or return from the `QuickSort()` function to await the next assignment.

> **NOTE**
>
> You can put the test for the pool termination flag in the `while` loop conditional expression. However, this is unlikely to catch all pool threads before they go back to get more work from the queue. You will still need to set the semaphore value in order to wake up threads that entered the `while` loop body before the pool termination flag was set.

If we use the TBB `concurrent_queue` container, threads executing a `pop()` in hopes of finding items in an empty queue can't be forcibly interrupted. If we have threads waiting for additional index pairs that won't arrive, we would modify the legal set of items that are put into the queue. In addition to the index pairs used for identifying partitions for sorting, we could add a special flag pair to let threads know when sorting is done. The easiest pair I can think of is $(-1, -1)$, since no array slot will have a negative index. After being signaled, the external thread loads up the queue with enough copies of the special pair for each thread to get one. Upon returning with a pair from the queue, threads first check to determine whether it is a valid index pair or the termination flag pair. If it is the latter, threads can exit the QuickSort() function.

Final Threaded Version

Example 8-17 contains the code for the threaded QuickSort() function using Windows Threads.

EXAMPLE 8-17. Final threaded version of QuickSort() function

```
unsigned __stdcall QuickSort(LPVOID pArg)
{
  int p, r, q;
  qSortIndex *d = NULL, *d1, *d2;
  long t;
  int N = *((int *) pArg);

  while (1) {
    WaitForSingleObject(hSem, INFINITE);
    if (Done) break; //external signal to terminate threads
    dequeue(Q, d);
    p = d->lo;
    r = d->hi;
    free(d);
    if (p < r)
    {
      q = Partition(p, r);
      InterlockedIncrement(&tCount);
      d1 = new qSortIndex; d1->lo = p; d1->hi = q-1;
      enqueue(Q, d1);
      d2 = new qSortIndex; d2->lo = q+1; d2->hi = r;
      enqueue(Q, d2);
      ReleaseSemaphore(hSem, 2, NULL);  // Two items added to queue;
    }                                   // increment semaphore count by 2
    else if (p == r) {
      t = InterlockedIncrement(&tCount);
      if (t == N) SetEvent(tSignal);   // Signal that sorting is done
    }
  }
  return 0;
}
```

Assume the variables tCount (of type long) and Done (of type BOOL) have been declared in the scope of all pool threads and have been initialized with zero and FALSE, respectively. This code uses the InterlockedIncrement() intrinsic to perform an atomic increment of the tCount counter. This increment is done after each call to Partition() and when a partition with a single element (p == r) is detected. In the latter case, there is the chance that this is the last element to be sorted. If tCount has reached the total number of elements to be sorted, the thread that detects this fact sets the event tSignal. An external thread will be waiting for the sort to complete by waiting on tSignal. See Example 8-18.

EXAMPLE 8-18. Code fragment for calling threaded QuickSort()

```
e1 = new qSortIndex;
e1->lo = 0; e1->hi = NumToSort-1;
enqueue(Q, e1);

// Initialize semaphore with 1 item on the queue
hSem = CreateSemaphore(NULL, 1, NumToSort, NULL);

for (i = 0; i < NUM_THREADS; i++)
  hThreads[i] = (HANDLE) _beginthreadex(NULL, 0, QuickSort, &NumToSort, 0, NULL);

WaitForSingleObject(tSignal, INFINITE); // Wait for signal

Done = TRUE;
ReleaseSemaphore(hSem, NUM_THREADS, NULL);
```

After the signal confirming that the sorting task has been completed, the thread executing Example 8-18 will set Done to TRUE and increment the semaphore by the number of threads in order to wake up the pool threads waiting on the semaphore. The pool threads will break out of the while loop and then, in this case, terminate them by exiting the QuickSort() function. Instead of setting the semaphore value, we could explicitly terminate the threads with repeated calls to TerminateThread(), one per thread HANDLE (but you didn't hear that from me).

Design Factor Scorecard

How efficient, simple, portable, and scalable is the final concurrent version of the Quicksort code described earlier? Let's review the algorithm with respect to each of these categories.

Efficiency

The thread pool version of Quicksort is going to be much more efficient than spawning a new thread for each recursive call. Even in the thread pool version, you can restructure the code to place only one partition index pair into the queue while the other partition is held for further processing. Keeping one of the partitions will give the algorithm a better chance of having at least some part of the array within the cache of the core executing a thread. Changing the queue structure to a stack (LIFO) could provide some of this benefit, too, in cases where there is a shared cache among cores.

Another source of obvious overhead is the coordination needed to access the shared queue that was not part of the original iterative algorithm. As soon as the system has generated a number of partitions equal to the number of threads, it might be tempting to take the queue out of the algorithm, since each thread would then have a partition to process. This removes the overhead of coordination (i.e., use of the semaphore and synchronization needed to ensure a thread-safe queue), but can lead to a load imbalance. If the chosen pivot elements always fall at or near the midpoints of the subarrays calling Partition(), the loads will be balanced. Unfortunately, we can't know which element will be the midpoint of a subarray unless we sort it or run the Selection code on it. The overhead of using the queue to distribute work is offset by having a better guarantee that the load balance of the sort will be equitable.

Simplicity

Once you understand the iterative algorithm, the parallelization is straightforward. The only tricky bits of the threaded code shown earlier are the use of the semaphore to throttle access to the shared queue and setting up the pool of threads to be terminated. Using the count of the number of elements that have been placed in their sorted position to determine that the sort has completed is probably not the most intuitive means of checking for completion. However, once explained, I hope it made sense. Even after all these changes, you can still find the original iterative algorithm in the threaded version.

Portability

Implementing this algorithm in Pthreads is quite easy, and requires the following:

- Split the single ReleaseSemaphore() call into two separate sem_post() calls, one after each enqueue() call.
- Use a condition variable to signal the external thread upon sort completion.
- Set up the atomic increment of the counter.

A pthread_mutex_t object would be too heavy for the atomic increment. I would recommend using the TBB atomic fetch_and_add() operation. Be aware that the return value for this method is the previous value of the variable, so you will need to compare it to N-1, rather than N, to know when the final count is reached.

This is not a good algorithm for use with OpenMP as a data parallelism solution. There is no loop on which to attach a loop worksharing construct. However, if you have a compiler that supports the OpenMP 3.0 standard, you can go back to the recursive algorithm and the idea presented in Example 8-13. Instead of creating a new thread for each new partition to be sorted, though, you can spawn a new task. Unfortunately, as of this writing, I've not had the chance to work with the task constructs in OpenMP, so there may be other details and traps to implementing Quicksort with OpenMP tasks that I can't even warn you about. (A colleague has implemented Quicksort using the nonstandard taskq extensions to OpenMP available within Intel compilers, so I'm confident that you will find a way to utilize the officially approved task constructs.)

A distributed Quicksort implementation for both a mesh and a *d*-dimensional hypercube are described in *Introduction to Parallel Computing: Design and Analysis of Parallel Algorithms* (Benjamin Cummings, 1994) by Kumar et al. The idea in the case of the hypercube is to repeatedly split the cube network into two smaller subcubes. After choosing a pivot value, one of the processes broadcasts it to all other processes. Processes partition the data in their local memory into two subarrays around the pivot value. Subarrays are then exchanged between the processes that share a link across the hypercube split, and each subcube picks a new pivot element to broadcast within the subcube. The process of splitting the cubes into smaller subcubes and exchanging subarrays across the network dimension proceeds recursively until each node is alone within its own subcube. The data is sorted locally and the order of the nodes is used for the overall order of data from one node to another.

Scalability

This version of concurrent Quicksort is very scalable. With each creation of two partitions to be sorted, there is a chance for another thread to be assigned work. With finite resources, the execution will reach a point where all threads in the pool have been assigned an initial partition and no more threads will be sitting idle. As the sorting progresses, the size of the partitions will continue to get smaller. Decreasing amounts of computation to the fixed overhead required to enqueue and dequeue index pairs will eventually yield adverse performance. Before the granularity of sorting a partition becomes too fine, you should execute a "short-circuit" sort. That is, when a partition gets too small to afford further concurrent execution, you should use a serial sort to finish the partition (the number of elements sorted here needs to be correctly reflected in the variable keeping count of sorted items).

There is a very real chance of load imbalances due to the pivot selection leading to very small partitions. You could implement an algorithm to choose a pivot that is more likely to be the median of the data. The dynamic assignment of tasks to threads through the shared queue helps to alleviate the impact of such imbalances. Increases in the data size for a fixed number of threads will yield more opportunities for smoothing out the load balance between threads in the algorithm, too.

Radix Sort

Radix sort uses the binary structure of keys to sort data. If that binary representation of keys can be interpreted as an unsigned integer, you can use a radix sort. The unique method of comparison between parts of keys, rather than the key as a whole, gives radix sorts a linear time asymptotic complexity, as opposed to the polynomial complexity of the other (compare-exchange) sort algorithms we've looked at in this chapter.

There are two methods of processing the binary keys that define two distinct radix sorts. Looking at bits from most significant to least significant (left to right) gives us the *radix exchange sort*. Processing bits from least to most significant (right to left) is known as *straight radix sort*. We'll look at each of these methods and how to thread them.

Radix Exchange Sort

Consider the most significant bit of a set of keys. There are only two possibilities for the value of this bit: 0 or 1. After sorting the entire data set, all keys that start with 0 will appear before all keys that have a 1 in this initial bit position. Thus, we can partition the data into two sets, those whose keys begin with 0 and those whose keys begin with 1, where the former set will precede the latter set.

If you consider the next most significant bit in the data subset of keys with a leading 0, there are two possibilities for the value of this bit: 0 or 1. In the final sorted order, all keys that start with 00 will be listed before all keys that start with 01. Thus, we can partition the data from the leading 0 subset into two sets based on the value of the second most significant bit. Figure 8-8 illustrates the partitioning of keys I've just described through the first two bit positions.

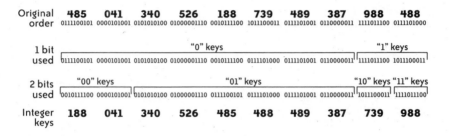

FIGURE 8-8. Radix exchange sort—two phases

If you've read the previous section of this chapter, you should recognize the description just given as being very similar to the Quicksort algorithm. However, rather than partitioning the data based on the relationship of keys to a pivot element, the radix exchange sort partitions data into two separate and independent sets based on the value of a single bit within each key. I hope you've already imagined a recursive solution for the radix exchange sort, as well as an equivalent iterative solution. Example 8-19 shows an iterative serial implementation of the radix exchange sort with the adapted `Partition()` function.

EXAMPLE 8-19. Serial version of radix exchange sort

```
int Partition(int *A, int p, int r, int bPos)
{
  int k = p-1;
  int l = r+1;
  int t;

  do k++; while ((k < r) && (bits(A[k],bPos,1) == 0));
  do l--; while ((l > p) && (bits(A[l],bPos,1) == 1));
```

```
  while (k < 1) {
    t = A[k];   A[k] = A[l];   A[l] = t;
    do k++; while (bits(A[k],bPos,1) == 0);
    do l--; while (bits(A[l],bPos,1) == 1);
  }
  return l;
}

int RadixExchangeSort(int *A, int p, int r, int b)
{
  int q = 0;
  qParams *d, *d1, *d2;
  int bPos = b;

// initial partition to prime the queue
  d1 = new qParams;
  d1->lo = p; d1->hi = r; d1->bitPosition = bPos;
  enqueue(Q, d1);

  while (notEmpty()) {
    dequeue(Q, d);   //pull out next index pair, unless queue is empty
    p = d->lo;
    r = d->hi;
    bPos = d->bitPosition-1;
    free(d);

// if there is one or more things to sort and more bits to process...
    if ((p < r) && (bPos >= 0)) {
      q = Partition(A, p, r, bPos);

// encapsulate the indices for the lower portion of the partition and enqueue
      d1 = new qParams;
      d1->lo = p; d1->hi = q; d1->bitPosition = bPos;
      enqueue(Q, d1);

// encapsulate the indices for the upper portion of the partition and enqueue
      d2 = new qParams;
      d2->lo = q+1; d2->hi = r; d2->bitPosition = bPos;
      enqueue(Q, d2);
    }
  }
  return 0;
}
```

The arguments to the RadixExchangeSort() function are the array of items to be sorted (A), the low (p) and high (r) index values of the portion to be sorted, and the number of bits within the keys (b). If the keys are 4-byte integers, the initial value of b will be set at 32. The function declares some qParams object (a user-defined struct) to hold partition information within the queue. Each object will contain the two indexes of a partition and the bit position within the keys that was used to create the partition. When a qParams object is pulled out of the queue, the bit position value contained within is decremented to find the bit position of the current partitioning. The Partition() function includes a bit position argument, bPos.

The bits() function, used in Partition(), extracts and returns the nbits bits from the key starting from the position bit position. The position parameter is the most significant bit position to consider from the key. For the radix exchange sort, we need only a single bit from the desired position within the key; for straight radix sorting, we will use multiple consecutive bits. The implementation details of bits() will differ depending on what bit manipulation functionality is available within the programming language you are using and the endian orientation of your processor.

We could thread the code from Example 8-19 in the same manner that we threaded the code in Quicksort. Similarly, the empty queue is used as a signal for the serial function to terminate with the input data in sorted order. For the concurrent version, we need to add a counter to be incremented when elements are in their final sorted positions. There are two ways to tell when elements are in their sorted positions:

- The partition contains a single item.
- The next bit position to be examined lies beyond the least significant bit (the bit position "index" has gone below zero).

When all bit positions have been used to partition keys, the keys that remain within a partition are equal, and those keys are in the proper sorted positions. In this case, we need to count the number of keys in the partition and add this to the global count.

One other difference between the radix exchange sort algorithm and Quicksort is that there is no pivot element in the radix exchange sort. Thus, in the Partition() function, there is no final swap of the pivot item with the item at the point in the array where the two index pointers have met. This means that the global counter in our threaded version is not incremented after each call to Partition().

Straight Radix Sort

The straight radix sort is the version of radix sorting that most everyone is familiar with. This algorithm was used in sorting decks of Hollerith cards on a card-sorting machine. Starting with the column at the far right of the key (least significant digit), the card-sorting machine would read the column and deposit the card into a bin based on the digit found. This process partitioned cards into classes based on the digit of the keys under consideration. The cards were gathered up, kept in the same relative order of the bins they fell into, and the next column to the left was used to sort the same deck. The deck of cards was repeatedly passed through the machine, with columns progressing to the left for each pass, until all the key columns of the cards had been used for partitioning.

When first encountered, the algorithm is counterintuitive. The key piece that makes the algorithm work is the stability of the order in which the cards are deposited in each bin and gathered up in order to make the next pass with the next significant column.

NOTE

A sorting algorithm is *stable* if records with equal keys end up in the same relative positions to each other that they started in before sorting.

Figure 8-9 gives an example of the straight radix sort algorithm. In this example, we are sorting three-digit keys, at a rate of one digit per pass. The bar (|) is placed to the left of the digit being sorted on. Notice that the keys with the same digit of interest (e.g., the 8 after the second pass) are in the same relative positions as they were from the previous pass.

Original list	After 1st pass	After 2nd pass	After 3rd pass
485	34|0	5|26	|041
041	04|1	7|39	|188
340	48|5	3|40	|340
526	52|6	0|41	|387
188	38|7	4|85	|485
739	18|8	3|87	|488
489	98|8	1|88	|489
387	48|8	9|88	|526
988	73|9	4|88	|739
488	48|9	4|89	|988

FIGURE 8-9. Straight radix sort using decimal digits

The straight radix sort can use multiple bits for each pass. If we assume that the keys in Figure 8-9 were represented as a string of characters, the example would have accessed a full byte of the keys at each pass. The number of bits examined within each key for each pass should be a divisor of the key length; otherwise, the final pass will need to deal with a different number of bits than all the other passes. The number of passes required is, of course, the number of bits in the keys divided by the number of bits used per pass. Example 8-20 shows a serial implementation of a straight radix sort of integer keys (32 bits) examined in 4-bit chunks at a time.

EXAMPLE 8-20. Serial version of straight radix sort algorithm

```
#define mbits 4
#define M 16

void StraightRadixSort(int *A, int N, int b)
{
  int i, j, pass, tBits;
  int count[M];
  int *tA = new int[N];
  int *tempPtr;

  for (pass = 0; pass < (b / mbits); pass++) {
    for (j = 0; j < M; j++) count[j] = 0;
    for (i = 0; i < N; i++) {
      count[bits(A[i],pass*mbits, mbits)]++;
    }
    count[0]--;
    for (j = 1; j < M; j++) count[j] += count[j-1];  // prefix sum on counts
    for (i = N-1; i >= 0; i--) {
      tBits = bits(A[i], pass*mbits, mbits);
      tA[count[tBits]] = A[i];
      count[tBits]--;
    }

// swap pointers to swap arrays to sort in next pass
    tempPtr = tA; tA = A; A = tempPtr;
  }
  free(tA);
}
```

The outer for loop iterates over the number of passes to be made. Each iteration of this loop examines the mbits bits of interest within each key using the bits() function described in our implementation of the radix exchange sort. Rather than spending the overhead to move data into lists that would mimic the bins of a card-sorting machine, a count of the number of keys matching each bit pattern is kept (in elements of the count array indexed by the key value). After examining all keys, the code uses a prefix scan to sum the counts (after decrementing the count[0] value to account for zero indexing). The algorithm uses the scan results to put keys with the same bits of interest together into consecutive slots of a different array (tA), which is very much like how we've seen prefix scan used to pack an array in Chapter 6 and in the sidebar "Array Packing with Prefix Scan" on page 120. After copying all the records to the new array based on each key's bits of interest, the code performs the next pass with the next most significant mbits of keys. Figure 8-10 shows highlights of the computation and data movement from the first pass on 10 integer keys with mbits set to 3. Keys are displayed in both their decimal and binary interpretations.

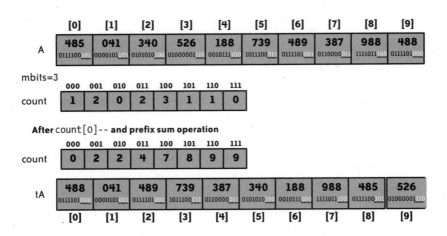

FIGURE 8-10. Straight radix sort code execution

The number of times each data record is moved is equal to the number of passes executed (number of iterations in the outermost loop). The number of passes depends directly on the size of the keys and the number of bits (mbits) examined in each pass. You can tune these parameters during development to find an efficient value for mbits.

Using prefix scan to gather keys

The results of the prefix scan on the number of occurrences of each bit pattern of interest will hold the value of the last index of the new array that will hold those keys with the same bits of interest. Once these final index positions are known, the algorithm traverses the list of keys in reverse order. It finds the new position of each item by indirect addressing using the count array value indexed by the bits of interest within the key. After moving an item, the algorithm decrements the element from the count array for the next key with matching bits of interest.

Even with the picture in Figure 8-10 being worth a thousand words, I'd like to expend a few more to illustrate how the prefix scan determines where records are copied into the new array. I'll do this by following the movement of elements with key bits of interest, 100. There are three such keys in the original array A: 340, 188, and 988. Once the keys have been counted, Figure 8-10 shows a 3 in the count['100'] array element. After the prefix scan operation, the count array corresponding to the 100 key bits contains 7. This is the index within the new array, tA, to receive the rightmost (highest index) element with a matching key portion.

Starting from A[9] and scanning from right to left, we find that the first key with 100 in the bits of interest is the 988 key in A[8]. This record is copied into tA[count['100']] or tA[7]. The algorithm decrements the value in count['100'] to 6, and continues with the traversal of A. The next 100 key encountered is 188 in A[4]. The code copies the record into tA[6] and decrements the value in count['100'] to 5. The last 100 key record, 340, is found in A[2] and copied into tA[5]. Of course, the data movement portion copies each element from A to tA when it is encountered during the traversal from high to low index.

Keeping data movement stable

There is an unremovable dependency between iterations of the outermost loop, due to the stability requirement of the algorithm. We must use less significant bits of keys before we can consider more significant bits. We can use a data decomposition scheme within each pass through the keys to convert the straight radix sort algorithm in Example 8-20 to a concurrent version. The examination and count of the bits of interest from each key are all independent as long as updates to each of the counters are atomic or protected. We can easily perform a prefix scan, too. Unfortunately, movement of data will be much trickier.

If the keys have been split up among threads, determining where any given record will be copied requires knowing how many records will fill positions in the receiving array prior to the desired record. If we have a single global array holding the prefix scan of bit value counts, only the thread processing the final chunk of the array of records is certain where its records are to be copied. If we use the ideas from the serial algorithm described in the previous section (decrementing the corresponding count element after an item is copied), the thread assigned the second-to-last array chunk would only know where to copy its records after the thread handling the last array chunk has moved all of its records. This serial data movement will certainly preserve the stability of the keys. But, since this is a book about concurrency, we should want concurrent data movement. Copying one element from here to there is independent of the movement of another item, as long as we can guarantee no two elements will try to occupy the same slot. To achieve this, we'll need more processing or recordkeeping.

NOTE

Alternatively, after computing the prefix scan of count, the implementation can assign chunks of the count array to threads. For each different element of count assigned, a thread will have a different key bit pattern and all the records with keys matching the pattern that it will be responsible to move. A thread scans backward through the array of records and tests each key. For those that match any of the assigned bit patterns, the thread moves the record to a slot in the receiving array using the corresponding count scan value, which is decremented after use. This scheme is only scalable to the number of different bit patterns used (mbits squared) and requires all threads to read all data keys.

Kumar et al. give a distributed radix sort algorithm that requires a number of processors equal to the number of records to be sorted in *Introduction to Parallel Computing: Design and Analysis of Parallel Algorithms* (Benjamin Cummings, 1994). With each pass examining a different mbits section of keys, an inner loop iterates over all potential values of the mbits-sized bit sequence. During each iteration, the processor examines its one assigned key to determine whether the relevant portion of the key is a match for the current bit sequence being considered. If the key matches, the processor sets a local flag to 1. Then, a prefix scan is executed over all the flag variables across the processors, and for those nodes whose local flag was set, the local value of the prefix scan is added to an offset (initially 0 for each pass) to find the destination (rank of a processor) that will receive the local record. A parallel sum on the flag values updates the offset before the processors examine the next pattern in the next inner loop iteration.

Since each processor executes the parallel sum and prefix scan operations, regardless of the current flag value, they are synchronization points and guarantee that each potential bit pattern is handled by all processors before the next possible pattern is considered. Before each check of the next possible bit pattern, the nodes reset all local flags to 0 so that the prefix scan across the processors is correct for the current pattern under consideration. Once all possible bit patterns have been addressed and all the keys in all the processors have a unique destination, each processor sends its local record to the destination processor. The processor also receives a single record before moving to the next most significant bits within the key and repeating the process of matching against possible bit patterns, setting the flag, and going through the prefix scan and parallel sum operations.

To illustrate this distributed algorithm, imagine a line of P people sitting in consecutively numbered seats (1..P). Each person has been given a random nine-digit identification number. Starting at the least significant digit, we ask everyone whose ID number ends in 0 to raise their hands. We walk down the line and give each of those people a number, in consecutive order, that starts with 1 and corresponds to the seat labels. Upon receiving a number, each person lowers his hand. After that, we ask for everyone whose last digit is 1 to raise a hand. Starting with the lowest unassigned number, we give out a seat number to anyone holding up a hand. We repeat this for the digits 2 through 9. Once we have given out all P seat numbers, we instruct everyone to get up and go sit in the seat number they have been given. After everyone has settled into their new seats, we do the same thing over again with successive digits of the ID number, initiating a movement of people for each digit position, until the most significant ID digit has been processed. At this point, the line of people is now in sorted order according to ID number.

We can mimic this algorithm by spawning a number of threads equal to the number of records to be sorted. This seems like it would be way too much overhead and, for very large amounts of data, would require a large investment in system resources just to set up and manage the threads. Since we will have a finite number of cores available, a better method, as we've seen, is to create a pool of threads and modify the algorithm to fit this thread pool.

Before I jump into the thread pool version of this algorithm, let's first look at how the serial code works for this approach. If we can understand the serial algorithm, it will allow us to achieve better insight into structuring the concurrent code. Example 8-21 shows code to implement a serial variation of the distributed straight radix sort algorithm described earlier.

```
#define mbits 4
#define M 16

void SerialStraightRadixSort(int *A, int N, int b)
{
  int i, j, pass;
  int offset, rank;
  int count;
  int *tA = new int[N];
  int *tempPtr;

  for (pass = 0; pass < (b / mbits); pass++) {
    offset = -1; //for 0-base index
    for (j = 0; j < M; j++) {
      count = 0;
      for (i = 0; i < N; i++) {
        if (bits(A[i],pass*mbits, mbits) == j) count++;
      }
      rank = offset + count;
      for (i = N-1; i >= 0; i--) {
        if (bits(A[i], pass*mbits, mbits) == j)
          tA[rank--] = A[i];
      }
      offset += count;
    }
// swap pointers to swap arrays to sort in next pass
    tempPtr = tA; tA = A; A = tempPtr;
  }
  free(tA);
}
```

The pass loop in Example 8-21 runs over each mbits-sized group of bits, from least to most significant, within the key of each record. The offset variable keeps track of the next open position in the tA array that will receive keys with matching mbits values. The j loop loops over all possible patterns of mbits bits. The inner i loop body cycles through each key in A to count the number of keys with matching bit patterns. Instead of a flag variable, we use a counter (count) to tally up the number of keys with bits of interest that match the pattern under consideration. Once we have this value, we can determine where the record with the highest index and matching key portion will be copied into the tA array (rank = offset + count;), and then traverse the records in reverse order to move those with keys that were counted in the previous traversal. We update the offset variable for the next bit pattern to be searched for within the keys. As before, we swap array pointers to prepare for the next pass with the next most significant mbits of the keys.

This version of a serial straight radix sort is more amenable to transformation into a concurrent version. Unfortunately, we still have an issue, in that the single count variable is not capable of easily determining where threads are to copy records. As we've done before, in order to compute the global count value, we can keep a local count and do a reduction sum on each local copy into a global copy after all assigned keys have been examined (since not every key will contain the bit pattern of interest, we might get away with a single global count and atomic updates without too much contention between threads).

If I tilt my head 90 degrees to the right and look at this problem from a slightly different angle, an idea pops into my brain. Rather than doing a reduction operation, what if we did a prefix scan over the threads' count variables? With the value in the "local" copy of count after the prefix scan, each thread would have the index of the last element in the receiving array (localRank = offset + localPrefixSumCount) into which it would copy the assigned records having keys matching the pattern under consideration. Thus, each thread would be able to concurrently move records that contain the current bit pattern of interest.

We can use a global array of count variables, one element per thread, to make the prefix scan computation easy. Regrettably, there are a couple of execution dependences with the concurrent algorithm. Before we do the prefix scan computation, we must be sure that all the counts have been tallied. Likewise, before we start moving records, we must be sure the prefix scan operation is complete. We're going to need a barrier between counting keys that match a bit pattern and another before moving the records whose keys matched.

OK, so we've got an algorithm sketched out from the serial code (Example 8-21) and the use of a prefix scan over count values computed in each thread. Thinking about Simple Rule 5, you may ask yourself, "Which threading model will be easiest to implement all the algorithmic features needed?" The code is loop-based and needs barriers. OpenMP handles parallelization of loops and has a barrier construct. In fact, there is an implicit barrier at the end of loop worksharing constructs that might give us one of the needed barriers "for free." The match counting loop and the data movement loop cover the same range of elements from the data array, but they run through the index values in a different order (the record movement loop runs backward through the assigned chunk). The coding and debugging of the algorithm will be simpler if we can guarantee that each thread counts the matches and moves records from the same block of the array. I'm not sure if we can make that guarantee with OpenMP loop worksharing constructs on loops that run in opposite directions of each other. We can use OpenMP with thread IDs to explicitly decompose the array into blocks and assign blocks to specific threads, but this defeats the spirit of OpenMP coding. Dividing the array of records into blocks by thread IDs is standard operating procedure in an explicit threading model, but these libraries don't have a native barrier operator. Should we mangle OpenMP around and use it like an explicit thread model just to get the barrier, or should we use a handcoded barrier operator within an explicit threading model?

Before I answer that last question, I want to address a bigger performance issue with the algorithm under consideration.

Reducing the number of data touches

The code in Example 8-21 ensures that all the records with keys containing 0000 are copied before records with keys containing 0001. The use of prefix scan across the count values local to each thread ensures that the concurrent algorithm (described earlier) will keep the stability of the relative order of records whose keys have equal values in the bits of interest.

Each record is moved only once per pass through the data to be sorted, but the number of times each key is examined is based on the size of the bit pattern of interest. For example, if we set mbits to 4, there will be 16 traversals of the array block elements for counting matching keys, and 16 traversals to determine which records are to be moved. Plus, there will be 32 barriers that each thread must pass through. And this will be repeated again for every separate mbits-sized section of the keys. Algorithmically, we're still in the realm of a constant asymptotic upper bound on the number of times keys are examined and data is moved. Even so, it still seems like a lot of extra processing.

Given a key with a pattern of 0110 in thread M, what information do we need in order to compute where the record with this key will be copied? Thread M requires the following information:

- The total number of records that have keys with patterns from 0000 to 0101.
- The number of records that have the 0110 pattern in threads 0 to $M-1$, plus any local records that precede the record of interest within the block of data assigned to thread M.

We can use the sum of these two values to index the receiving array to locate positions for copying records.

The first required value is kept in the offset variable in Example 8-21, but it's only relevant once the previous key bit patterns have been handled. Looking back at Example 8-20, notice that, after the first i loop executes, the count array holds the number of corresponding key bit patterns, all within a single traversal of the keys. If we performed an exclusive prefix scan on count, the value of each item in the scanned array would be the number of records with preceding key bit patterns. That is, after the exclusive scan, the value in the 0110 indexed element of the count array holds the number of records for keys with patterns from 0000 to 0101.

With multiple threads, we can execute a single traversal of the data array, counting how many of each key bit pattern is found, and then combine all the local count array results into a separate global array, gCount. Running an exclusive prefix scan on the gCount array will give us the total number of keys with bit patterns of lower values in the entire data set. This is the first value we need.

We can compute the second value by running a prefix scan across corresponding elements of the count arrays in thread ID order. If you imagine each thread's count array as a row within a 2D array, arranged by increasing thread ID, a prefix scan down individual columns will compute the number of keys with the same bit pattern in the local thread and all threads with a lower thread ID. If you include the gCount array—set above the threads' count arrays in our 2D arrangement—as part of this prefix scan, each thread's count array will be the sum of the two required values identified previously. We can use this result to directly compute the index of all records that have been assigned to a thread, and, with one traversal, all records can be moved to the proper location in the receiving array.

Did you get lost in those last three paragraphs? It's a complex algorithm to try and understand with just words. Whenever I'm designing a new algorithm, serial or concurrent, I like to draw pictures in order to visually understand and check the data processing. So, I've included Figure 8-11, which shows the scans I've just described and data movement from the first pass (least significant digit) on a set of two-digit keys with four threads.

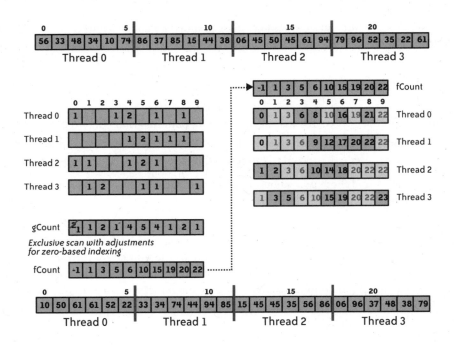

FIGURE 8-11. Straight radix sort concurrent algorithm

The division of keys among the threads is shown at the top of Figure 8-11. On the left side of the figure are the count arrays, one per thread, for all possible digit patterns (0 to 9) of the least significant digit (blank entries are 0 values). The gCount array is the result of the 10 reductions (parallel sums) between corresponding elements of the count arrays. The gCount[0] element is decremented by 1 to account for the 0-based indexing of the C language. The array shown immediately below the gCount array, labeled fCount, is the result of performing an exclusive prefix scan of the gCount elements and then setting the gCount[0] value to −1 for the 0-based indexing. This array then "primes" the 10 prefix scans of the collected count arrays for each thread. The results of these scans are shown on the right (the gray entries are the original 0 values and won't be used in the data movement portion of the algorithm).

Along with the final prefix scan results (that used fCount), each thread traverses its assigned block of the array in reverse order. For each key, the record is moved to the location in the receiving array indexed by the value stored in the "local" version of the count array, indexed by the key bit pattern. The local count element is then decremented for the next key that has the same bit pattern. The array of keys shown at the bottom of the figure is the receiving array after all threads have moved their records concurrently. This array will be used for the next pass on the next most significant digits in the key.

A bit Gordian, yes? Maybe a little, but it doesn't use anything you haven't seen before (you did read Chapter 6 before this, right?). Is it better? I think so. With the above counting and data movement algorithm, the number of traversals required for each pass loop iteration will be two, no matter how many bits are used for key bit patterns. This is much fewer than the 32 traversals for mbits set to 4. Use of this algorithm is a case where we would be willing to trade a simpler code implementation with one that is more efficient.

The Concurrent Straight Radix Sort Solution

Example 8-22 shows the threaded ParallelStraightRadixSort() code that incorporates the counting and data movement algorithm demonstrated in Figure 8-11. As you can see, this example uses Pthreads.

EXAMPLE 8-22. Pthreads version of improved straight radix sort

```
#define mbits 4
#define M 16

void *ParallelStraightRadixSort(void *par)
{
  tParams *lpar = (tParams *) par;
  int N = lpar->num;
  int b = lpar->keylength;
  int tNum = lpar->tid;

  int i, j, pass, tBits;
  int *tempPtr;
  int start, end, offset;

  start = ((float)N/NUM_THREADS) * tNum;
  end =   ((float)N/NUM_THREADS) *(tNum+1);
  if (tNum == NUM_THREADS-1) end = N;

  for (pass = 0; pass < (b / mbits); pass++) {
    for (j = 0; j < M; j++) lCount[tNum][j] = 0;
    for (i = start; i < end; i++)
      lCount[tNum][bits(A[i], pass*mbits, mbits)]++;
```

```
      pth_barrier(&b1);
      if (tNum == 0) { // one thread computes sums

// sum for each bit pattern from lCount totaled into gCount
      for (i = 0; i < M; i++) {
        gCount[i] = 0;
        for (j = 0; j < NUM_THREADS; j++)
          gCount[i] += lCount[j][i];
      }

// exclusive prefix of gCount into fCount
      fCount[1] = gCount[0]-1;
      for (i = 2; i < M; i++)
        fCount[i] = fCount[i-1] + gCount[i-1];
      fCount[0] = -1;

// prefix scan for each bit pattern from fCount through lCount
      for (i = 0; i < M; i++) {
        lCount[0][i] += fCount[i];
        for (j = 1; j < NUM_THREADS; j++)
          lCount[j][i] += lCount[j-1][i];
      }
    }
    pth_barrier(&b2);  // other threads wait for all sum computations

    for (i = end-1; i >= start; i--) {
      tBits = bits(A[i], pass*mbits, mbits);
      tA[lCount[tNum][tBits]] = A[i];
      lCount[tNum][tBits]--;
    }
    pth_barrier(&b1);
    // swap pointers to swap arrays for next pass
    if (tNum == 0) { tempPtr = tA; tA = A; A = tempPtr; }
    pth_barrier(&b2);
  }
}
```

For me, the division of the array of records and addressing those elements with the explicit threads (Pthreads) in Example 8-22 easily outweighs the implicit and explicit barrier functionality of OpenMP. Plus, trying to guarantee that the same thread is assigned to a given block of the array would make the OpenMP code more complex and less obvious.

In Example 8-22, the first i loop tallies the number of occurrences of all possible bit patterns while traversing the assigned keys exactly once. At the end of each pass, the final i loop traverses the assigned block of keys once more, in reverse order, and uses the prefix scans results to index the receiving array. Between these two parts is the code that does the sums and prefix scans of the counts (lCount) that are computed by each individual thread. The lCount 2D array uses the first index to determine the thread that has access to that row. The second index ranges over the number of bit patterns possible based on mbits. The thread, whose assigned tNum is 0, uses the gCount array to hold the sums of counts (from lCount) for each bit pattern and assigning fCount the results of the exclusive prefix scan on gCount. Once the fCount array has been computed, this array will serve as the initial value of a prefix scan for each bit pattern (down the columns) held in the lCount array.

Before and after these summation operations are two barriers (pth_barrier()). The first barrier (b1) ensures that all threads have completed tallying their local counts, and the second (b2) ensures that the computations of the sums and scans have completed before each thread starts to copy records into the receiving array. Since the number of threads and the number of bit patterns should be relatively small, the code uses only one thread to make all the summation computations. If there is an increase in either the number of threads or the value of mbits, there would be a point where execution of this part of the algorithm might be able to run with multiple threads.

Finally, this example reuses the two barriers around the swap of the A and tA array pointers (both now global arrays) and restricts the swap to be executed by one thread. This was done in observance of Simple Rule 6. We can't guarantee that all threads will be ready for the array swap at the same time. Without the first barrier, some threads may be still copying records within the for loop that precedes the pointer swap. The second barrier ensures that the arrays have been swapped before the next pass takes place. Even with the two barriers in place, restricting the array swap to a single thread ensures that the swap is done once.

> **NOTE**
>
> I hate to admit that I originally didn't have the protections on the swap code. The sort worked fine with one thread, but would never get close to a correct answer with two or more. This bug plagued me for two hours. Once I figured out what should have been so obvious, I wished someone had been around to smack me across the nose with a rolled-up newspaper.

Looking back, you may realize that the concurrent version given in Example 8-22 is closer to the algorithm given in Example 8-20 than you might have expected. Both traverse the keys twice per pass: once to count how many times each key bit pattern appears, and once to move keys. It's never a bad thing to get inspiration from other sources when designing concurrent algorithms. In this case, going through the distributed-memory algorithm led to the insight of using parallel sum and prefix scan. Ending up at a place that we can easily relate back to the original serial code can give us confidence that we've done something right with this design and implementation.

Design Factor Scorecard

How efficient, simple, portable, and scalable are the concurrent radix exchange sort algorithm and the final straight radix sort code described earlier? Let's review both algorithms with respect to each of these categories.

Efficiency

When keys can be interpreted (at the bit level) as integer values, radix sort algorithms are capable of delivering efficient sorting with the number of operations (compares and movement of data) in linear proportion to the number of records to be sorted. All of the other sorting algorithms we considered in this chapter require a number of operations that is proportional to a polynomial function of the number of records to be sorted.

The examination and movement of data in the radix exchange sort is similar to that of Quicksort. As the algorithm proceeds, the range of array elements over which the records may be examined and moved becomes smaller and smaller, and, consequently, the required amount of cache decreases. The straight radix sort carries out the traversal of data to count bit pattern occurrences within keys, all within a contiguous range of memory. This yields a good chance of prefetching data and minimal cache collisions, but once the keys have been counted, the records are only examined once more per pass in order to determine where to copy the records. Of course, records are moved to positions within the receiving array without regard to any kind of efficient use of cache or memory access.

The low number of passes through the data versus the unpredictable memory access pattern when copying records is the tradeoff for use of straight radix sort. This is true for both the serial and concurrent versions of the algorithm. There is one faint ray of hope for the problem of random data movement and potential cache thrashing between threads. If the size of records is a multiple of the cache line size, then threads won't share cache lines when moving records.

Simplicity

Radix exchange sort is as simple as Quicksort. The only major difference is how the Partition() function determines where a record is placed for the next bit position to be examined. The straight radix sort shown in Example 8-22 is a straightforward parallelization of the first serial code given (Example 8-20). We've implemented a more complex summation of counts in order to determine the index positions within the receiving array of each key held. This is an example of possible tradeoffs between design factors. This more complex (and serial) summation process allows us to realize a reduction in the number of traversals required to count key bit patterns within a thread. This is much more efficient than the code shown in Example 8-21, which counts only keys that match a specific bit pattern before moving those matching records and traversing the keys for the next bit pattern.

Portability

OpenMP and TBB are not well suited for implementing the concurrent version of straight radix sort. The algorithm requires that, within each pass, the key bit pattern counts computed for a given block of records remain associated with that block for the summation operations and the movement of records. You can use OpenMP code with API calls to have the same thread execute on the same array elements for each pass. Doing this would require all the logic and overhead computation of start and end index values that are required for an explicit threaded implementation. For efficiency, TBB parallel algorithms don't make available this level of association of data to threads. We could use the task facility within TBB, but again, the structure of the code would be so similar to an explicit threading solution that it doesn't seem worth the confusion and hassle of trying to bend one means of threading into a completely different one.

You can convert the threaded version of a straight radix sort to a distributed version. Locally counting bit patterns within keys is easy enough. You can use broadcasts and scatter/gather (or some other communication methods) to carry out the summation across distributed nodes. Also, if each node knows the layout of the records across the nodes, you will be able to compute the rank of the receiving node and the index within that node for each record to be moved. The only really tricky bit is making sure that the receiving node understands where to place the records that will be sent to it. We can resolve this by including, within the message, the internal index that will hold the record being received. If the communication API has the ability for one-way communication, the sending node can simply "write" the records to be moved into the separate receiving array on each node.

Scalability

The two radix sort algorithms that we have discussed are readily scalable. Radix exchange sort has the same scalability properties as Quicksort, and while straight radix sort has memory issues, those issues won't get better, but they won't get worse with more threads or more data.

CHAPTER NINE

Searching

As I mentioned at the beginning of Chapter 8, it has always been a popular claim that more than 80% of all computing cycles are devoted to the process of sorting. This was especially true when mainframes were just about the only computers around and a majority of these were doing business-centric computations. Querying and managing databases, payroll, loan applications, medical billing, and other such processing had names and ID numbers associated with records that needed to be sorted.

Today, there is still quite a bit of sorting going on all the time (you still want to collect your paycheck, and the security device supplier still needs to know how many THX-1138/GL steam-powered tasers are on hand). With the advent and popularity of search engines on the Internet, I think that searching has certainly become more high-profile and also accounts for a bigger slice of the total computing cycle pie.

In this chapter, I'll discuss two algorithms you can use to search through a collection of data and how to make them concurrent to decrease the time needed to locate items of interest. For simplicity, I will assume that all keys within a data set to be searched are unique. Strategies for dealing with multiple duplicate keys will be mentioned, but the implementation details are left to you. More complex or proprietary searching techniques (e.g., Google, Lucene), while interesting, are outside the scope of this book (and are typically corporate trade secrets that I couldn't discuss even if I knew them).

Unsorted Sequence

There are two types of data: sorted and unsorted. Let's consider unsorted first. A stack of books that has fallen over into a pile, words in a letter to the editor, or a group of people at a party are all examples of unsorted data sets. If you wanted to find your copy of *The Time Machine*, you would start checking titles of books one at a time from the pile; if you wanted to know whether the phrase "fiscal conservative" was in a letter, you would start reading from the beginning and look for that phrase; or, if you wanted to find out who owned the SUV blocking your car when you're ready to leave the party, you would approach each person and ask him if he was the owner. (Sure, in this last example you could make a big, loud announcement calling for the identity of the owner, but let's assume you want to leave discreetly and not let the hostess know you are ducking out early.)

In each case, the algorithm is to simply start at one end of the data set and examine each item in the set to determine whether it is the one you are interested in locating. If it is not, you go on to the next item in sequence until you either find the item or run out of things to search. If you forgot that you loaned your copy of *The Time Machine* to a friend, you look through all of the books in the pile only to discover that your copy is not there.

Example 9-1 contains the LinearSearch() function to examine an array of integers (like so many simple examples before this) to determine whether a specific value (key) is contained in the array (A). The function will return the index (position) of a found element or a value of −1 in the case that the key value is not contained in the array. The value −1 signifies that an item does not have a matching key, since 0 is a valid index. Any integer index value not within the bounds of the search array would work.

EXAMPLE 9-1. Linear search code to look through unsorted data

```
void LinearSearch (int *A, int N, int key, int *position)
{
  int i;
  *position = -1;  // assume not found

  for (i = 0; i < N; i++) {
    if (A[i] == key) {
      *position = i;
      break;
    }
  }
}
```

To write a concurrent version of the linear search algorithm, we'll use a data decomposition approach. The problem involves a large collection of data, and each element of the data is to be handled in exactly the same way: compared against the search key for a match. From the simple code in Example 9-1, we can divide the array into some number of chunks. Each chunk would be assigned to a thread that would compare keys to the search key and update the global position variable if the comparison ever found a match. Example 9-2 shows a concurrent version of LinearSearch() using OpenMP.

EXAMPLE 9-2. OpenMP version of linear search algorithm

```
void LinearSearch (int *A, int N, int key, int *position)
{
  int i;
  *position = -1;  // assume not found

#pragma omp parallel for
  for (i = 0; i < N; i++) {
    if (A[i] == key) {
      *position = i;
    }
  }
}
```

There are two things to note about the code in Example 9-2. The first is that there is no added synchronization to protect access to the position variable, even though this shared memory location is being updated within a parallel region. Do we need to add such protection? Only if there is potentially more than one instance of an array item matching the search key. Since I've stated at the beginning of the chapter that each key within the example data sets will be unique, we know that, at most, only one array item matches my search and only one thread will be given the data chunk containing that key. Thus, no protection of the update to position is needed.

What if duplicate keys were allowed and we wanted to find the lowest indexed item that contained such a key? The serial code in Example 9-1 already solves this problem. With the OpenMP version given in Example 9-2, we have the chance that multiple threads will want to update position (or the same thread may attempt to update the variable multiple times). Certainly, without synchronization of any kind, there is no way to guarantee that the last value deposited into position will be the value of the lowest index containing a matching key. Even if access to position were synchronized, any simple locking object is not going to guarantee that the correct value is the final or only value written. We need something a little more sophisticated.

One solution that comes to my mind is to create a "local" version of position for each chunk that is updated only when a matching key is found in the data chunk and no previous match has been seen in the chunk. After searching all the chunks concurrently, we can run a reduction on the "local" position variables to find the minimum positive value. This minimum positive value will be the first instance of an array element with the matching key. If all the position values are −1, the key was not found.

The second point to notice in Example 9-2 is that the break statement from the serial version has been taken out of the loop body. If it is there to be found, you invariably find what you are seeking in the last place you look. The break stops the serial search when a match is located. Unfortunately, the OpenMP loop worksharing construct is only valid on loop bodies that are structured blocks (one entry, one exit). The break statement gives the loop body two exit points, which no longer qualifies it as a structured block. Once the matching record is found, the OpenMP thread will continue to search through the rest of the assigned chunk. Is this a bad thing?

Well, if you have an array of N items to be searched, the serial code will look through only the number of items needed until a matching key is found, or the entire array if there is no match. On average, this will execute $N/2$ comparisons. The OpenMP version looks through all data items regardless of the data size or location of a match. With multiple threads and a separate core for each one, say p of them, the elapsed time for executing the parallel search will be on par with the time needed to perform N/p serial comparisons. If the number of cores is larger than 2, the OpenMP algorithm will, on average, give better overall performance, especially as the size of the data set, N, gets bigger.

Curtailing the Search

Consider the case where your application will be running the search repeatedly. If a large majority of searches are locating items somewhere in the first 10 slots of a 10,000-item array, the concurrent code given in Example 9-2 will not compare favorably with the serial version. You might want a version that can halt the search of the thread that locates the item to be found and that will then inform all other searching threads of the discovery so that they might quit early, too. To do this, we'll use a global flag (similar to the thread pool termination flag we used in the Quicksort algorithm in Chapter 8) to signal that the search can be terminated early.

Once a thread has found the array element with the matching key, that thread can set the global flag. All threads should look first at the global flag before doing a comparison of the search value and the key of the next array element under consideration. If the flag has been set, there is no need to do any more comparisons and the thread can stop searching; if the flag is not set, more searching is required and the threads must do the current key comparison. Since OpenMP doesn't make it easy to prematurely terminate threads in the team, I'm going to switch over to Windows Threads for the implementation.

I've spread out the relevant code segments for this example in three parts. The first, Example 9-3, displays the global declarations. Example 9-4 has the code for the linear searching function as well as the helper function to assist in unpacking the function parameters. Example 9-5 shows the code that creates the threads and determines the results of the search.

EXAMPLE 9-3. Global declarations used for concurrent linear search

```
typedef struct {
  int *A;          // pointer to the array to be searched
  int num;         // total number of items in the array
  int key;         // search key value
  int threadID;    // thread ID
} sParam;

BOOL Done = FALSE; // initialize to NOT FOUND
```

The global declarations in Example 9-3 include only two things. The first is the definition of the struct to hold the parameters needed to execute the concurrent linear search. These include a pointer to the array to be searched (A), the number of items in the array (num), the key value of interest (key), and the ID number of the thread (threadID). If you compare the contents of this struct to the list of actual parameters in Example 9-1, you will notice that the first three are the same, but we've replaced position with the thread ID. We could have easily added a position field in the struct in order to return the index of an array element found to have a key match. However, I've got another idea about how to return this value to the point where the search was initiated, which I'll discuss in a page or two.

The second item shown in Example 9-3 is the flag (Done) used to signal when the record with a matching key is found so that all threads can terminate the search before all elements within the assigned chunk have been examined. This is a BOOL variable that is set to TRUE whenever a thread finds the matching record. Example 9-4 shows how to use this flag to cut short the search across multiple threads.

Like many previous examples, we're going to assume that the number of threads has been defined (NUM_THREADS) or would be assigned to an appropriate global variable. We will also assume that the number of elements in the array has been determined before threads are created and the search is initiated. Example 9-4 does not show the definition of these two values.

EXAMPLE 9-4. *Linear search function and helper function to be threaded*

```c
void LinearPSearch (int *A, int s, int e, int key, DWORD *position)
{
  int i;

  for (i = s; i < e; i++) {
    if (Done) return;
    if (A[i] == key) {
      *position = i;
      Done = TRUE;
      break;
    }
  }
  return;
}

unsigned __stdcall pSearch (LPVOID pArg) // Helper function
{
  sParam *inArg = (sParam *)pArg;
  int *A = inArg->A;
  int N = inArg->num;
  int key = inArg->key;
  int tNum = inArg->threadID;

  int start, end;
  DWORD pos = -1;

  start = ((float)N/NUM_THREADS) * tNum;
  end   = ((float)N/NUM_THREADS) *(tNum+1);
  if (tNum == NUM_THREADS-1) end = N;

  LinearPSearch(A, start, end, key, &pos);
  free(pArg);
  ExitThread(pos);
}
```

Example 9-4 contains the function that performs the linear search (LinearPSearch()) and the function that is called when threads are created (pSearch()). The helper function pSearch() has no equivalent in the serial code. The purpose of this function is to unpack the parameter list from the single allowed parameter, to call the function that actually does the search (LinearPSearch()), and to ensure that the results are made available to the code that will use those results.

The four parameter values arrive to the pSearch() function in a struct of type sParam. The four parts of the struct are assigned to local variables of the appropriate type. Also declared locally are a start and end to define the chunk of the data array that will be statically assigned to the thread, and a variable to hold the position (pos) of the array element that has a matching key value. Once the parameters are unpacked, the helper function computes the bounds for the chunk of the array that the thread should search. The values assigned to start and end are based on the thread ID number (threadID), the number of threads (NUM_THREADS), and the number of elements in the array (N). The linear search function is then called.

Upon termination of LinearPSearch(), the thread returns the value of pos through ExitThread() from pSearch(). If the thread found a key match, that index position will be returned. Otherwise, the initial value of −1 will be returned to indicate that the thread did not find the key value within the chunk of array assigned.

The LinearPSearch() function has three differences from the serial version of the algorithm shown in Example 9-1. The first is that the variable to hold the position index, if needed, is not initialized here. This variable was initialized in the helper function. The second is that the parameter for the number of items within the array has been replaced by the start and end index values computed in the helper function.

Finally, the test and setting of the Done variable has been added in order to signal all threads when the search has yielded a positive match and can be halted. Before each comparison of the search key and a new item from the array, the status of the Done flag is tested. If it is set to TRUE, the item has been found and the thread simply exits the LinearPSearch() routine to return processing back to the helper function. If Done is still FALSE, a key comparison is made; if that key comparison finds a match, the position of the matching item is stored in pos and the value of Done is set to TRUE.

Do we need to protect access to Done? We have not added any mutual exclusion code around the code that reads or writes the Done value. We've got all threads reading the contents of this variable during the search. If there is no matching item in the array, there is no race condition. However, if there is a match, one of those threads will update the value of Done to TRUE. Won't this screw up any of the threads that are only reading the contents of Done?

Fortunately, it won't. This is another example of a benign data race. The worst that could happen would be one or more of the reading threads not seeing that the value of Done had changed before executing another iteration of the search loop. These threads would, however, pick up on the fact that Done was set to TRUE on that next iteration. Thus, some threads might execute one unnecessary loop iteration and examine one more element from the array than needed. The fix to correct this data race will be much worse than the consequence of one superfluous key comparison.

EXAMPLE 9-5. Code segment to create threads and examine results of search

```
for (i = 0; i < NUM_THREADS; i++) {
  sParam *pArg = new sParam;
  pArg->A = S;
  pArg->num = NumKeys;
  pArg->key = sKey;
  pArg->threadID = i;
  tH[i] = (HANDLE) _beginthreadex(NULL, 0, pSearch, (LPVOID)pArg, 0, NULL);
}
```

```
WaitForMultipleObjects(NUM_THREADS, tH, TRUE, INFINITE);

for (i = 0; i < NUM_THREADS; i++) {
  GetExitCodeThread(tH[i], (LPDWORD) position);
  if (*position != -1) {
    printf("key = %d found at index %d\n", sKey, *position );
    break;
  }
}
if (*position == -1) printf("key = %d NOT found.\n",sKey);
```

The code in Example 9-5 is just enough to demonstrate how the declarations in Example 9-3 and the two functions in Example 9-4 could be used. At the entry point to this code segment, I have assumed that we have initialized the array to be searched (S) with numKeys keyed items and that we have decided on which key value to search (sKey). The first for loop allocates a new sParam object and loads the fields with the appropriate values. Next, a thread is spawned on the pSearch() function with a pointer to the newly allocated and loaded sParam object as the single parameter.

After all search threads have been launched, the thread executing the code in Example 9-5 waits for the termination of all the search threads. It examines the return code from each search thread to determine whether any of the threads found a key matching the search key. The GetExitCodeThread() function retrieves the return code of a thread. If any of the search threads returns a value other than −1, this will be the index of the found item within the array; if all threads return a −1 value, there is no record in the array that has a matching key. This simple example just prints the results of the search. I expect that the location of the search item will be used for something more substantial within an actual application.

Design Factor Scorecard

How efficient, simple, portable, and scalable is the concurrent version of the linear search code described earlier? Let's review the algorithm with respect to each of these categories.

Efficiency

The static allocation of chunks of the array to be searched will be good for cache utilization within each thread. The access pattern per thread is very regular, as it was in the serial version, and could take advantage of any cache prefetching technology that exists on the processor. Plus, there are no updates to the search data, so there would be no false sharing overheads from the search.

The overhead introduced by adding the helper function should be minimal. This routine is called only once (when each thread is created) and simply pulls out parameters from a struct and ensures that the search results from the LinearPSearch() function are propagated correctly.

There is one glaring bit of added overhead, though. This is the additional test to determine whether a different thread has found a match. As the code stands in Example 9-4, there are two conditional expression evaluations per loop iteration, as opposed to the one needed in the OpenMP version (Example 9-2). Of course, the extra evaluations will save the execution of unneeded iterations. There is a threshold that is used to decide whether you can reduce execution time by terminating the search as early as possible (with all the additional time needed for the extra tests) versus just running through all assigned records. I can't tell you where that line sits or how to figure out where it might be in every case. You could do some analysis about average cases and number of iterations executed per thread to get some kind of idea about what to expect. Nevertheless, the analysis results would change with the number of threads or the size of the data or the relative execution times for each type of comparison, among other factors.

Accessing a global variable (Done) that other threads are accessing could take more time than accessing values within a core's local cache, which are not being touched by other threads. Thus, we should cut down on the number of times a thread accesses global variables, which is never a bad idea anyway. For the LinearPSearch() function, one obvious modification would be to perform the search-terminating test at regular intervals larger than once per iteration. For example, every 10th iteration might be a good time to test. The code in LinearPSearch() would have a nested loop, where the inner loop would test for the key matches on 10 consecutive array items and the outer loop would choose the index of every 10th item for the inner loop to start from (we've got to be sure to include code that will pick up those spare iterations for when the original chunk size is not evenly divisible by 10). Before the inner loop executes, a thread tests to see whether another thread has already found a matching item. At worst, each thread might then waste up to 10 search comparisons, but we've cut the extra conditional expression evaluations to 10% of what they were.

If you implement the scheme just described, I would recommend that you use a tunable parameter for the number of iterations to be executed per early termination test. Not every set of data and number of threads will get the best performance with the same fixed value. Either computing this value based on the execution characteristics or tuning by hand to find an acceptable value will help your application maintain good execution performance across a wide range of situations.

Simplicity

Besides the purpose just stated, one other reason to use a helper function is to keep the code doing the actual computations as close as possible to the serial algorithm. Even if we required wholesale changes in the source code of the computation function, the helper function can at least reduce the clutter of unpacking the parameters from a struct. Any chance to keep code as similar to the original serial code—like being able to retain the actual parameter list of a function—will reduce the number of maintenance hurdles that we need to overcome later in the life of the application.

As I was going over the code in Example 9-4, I realized that the break statement is redundant here since the next iteration of the loop will force a return from the function based on the value of Done. However, since it is included in the serial code, I elected to keep it in the threaded version. It will cut out a few processing cycles, but, more importantly, it keeps the code as close to the original serial version as possible. My hope is that this will allow a more rapid understanding of the concurrent code by some future programmer charged with making updates to the application.

Portability

You can easily translate the Windows Threads code to POSIX threads. You could use a global flag to prevent unnecessary key search comparisons within an Intel TBB parallel_for algorithm, too.

Trying to terminate a search early within a message-passing environment would be a performance nightmare. Once the search key was broadcast to each process, keeping an eye out for a signal from another process would require some form of collective communication function call, and the time needed to do that compared to the time to continue searching locally would be prohibitive. It will be much more efficient and scalable to do all local searching and then use some form of reduction communication in order to identify the process and location of an item with the matching key.

Scalability

As with other algorithms presented, there is a point of diminishing returns on fixed data set sizes and increasing numbers of cores and threads. However, the scalability of the algorithm is very good, since the search computations are all independent of each other. The early termination tests on the Done variable, as discussed earlier in "Efficiency", would be the biggest potential drag on performance with an increase in the number of threads. Fortunately, there is no need for mutually exclusive access to the variable, since no more than one thread will update the value. Needing some form of lock object in order to access (read and write) Done would not have been acceptable with regards to maintaining scalable performance.

A coding change that you could implement for a small improvement in scalability of the code given in Example 9-5 is to first look to the Done variable before looking at the return codes from each thread. If Done is still FALSE, no matching item was found and there is no need to examine the return codes. If Done is TRUE, a run-through of the return codes is executed. Alternately, if Done were an integer, you could use it to indicate which, if any, thread found the search item by returning the thread ID, which is the index into the thread handles array, tH.

Binary Search

If your data collection is sorted on a key, you can do better than simply starting at one end of the array and looking at each key until you either find what you are looking for or reach the end. Binary search examines the key of the element at the midpoint of the array to be searched. If there is a search key match, the algorithm returns the index of the matching item. If there is no match, the search key will be either greater than or less than the midpoint key value. Whichever condition holds determines which half of the search array will contain the matching key, if such a record exists. A binary search is executed on the chosen half. If there is only one element in the search array and it doesn't match the search key, a matching item is not contained in the array. Example 9-6 gives a serial version of the binary search algorithm on an array of integers.

EXAMPLE 9-6. Iterative version of binary search algorithm

```
void BinarySearch (int *A, int lo, int hi, int key, int *position)
{
  int mid;
  *position = -1;  // assume not found

  while (lo <= hi) {
    mid = (lo + hi) / 2;
    if (A[mid] > key)
      hi = mid - 1;
    else if (A[mid] < key)
      lo = mid + 1;
    else {
      *position = mid; // found
      break;
    }
  }
}
```

The parameters lo and hi are the lower and upper index values of the initial search array. These values are modified as the algorithm proceeds to pare down the current bounds of the search array. If the search array becomes empty, the while conditional expression is false and no matching item was found. Otherwise, the midpoint index is computed and that element is tested against the key value. Depending on the results of the comparison against the search key, either hi or lo will be updated or the array item with a matching key has been found. In the latter case, the break statement prevents any more key comparisons after the mid value has been stored in position.

We could write a recursive version of BinarySearch(). However, since recursive codes are typically not easy to translate into concurrent equivalents, we've started with an iterative version.

To write a concurrent version of binary search, we can take the same approach we did with linear search in Examples 9-3 through 9-5. We can take the large data set, divide it into nonoverlapping chunks, and assign each chunk to a thread for a local binary search. As in Example 9-4, a helper function will take a single struct parameter and pull out the component parameters for the search function, determine the lo and hi index points for each chunk, set the initial guess of position to −1, and call BinarySearch() on the assigned chunk. Since binary search is so much faster than linear search, $O(\log_2 n)$ versus $O(n)$, we don't need to bother with any additional code to halt external searches once a thread has found the matching item.

Of course, only one thread will find a matching item. All others will simply run through the algorithm on the assigned chunk and not find a match. If this implementation scheme is enough for you, you can stop reading this chapter and go on to the next one. Before starting that next chapter, take some time to stretch and get something to drink. Your legs will appreciate it.

Now, for those of you who have chosen to keep reading, I'm going to present a different usage of multiple threads to perform a binary-like search. However, you might also want to take a moment to stretch and get something to drink before we go on.

If we have N threads available, we can develop a concurrent N-ary search. This search identifies N well-spaced points within the search array bounds and compares the key of the corresponding records to the search key. Each thread does one of the N comparisons. There are three possible outcomes from these comparisons. The first is that the item of interest is found and the search is complete; the second is that the item key examined is less than the search key; the third is that the item key examined is greater than the search key. If no search key match is found, a new, smaller search array is defined by the two consecutive index points whose record keys were found to be less than the search key and greater than the search key. The N-ary search is then performed on this refined search array. As with the serial version of binary search, the process is repeated until a match is found or the number of items in the search array is zero. A pictorial description of this algorithm is shown in Figure 9-1.

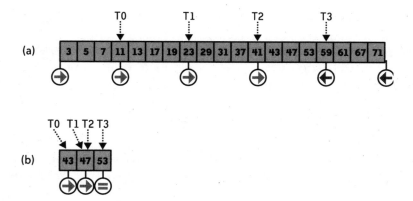

FIGURE 9-1. N-ary search example with four threads

Given the sorted array of prime numbers in Figure 9-1 (a), let's say we want to determine whether the value 53 is in the array and where it can be found. If there are four threads (T0 to T3), each computes an index into the array and compares the key value found there to the search key. Threads T0, T1, and T2 all find that the key value at the examined position is less than the search key value. Thus, an item with the matching key value must lie somewhere to the right of each of these thread's current search positions (indicated by the circled arrows). Thread T3 determines that the examined key value is greater than the search key, and the matching key can be found to the left of this thread's search position (left-pointing circled arrow). Notice the circled arrows at each end of the array. These are attached to "phantom" elements just outside the array bounds.

The results of the individual key tests define the subarray that is to become the new search array. Where we find two consecutive test results with opposite outcomes, the corresponding indexes will be just outside of the lower and upper bounds of the new search array. Figure 9-1 (a) shows that the test results from threads T2 (less than search key) and T3 (greater than search key) are opposite. The new search array is the array elements between the elements tested by these two threads. Figure 9-1 (b) shows this subarray and the index positions that are tested by each thread. The figure shows that during this second test of element key values, thread T3 has found the element that matches the search key (equals sign in circle).

Consider the case where we want to find a composite value, like 52, in a list of prime numbers. The individual key results by the four threads shown in Figure 9-1 (a) would be the same. The subarray shown in Figure 9-1 (b) would have the same results, except that the test by T3 would find that the key value in the assigned position was greater than the search key (and the equals sign would be a left-pointing arrow). The next round of key comparisons by threads would be from a subarray with no elements, bounded by the array slots holding the key values of 47 and 53. When threads are confronted with the search of an empty search space, they know that the key is not to be found.

This is obviously more complex than a simple binary search. The algorithm must coordinate the choices of index positions that each thread needs to test, keep and store the results of each test such that multiple threads can examine those results, and compute the new search array bounds for the next round of key tests. From this quick description, it's clear that we'll need some globally accessible data and, more importantly, we need a barrier between the completion of the key tests and the examination of the results of those tests.

But First, a Serial Version

Though it doesn't make much sense to implement the N-ary search algorithm in serial, we're going to do it anyway. By examining the serial version first, we can identify all the pieces and parts of the algorithm, which is an adaptation of the CREW SEARCH algorithm from Selim Akl's *The Design and Analysis of Parallel Algorithms*. Once you've got that down, creating a concurrent version using OpenMP will be very straightforward. (Oops! I've wrecked my reveal.) Example 9-7 contains a serial version of N-ary search.

EXAMPLE 9-7. Serialization of N-ary search algorithm

```
void NarySearch (int *A, int lo, int hi, int key, int Ntrvl, int *pos)
{
  float offset, step;
  int *mid = new int[Ntrvl+1];
  char *locate = new char[Ntrvl+2];
  int i;

  locate[0] = 'R'; locate[Ntrvl+1] = 'L';
  while (lo <= hi && *pos == -1) {
    int lmid;
    mid[0] = lo - 1;
    step = (float)(hi - lo + 1)/(Ntrvl+1);
    for (i = 1; i <= Ntrvl; i++) {
      offset = step * i + (i - 1);
      lmid = mid[i] = lo + (int)offset;
      if (lmid <= hi) {
        if (A[lmid] > key)
          locate[i] = 'L';
        else if (A[lmid] < key)
          locate[i] = 'R';
        else {
          locate[i] = 'E';
          *pos = lmid; } // found
      }
      else {
        mid[i] = hi + 1;
        locate[i] = 'L';
      }
    }
    for (i = 1; i <= Ntrvl; i++) {
      if (locate[i] != locate[i-1]) {
        lo = mid[i-1] + 1;
        hi = mid[i] - 1;
      }
    }
    if (locate[Ntrvl] != locate[Ntrvl+1]) lo = mid[Ntrvl] +1;
  }
}
```

The parameters to the NarySearch() function are the array to be searched (A), the initial index bounds of the search space (lo and hi), the value of the key the algorithm is attempting to find (key), the number of intervals to divide the search array into each round (Ntrval), and the pointer to return the index position of a record with a matching key (pos). The code assumes that the pos value has been initialized to −1 before calling this function. The Ntrvl parameter is likely going to be the number of threads; I will explain why we're implementing the function with this parameter when I discuss the concurrent solution.

This function declares two arrays. These will hold the index of the key test element (mid) and the results of the corresponding key comparison (locate). I've chosen to use a character array for the latter to denote whether the element's key is too big, too small, or just right. The letters indicate that the desired element with the matching search key will be found to the right (R) or to the left (L), or that the search and item keys are exactly equal (E). Any three values can be used here, as long as two consecutive elements, when compared, are found to have either the same value or different values. The locate array has two more slots than the number of intervals to be used. The first and last elements mimic the key comparison results from the phantom array slots just outside the bounds of the search array and are initialized to R and L, respectively.

The while loop continues to iterate a new search round as long as there is at least one array item to be searched and no element of the array has been found to have a matching key. The mid[0] element holds the index of the leftmost bound of the search array, and step is the number of slots between each element to be tested in the current round. Note that the code declares step as a float rather than an integer. By computing indexes with floating-point numbers and truncating any fractional parts before utilizing the value, we can ensure that the computed key test indexes are more equitably spread out within the search array (we used the same scheme for computing chunk boundaries within the reduction algorithm in Chapter 7). In addition, this code includes the lmid variable to give threads a local value for holding the index value of a key to be compared against the search key. This addition follows Simple Rule 7.

The body of the while loop has three separate parts. The first for loop computes an offset into the search array for each interval and stores the computed index into the corresponding element of mid (if the computed index is outside of the search array, the saved value is hi + 1 and this will be treated like the rightmost phantom element). Next, the key found at each of these positions is compared to the search key and the relationship of the location of the search key to the element key is recorded in the corresponding locate element. If there is a match on the search key, the value of pos is updated with the index of the matching element.

Once all of the test indexes are computed and the results of the key comparisons have been noted, the second for loop checks all consecutive pairs of elements from the locate array to see whether the characters stored there are different. As shown in Figure 9-1, this difference indicates that the record that matches the search key will lie between the two corresponding index points in the search array. When such a difference is found, the values of lo and hi are updated to set the bounds of the search array for the next iteration of the while loop. The third part of the while loop body does this same locate element test, but it does so with the rightmost phantom index (Ntrvl + 1). If this value is different from the locate element of the final computed test index, then only the lower bound of the search array needs to be updated.

Could there be more than one difference in the locate array? If the search key doesn't match any of the keys at the test index positions, the locate array will have only R and L characters. This is shown in Figure 9-2 (a). In fact, there will be one or more Rs followed by one or more Ls. Because the keys in the search array are sorted, all positions in locate to the left of the rightmost R must also be Rs, and all positions in locate to the right of the leftmost L must be Ls. If the search key is found, though, there will be two differences in the locate array, as shown in Figure 9-2 (b). While this will cause the serial algorithm to update the lo and hi bounds twice, when the algorithm expects this to be done only once, the next while conditional expression evaluation will yield FALSE. Thus, this extra bounds update will simply be discarded as the NarySearch() function returns from a successful search.

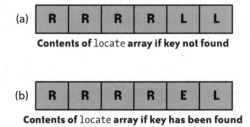

(a) Contents of locate array if key not found

(b) Contents of locate array if key has been found

FIGURE 9-2. Example of the locate array contents for two different cases

At Last, the Concurrent Solution

Example 9-8 contains the OpenMP version of *N*-ary search. The main reason that we're using OpenMP for the concurrent version of NarySearch() is because of the need for two barrier synchronizations. We need the first between the determination of the location of the matching element from the data array and the search through the locate array to identify the difference between two consecutive items. We need the second barrier between the update of lo and hi and the start of the next iteration of the while loop. Of course, the decision to use OpenMP is helped along by the fact that the algorithm has a data decomposition solution and uses for loops for iteration within the while loop. The additions to the code from Example 9-7 have been highlighted in bold.

EXAMPLE 9-8. OpenMP implementation of concurrent N-ary search algorithm

```
void NarySearch (int *A, int lo, int hi, int key, int Ntrvl, int *pos)
{
  float offset, step;
  int *mid = new int[Ntrvl+1];
  char *locate = new char[Ntrvl+2];
  int i;

  locate[0] = 'R'; locate[Ntrvl+1] = 'L';
#pragma omp parallel
  {
  while (lo <= hi && *pos == -1) {
    int lmid;
#pragma omp single
    {
      mid[0] = lo - 1;
      step = (float)(hi - lo + 1)/(Ntrvl+1);
    }
```

```
#pragma omp for private(offset) firstprivate(step)
    for (i = 1; i <= Ntrvl; i++) {
      offset = step* i + (i - 1);
      lmid = mid[i] = lo + (int)offset;
      if (lmid <= hi) {
        if (A[lmid] > key)
          locate[i] = 'L';
        else if (A[lmid] < key)
          locate[i] = 'R';
        else {
          locate[i] = 'E';
          *pos = lmid; } // found
      }
      else {
        mid[i] = hi + 1;
        locate[i] = 'L';
      }
    }
#pragma omp single
    {
      for (i = 1; i <= Ntrvl; i++) {
        if (locate[i] != locate[i-1]) {
          lo = mid[i-1] + 1;
          hi = mid[i] - 1;
        }
      }
      if (locate[Ntrvl] != locate[Ntrvl+1]) lo = mid[Ntrvl] +1;
    } // end single
  }
 } // end parallel region
}
```

The parallel region encloses the while loop, which means that each thread on the team will be executing all iterations of the while loop (the curly braces on the parallel pragma aren't strictly needed, but they serve to point out the extent of the parallel region). For threads to keep in sync with these iterations, the variables for lo, hi, and pos must be globally accessible to each thread. This will ensure that the results of the while conditional test are the same in all threads and that the threads will end the parallel region at the same time.

All threads share the step variable before the OpenMP loop worksharing construct begins, but the initial assignment of step and mid[0] must be done in serial. The firstprivate clause will create a private copy of this variable for each thread and initialize that copy with the value computed outside of the worksharing construct. Having a local copy of step is useful if there are fewer threads than intervals to check by avoiding multiple accesses of the global step by each thread.

The computation of the test key indexes and the discovery of the correlation of key values found at those points are all independent. Thus, the loop worksharing construct will divide up the intervals (via division of the loop iterations) among the threads of the team. If the number of intervals (Ntrvl) is equal to the number of threads, we will get one interval per thread; if there are more intervals than threads, multiple intervals will be assigned to threads. By including the interval parameter (Ntrvl), we can better control the granularity of computations assigned to each thread.

You may find that the overhead of doing only one interval per thread is too high versus the amount of computation. So if you specify, say, 10 intervals per thread, there is relatively less OpenMP overhead per computation per iteration of the outer while loop per thread. In addition, you execute fewer iterations of the while loop with 80 intervals than with 8. This assumes that you have a data set large enough to benefit from probing 80 locations.

Using the single worksharing construct makes certain that the second for loop and the last boundary check of the algorithm will be executed in serial. We're using single rather than master for the implicit barrier to ensure that values for lo and hi are updated before threads undertake the next iteration of the while loop. Actually, only the last boundary check is a serial operation. We could put the second for loop in a loop worksharing construct, especially if we have more intervals than threads. However, for a small number of intervals, there will be less memory traffic into cache lines holding the locate array if one thread alone does the check.

Since only one interval test will find a difference in consecutive locate elements, only one thread will update the lo and hi values. As a result, even if we ran the second for loop concurrently, there would be no need for mutually exclusive access and no need for any synchronization objects. This is true even when a matching element from the array is found and there are two differences in locate. Yes, this could lead to the situation of a race to store conflicting values into lo and hi, but the while condition test immediately after will halt the search, since the item of interest has been found.

Design Factor Scorecard

How efficient, simple, portable, and scalable is the concurrent version of the N-ary search code described earlier? Let's review the algorithm with respect to each of these categories.

Efficiency

You can use the Ntrvl parameter to affect the memory traffic of this algorithm by cutting out the need to share cache lines for updates. Elements from both the locate and the mid arrays are written during the first for loop. By setting the number of intervals, the loop iterations can be assigned such that no threads will share cache lines holding elements from the locate or mid arrays. There will be some overlap of cache line access in the second loop, but these accesses will be read-only (or done by a single thread).

The declaration of lmid within the while loop gives each thread a local copy. There are up to four read accesses of this variable within the body of the first for loop. If each of these accesses were to use the mid[i] location instead, there would be a potential false sharing conflict while other threads were attempting to update the mid array with a computed test index. Having the local computed value should reduce the chance of false sharing during this portion of the algorithm.

Since no synchronization objects are needed, the only other efficiency issue for this code is the granularity. The amount of work involved per for loop iteration and the number of iterations assigned to threads will be direct factors in the overall performance. As I've discussed, you can adjust these proportions by changing the value of the Ntrvl parameter. I don't have any advice on how to determine this parameter, except to say that this will depend on the size of the array to be searched and the number of threads and cores available. You should test different parameter values and use the ones that give the best results.

Simplicity

The concurrent solution presented here is as simple as the serial algorithm (and I hope the serial version is simple enough to understand). In the body of the first for loop, the computation of offset is based on the fixed value of step and the loop iteration variable, i. This makes each computation of offset independent of previous or future calculation of the offset into the search array. Keeping such details in mind when developing serial code that will ultimately be made concurrent, or when surveying serial code for concurrency opportunities, will make the transformation from serial to concurrent much easier.

> **NOTE**
>
> You might have realized that I could have coded the function in Example 9-7 to return an int and have a return of lmid when a key was found to be equal (at the "found" comment). If I were writing the algorithm only for serial, if I'd ever write a serial N-ary search, I would have done it that way. Since I was ultimately going to turn the code into a concurrent version, I deliberately put in the extra work that I knew would be handled by multiple threads. I guess this is an instance of Simple Rule 8 and also of developing and debugging in serial before parallelizing the code.

Portability

You could use the parallel_for algorithm from TBB to do the key tests that update the global mid and locate arrays. If the second for loop is not done in serial, you could use a second parallel_for algorithm. For an implementation with an explicit threads library, you would need global access to the mid and locate arrays, rather than declaring them within the NarySearch() function. Also, the lo and hi variables would need to be shared.

Distributed-memory platforms are going to be better off with each process doing the binary search on the local data. As a first test, the algorithm could test keys of elements at the lower and upper bounds of the assigned array chunk. If the key is not to be found between those items, then the process doesn't need to do anything more until the search is completed on the node that would contain the record with a matching key. Trying to implement something like the algorithm in Example 9-8 would lead to too much communication of data compared to the amount of computation that would be done.

Scalability

The granularity of the computations assigned to each thread will directly affect the execution time and performance. By divorcing the number of intervals from the number of threads, you can affect the granularity in a positive way by setting the number of intervals based on the current data set size and number of cores available. This will also make the algorithm more easily adaptable to different numbers of threads from one execution to another.

CHAPTER TEN

Graph Algorithms

A GRAPH IS A COMPUTATION OBJECT THAT IS USED TO MODEL RELATIONSHIPS AMONG things. For example, constituent atoms within a molecule, components within an electrical circuit, and nodes in a communication network are all things that you can represent and manipulate as graphs. Trees are graphs with special properties, so you could represent a hierarchical chart or family tree as a graph. There is a lot of terminology involved with graph theory. The next few paragraphs give a quick overview of the basic terminology needed to study concurrent algorithms to compute with graphs. If you're already familiar with graph theory terms, feel free to skip ahead a bit. Of course, if you've made it this far through the book, what's another page and a half between reader and author?

A graph is made up of two finite sets: a set of *nodes* (or *vertices*) and a set of *edges*. Each node has a label to identify it and distinguish it from other nodes. Edges in a graph connect exactly two nodes and are denoted by the labels of the pair of nodes that are related. If you have a graph of three nodes—A, B, and C—the two edges connecting A with B and B with C would be written as (A,B) and (B,C).

A graph is *directed* if all edge pairs are ordered. Directed edges represent a one-way relationship from one node to another. If the node pairs are unordered, the graph is *undirected*. A directed graph can be undirected if, for every edge (u,v), the graph contains the edge (v,u). Think of a two-way street where traffic can travel between two intersections in either direction, but only on the correct side of the street.

The most frequently used representation of a graph within a computer application is an *adjacency matrix*. Given a graph of n nodes, the adjacency matrix is an $n \times n$ binary matrix that represents the edges within the graph. Each row and each column of the matrix is assigned a node from the graph. If the edge (u,v) is present in the graph, a 1 is entered in the element at the intersection of the row representing u and the column representing v; otherwise, a 0 is stored to note that the edge is not within the graph. Figure 10-1 shows a representation of a directed graph (the circles are nodes with the assigned label near the node; the arrows are edges) and the corresponding adjacency matrix.

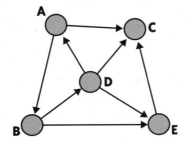

	A	B	C	D	E
A	0	1	1	0	0
B	0	0	0	1	1
C	0	0	0	0	0
D	1	0	1	0	1
E	0	0	1	0	0

FIGURE 10-1. Directed graph with corresponding adjacency matrix

There are cases when the relationship between nodes is associated with a real value, called the *weight*. When each edge of a graph has an associated weight, the graph is known as a *weighted graph*. For example, the weight of an edge might be the electrical resistance of the wire between two electronic components, the strength of the bond between atoms, or the bandwidth between communication nodes. While the interpretation of the value quantifying the relationship between nodes depends on what the graph represents, it is customary to talk of the weights in terms of length, as if the nodes were points along a system of roads represented by the edges. When I discuss weighted graphs, I will use this convention. Figure 10-2 shows an undirected weighted graph and the corresponding weight matrix representation.

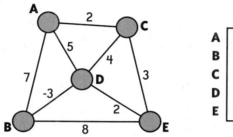

FIGURE 10-2. Undirected weighted graph and associated weight matrix

Note the symmetry of the matrix in Figure 10-2 across the main diagonal. With an undirected weighted graph, you only need to allocate memory to hold just under half of the weight matrix: either the lower triangular section below or the upper triangular section above the main diagonal.

How a weighted graph represents the case where there is no edge between nodes will depend on the intended usage of the graph. Typical values used are 0, some negative number, the maximum number that can be represented for the weight data type, or infinity. For the graph shown in Figure 10-2, the use of the infinity value (∞) indicates that there is no direct edge between the pair of nodes and 0 to indicate that no edge is required from a node to itself.

NOTE

If the graph has a maximum or fixed number of edges attached to each node, you can use a structure containing a fixed number of pointers to represent a node. The pointers mimic the edges of the graph by referencing (pointing to) those nodes that are connected to a given node. Trees are often represented in this way during computations because trees are graphs where (nonleaf) nodes likely have a set number of edges (e.g., binary trees) or some maximum number of edges (e.g., 2-3-4 trees).

A *path* within a graph is a sequence of nodes in which successive nodes are connected by edges in the graph, and a *simple path* has no repeated nodes. An example of a simple path from Figure 10-1 would be *ABDE*, since the edges (*A*, *B*), (*B*, *D*), and (*D*, *E*) are in the graph. A *cycle* is a path that begins and ends with the same node. The path *ABDA* is a cycle in the graph given in both Figures 10-1 and 10-2. A *tree* has no cycles. For weighted graphs, the *length* of a path is the sum of the weights assigned to the constituent edges. The length of the path *ABDE* in Figure 10-2 is $7+(-3)+2 = 6$.

We call a graph *connected* if there is a path from any node to any other node in the graph. The undirected graph in Figure 10-2 is connected. If a graph is not connected, it will be made of *connected components*—that is, a set of connected subgraphs with no shared nodes between any two subgraphs. A graph with a number of nodes and no edges is one extreme example of a graph built from connected components.

Depth-First Search

If the computation needs to visit every node in the graph, depth-first search is an excellent method for doing so. What kinds of problems can you solve by visiting every node in a graph? Well, you can tell whether an undirected graph is connected, or you can identify and label the connected components that make up the graph. You can also use a depth-first search to determine whether there is a cycle in the graph.

Discrete optimization problems have a finite or infinite set of states that can satisfy the constraints of the problem, and a cost function that yields a real number result for each possible state. You can formulate searches for a minimal cost solution through a subset of the state-space, since it is typically prohibitive to enumerate all possible states. For the computation, states are related to one another by some transformation rule that controls the move from one state to another. Depth-first searches can be used on the resulting portions of the state-space graph, which is constructed as the search progresses.

For me, the best example of such optimization problems is finding the next best move in zero-sum perfect-information games like tic-tac-toe, Awari, chess, or Go. The nodes of the state-space graph are board (game) positions, and the edges of the graph are legal moves that are possible to get from one position to another. Finding the next best move will start from a given board position and branch to other positions via all legal moves; your opponent's possible moves branch out from all of these nodes, and so on. The resulting graph is better known as a *game tree*.

NOTE

The *0/1 Knapsack Problem* is another instance of a discrete optimization problem. Given N things (each with a weight and value) to be placed in the knapsack (with a weight limit), there are 2^N possible solutions. The task is to find the set of items that will maximize the total value while making sure the total weight of the items does not exceed the sack's limit. Nodes in the graph will be the knapsack with or without each item; edges will correspond to adding an item that is absent or removing an item already in the knapsack. Starting with the empty sack, a depth-first search will go through each item, in some order, and either add it or keep it out of the knapsack. Once a possible solution has been reached, the search will return to previous partial solutions in the tree and try different combinations, determining whether each combination is a better solution or perhaps an impossible solution (too much weight for the sack to hold). The search continues until the best solution is identified.

The idea behind depth-first search is to visit a node and then visit one adjacent node. From this second node, the third node to visit is some node adjacent to the second node. Visualize a family tree where each successive generation is ordered from oldest to youngest children. Starting from the root couple, the next node selected is the eldest child of that couple. The search proceeds by visiting nodes on a path that goes from the root through the eldest children, initially ignoring brothers, sisters, cousins, aunts, uncles, nephews, and nieces, to the leftmost leaf of the tree. This "plunging straight to the depths" of the graph is where the algorithm got its name. When there is no other (previously unvisited) node adjacent to the just-visited node, the depth-first search returns to the parent node that preceded the just-visited node and will visit the next unvisited node from there. The numbers next to the nodes in Figure 10-3 show the order in which the nodes would be visited in a depth-first search of the undirected graph from Figure 10-2, starting from node A.

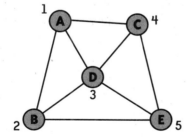

	A	B	C	D	E
A	0	1	1	1	0
B	1	0	0	1	1
C	1	0	0	1	1
D	1	1	1	0	1
E	0	1	1	1	0

FIGURE 10-3. Depth-first search example

Since node A is the start of the search, it is the first to be visited. The next node to visit is an unvisited node adjacent to A. Looking across the row of the adjacency matrix in Figure 10-3 corresponding to node A, the algorithm picks the first node that it encounters. Thus, it will visit node B. Looking across the node B row, we see that node A is the first adjacent node.

However, since the algorithm has already visited that node, it will look for the next adjacent node in line, which is node *D*. From node *D*, the algorithm will first try node *A*, then node *B*, and then visit node *C*. From node *C*, node *E* is the only adjacent node that has not yet been visited. Going through the node *E* row, the algorithm will find that all adjacent nodes have been previously visited, so it returns to node *C*. All possible adjacent nodes of node *C* have been accounted for, so the algorithm returns to node *D*. Picking up where the examination of the node *D* row left off, node *E* will be identified as the next possible candidate. Since this node has already been visited, there are no more nodes adjacent to node *D* and the algorithm will go back to node *B*. Since the algorithm has already visited all nodes adjacent to both *B* and *A*, the search finishes. If the graph were not connected, the algorithm would survey the nodes of the graph to find one that had not been previously visited and then resume the depth-first search from that node.

What does it mean to "visit" a node? What computation goes on during a visit? That will all depend on the reason for the search through the graph. It could be something as simple as labeling the nodes in a sequence for some external computation or checking for cycles by looking to see that no adjacent node has been previously visited. If you are searching a game tree, the node would first be checked to see if a winning (or losing) position had been reached, and, if not, the algorithm would generate the next set of legal moves from the current node's position.

A Recursive Solution

Even if you haven't studied depth-first search before this, I'm sure you've recognized that a recursive solution is the simplest way to "return" to a previous node once all the other adjacent nodes have been visited. Besides the adjacency matrix of the graph, the algorithm needs a method to keep track of which nodes it has visited. For this, we'll allocate an array with one element per node to serve as an indicator of a node having been visited. The code fragment in Example 10-1 gives some variable declarations needed within the recursive implementation of a depth-first search function, DFSearch(), and the associated function to perform the visit computations, visit(), on a selected node.

EXAMPLE 10-1. Serial implementation of depth-first search algorithm

```
int *visited; // notes when a node has been visited
int **adj;    // adj[][] is adjacency matrix
int V;        // number of nodes in graph

void visit(int k)
{
  int i;
  visited[k] = 1;
  /*
    Do something to VISIT node k
  */
```

```
  for (i = 0; i < V; i++)
  {
    if (adj[k][i])
      if (!visited[i]) visit(i);
  }
}

void DFSearch()
{
  int k;

  for (k = 0; k < V; k++) visited[k] = 0;
  for (k = 0; k < V; k++)
    if (!visited[k]) visit(k);
}
```

Nodes are associated with the rows and columns of the adjacency matrix adj. The values within adj are either 1 or 0, such that if adj[i][j] is 1, then there exists an edge between the node represented by row [i] and the node associated with column [j]; otherwise, the value is 0 to indicate that such an edge is not part of the graph. (For the rest of this chapter, I'm going to refer to nodes by their row or column index to avoid having to write "node associated with row/column" too much.) The code in Example 10-1 also assumes that the global integer, V, holds the number of nodes in the graph and, consequently, the number of rows and columns of adj.

The DFSearch() function first resets the visited array to all 0 entries, since none of the nodes in the graph have yet been visited. The for loop runs over all nodes in the graph. For any that are not visited, the visit() function is called. This for loop will work for graphs that are a collection of connected components. Once all the nodes of one component have been visited, the return from visit() to the DFSearch() function continues through the for loop, and the next unvisited node is chosen for the call to visit(). This will visit all the nodes in the associated component.

The actual computation to be done in order to "visit" a node is left unspecified in the comment of the visit() function. Before this computation is begun, the function marks the node as having been visited by setting the element of the visited array corresponding to the node. A scan through all the graph nodes is done. Any node that is adjacent to node k is tested for having been previously visited. If the node has not been previously visited, visit() is called on this adjacent, unvisited node.

Once a node has exhausted all the nodes in the graph that are adjacent to it, the visit() function returns to the location from which it was called. If this return is to a prior call of visit(), the for loop will resume the scan for adjacent nodes from the node that had prompted the just returned call to visit(). Through the combination of the for loop in DFSearch(), the recursion, and for loop in visit(), each node in the graph will be visited.

An Iterative Solution

We've seen from Quicksort (Chapter 8) that a recursive serial algorithm is not as easy to transform to a concurrent equivalent as an iterative algorithm. We can add a stack to the code and simulate the recursion by first pushing all nodes onto the stack within DFSearch(). Then, a while loop, on condition that the stack is not empty, will first pop() a node off the stack. If this node has not been previously visited, the visit computation is done, the node is marked as being visited, and all nodes adjacent to the newly visited node are pushed onto the stack. This modification is shown in Example 10-2, where the push(), pop(), and size() functions have been defined as you would expect for some stack data structure implementation. Though it really shouldn't matter to the search results, I've reversed the order in which the loops iterate their for loops to keep the same node order for visits as the recursive algorithm.

EXAMPLE 10-2. Iterative version of depth-first search algorithm

```
int *visited; // notes when a node has been visited
int **adj;    // adj[][] is adjacency matrix
int V;        // number of nodes in graph
stack S;      // stack of nodes (indices)


void DFSearch()
{
  int i, k;

  for (k = 0; k < V; k++) visited[k] = 0;
  for (k = V-1; k >= 0; k--) {
    push(S, k);
  }
  while (size(S) > 0) {
    k = pop(S);
    if (!visited[k]) {
      visited[k] = 1;
      /*
        Do something to VISIT node k
      */
      for (i = V-1; i >= 0; i--)
        if (adj[k][i]) push(S, i);
    }
  } // end while
}
```

The pushing of nodes onto stack S in the body of the while loop could also test whether or not the adjacent node has been visited prior to being pushed on the stack. As the search progressed, there would be fewer nodes placed on the stack. However, we still need to test whether or not a popped node remains unvisited at the top of the while loop body. There is always a chance that a node will be pushed onto the stack, popped off, and visited before a previously pushed instance is popped off and tested. For example, node *C* in Figure 10-3 will be pushed initially onto the stack when it is adjacent to node *A*, and then again when it is adjacent to node *D*. This last push() would lead to the first pop() that brings node *C* to be visited.

Not the Concurrent Solution, Yet

With Quicksort as an example, you should be able to transform the code in Example 10-2 into a concurrent version of depth-first search. The implementation will use a thread pool on a task decomposition design where the independent tasks are the visit computation of previously unvisited nodes. Some of the salient implementation points to keep in mind when designing such a solution are: find or implement a thread-safe stack, use a semaphore object to control and keep a count of the number of items in the stack, protect access to the shared visited array, and count the nodes as they are visited until the count reaches V to determine when the graph search is done. When threads find that the search has completed, the stack may still contain visited nodes; be sure to empty the stack to avoid a memory leak.

Hold on a minute—if this is just like the Quicksort code back in Example 8-17, why did I even include this algorithm in the book, let alone devote more pages to something that has essentially been done before? Depth-first search and Quicksort do have a similar concurrent algorithmic structure: tasks go into a shared structure where threads pull out and put in tasks before terminating (when all the work is done). However, depth-first search uses a visited array, which has no counterpart in the Quicksort algorithm. So, before we jump into the concurrent version of depth-first search, I want to address the details of handling this array, specifically issues concerning lock usage, that will come up during that implementation.

How many locks do we need?

In the concurrent implementation of depth-first search, the visited array needs to be shared, since all threads will need access to check on a node's visit history and update that history when the node is actually used. A single lock object on the entire array would be the easiest solution to regulate correct access to ensure that the same node is not visited by more than one thread. The biggest problem with this is the possibility of threads piling up awaiting access to the critical regions of reading or updating one element from the visited array. This will generate a very big overall performance hit and should be avoided if possible..

If we realize that the visited array will be updated once per node, but read by many threads during the course of the search, we might think about using *readers/writer locks*. This looks like the perfect situation for using such a synchronization object, since we can expect that the majority of accesses to visited elements will be for reading. Rather than having to queue up at a single monolithic lock on the entire array, all the reading threads can be given concurrent access. Surely, we should expect less of a performance hit than with a single lock.

Unfortunately, since the size of the critical region of code is so small, there will be no performance advantage. In fact, as Bryan Cantrill and Jeff Bonwick remind us in "Real-World Concurrency" (*Communications of the ACM,* 2008), since the state of the lock needs to be checked and updated atomically, the overhead associated with the readers/writer lock is going to be the same as using a single, ordinary lock. To be most effective, readers/writer locks need large critical regions to have the chance for multiple readers to be executing at the same time, which hides the latency of the lock overhead. Looking back to Example 10-2, there are, at most, only two lines of code (the if-test and the setting of visited[k]) accessing the visited array.

If you've got to pay the overhead one way or the other, you'll achieve the best performance by reducing or avoiding contention on the locking object. So, swinging from one extreme to the other, rather than having a single lock guard the entire array, we could have a lock for each individual array element. Access to an element of visited still has the same locking overhead, but, on average, there will be far fewer instances of multiple threads needing concurrent access to the same element in the array than there would be instances of multiple threads needing concurrent access to any element of the array protected by a single lock.

The drawback to the one element/one lock scheme (and you just knew that there had to be one, didn't you?) is that for a graph with V nodes, V lock objects will need to be allocated with the visited array. This is a tradeoff of space for performance. As the search state-space becomes larger and larger, this could quickly become a drain on platform resources. We need something between the two extremes to balance the contention and memory space issues.

My solution for such cases is to use *modulo locks*. If the multiple data items that require mutually exclusive access are indexed, you can allocate a fixed number of locks, and the result of the calculation of the item index modulo the number of locks is used to index the lock employed to regulate access to the given item. For example, if we allocate two lock objects, one of these will protect access to the even-indexed items and the other will control access to the odd-indexed items.

With a fixed number of lock objects, there is no problem with memory resources, even when the size of the data scales. In the case of two objects, we would expect that the contention on each lock would be cut in about half from what it would be with a single all-encompassing lock, which should yield some performance benefit. What is the optimal number of locks to use? As a rule of thumb, I think it's good to use a number of locks equal to the number of threads. If two locks cut the contention time in half, I figure that a number of locks equal to the number of threads should avoid all contention, with each thread never needing the same lock held by another thread. That won't happen, of course, but it is a good goal. Twice the number of threads should still be relatively small and will help spread out any anticipated contention even better.

The standard wisdom with critical regions is to keep them as small as possible. Remove any extraneous code that doesn't need to be protected in order to reduce the amount of time a thread spends in the critical region. This will lower the amount of time that threads spend waiting to gain access to the critical region code protected by a contended lock object. With the extra computation needed to perform the modulus calculation or the overhead of readers/

writer locks, it seems that a larger critical region will not be as detrimental, since both of these two synchronization options should greatly reduce the contention you would expect from use of a single lock object.

Locking a conditional expression evaluation

Another part of the code in Example 10-2 that concerns the use of locks protects the read access of visited[k] in the evaluation of the if conditional expression. You can't put a lock/unlock sequence in the conditional expression itself. However, you can read the value of the protected variable into a local variable and use the local variable's value within the conditional expression evaluation. Example 10-3 shows code that does just that. The Pthreads pthread_mutex_t object, Vmutex[j], protects the critical region on the read access of visited[k]. You must also use this object to protect the critical region that updates the visited[k] element, which you should realize automatically by now. The lVisited variable holds the local copy of the visited[k] value, and the local integer j holds the lock object index computed from the modulus operation.

EXAMPLE 10-3. Protecting access to variables within a conditional expression

```
j = k % NUM_LOCKS;
pthread_mutex_lock(&Vmutex[j]);
  lVisited = visited[k];
pthread_mutex_unlock (&Vmutex[j]);
if (!lVisited) {
  pthread_mutex_lock (&Vmutex[j]);
    visited[k] = 1;
  pthread_mutex_unlock (&Vmutex[j]);
  /*
    Body of if statement
  */
}
```

Now, let me throw another curve ball at you. The value of lVisited is only good as long as the execution is within the critical region. Upon doing a quick interleaving analysis, we find that we can have two threads, T0 and T1, approach the code in Example 10-3 with the same local values of k. T0 reads visited[k], sets the local value of lVisited, exits the first critical region, and is swapped out of the core, where T1 resumes execution. T1 enters the initial critical region and finds that the k node has not been visited and sets the local value of lVisited. In fact, if there are multiple cores, T1 can enter the initial critical region while T0 is testing its local value of lVisited. In either event, both T0 and T1 will execute the code to visit node k.

By using the same lock object around the read and around the update of visited[k], the code in Example 10-3 will protect the value of visited[k] from being changed while a thread is attempting to read it. However, if the values of protected variables can be changed before a copy of that value can be used, as shown earlier, we'll need to take steps to ensure that the retrieved value is utilized before the source of the value can be modified. Thus, it looks like we need to not only have both the read and write access of elements from visited protected by the same lock object, but also to have them in the same critical region.

With this in mind, Example 10-4 shows how we can modify the code from Example 10-3 to protect both the read and write access to visited[k] with a modulo lock and still have the results of the read control when a thread will execute the visit code in the body of the if statement.

EXAMPLE 10-4. Protecting both read and write of variable used in conditional expression

```
j = k % NUM_LOCKS;
pthread_mutex_lock(&Vmutex[j]);
  if (!visited[k]) {
    iWillVisit = 1;
    visited[k] = 1;
  }
pthread_mutex_unlock(&Vmutex[j]);
if (iWillVisit) {
  /*
    Body of if statement
  */
  iWillVisit = 0;
}
```

The code in Example 10-4 has only the one critical region and uses the local variable iWillVisit (initialized to 0, or FALSE) to preserve the results of the conditional expression evaluation. This is like buying a ticket for a seat at a concert. If there is an empty seat, you can purchase that seat. Once you have the ticket in your hand, you are the only one who can sit in that seat.

Also, within the critical region, if node k has not been previously visited, the visited[k] element is set to ensure that the thread setting this value is the only thread that will execute the visit computation for this node of the graph.

Now for the Concurrent Solution

Up to this point, we've only dealt with the locking requirements to protect access to the visited array. To complete the concurrent implementation of depth-first search, we will also need to find or implement a thread-safe stack, use a semaphore object to control access and keep a count of the number of items in the stack, and count the nodes as they are visited until the count reaches V to determine when the graph search is done. All of this should go into the section of code labeled Body of if statement in Example 10-4.

We can use the model of Quicksort to deal with the stack data structure and the associated semaphore. In addition, we'll need a critical region to protect the update of the global count, which will be incremented whenever a thread is to execute the code to visit a node. Since this is only incremented when a node finds an unvisited node, you might think we can protect the increment in the same critical region as the conditional expression evaluation. If we use a single lock to protect access to the entire visited array, this will work; if we use a modulo lock scheme, though, there can be cases where two threads with different modulo results will be granted concurrent access to the one counter. If we use a Windows Threads implementation, we can take advantage of the interlocked intrinsics to increment the counter, even when using modulo locks to protect the visited array.

If we are going to have a Windows Threads implementation, there is an alternative to the use of an explicit lock object to implement the critical region. Since we have to read the value of an element from the visited array and, based on that value, possibly update the value of that element, all in a mutually exclusive way, we could use InterlockedCompareExchange(). This intrinsic takes three parameters, d, e, and c. When called, this function stores the current value of d in a temp location and compares d to c. If the result of the comparison finds that the two values are equal, the intrinsic stores the value of e into d. Regardless of the comparison test, it returns the original value of d from the temp location. All of this is done atomically.

To use InterlockedCompareExchange() to replace the critical region algorithm from Example 10-4, we will set d to reference visited[k]. e will be 1 and c will be 0. If visited[k] is 0 (node has not been visited), comparing this to c will result in the equality test being TRUE, and the value in e will be stored in visited[k]. This atomically sets the status of the node to be visited, and the return of 0 from the originally stored value signifies that the node was previously unvisited. On the flip side, if visited[k] is 1, the comparison to c will not be equal, there will be no change made to the value stored in this array element, and the return of 1 signifies that the node has already been visited by a thread.

The code in Example 10-5 brings together all the ideas that we've examined over the previous few pages into a concurrent version of depth-first search using Windows Threads for the implementation. This includes the threaded function pDFSearch() and some global declarations that are different from earlier serial versions.

EXAMPLE 10-5. Concurrent implementation of depth-first search using Windows Threads

```
long *visited;
long gCount = 0;
stack S;

unsigned __stdcall pDFSearch(void *pArg)
{
  int k, i, iWillVisit=0;

  while(1) {
    WaitForSingleObject(hSem, INFINITE);  // Semaphore count of stack size
    if (gCount == V) break;
    k = pop(S);
    if (!InterlockedCompareExchange(&visited[k], 1L, 0L)) {
      iWillVisit = 1;
      InterlockedIncrement(&gCount);
    }
    if (iWillVisit) {
      /*
        Do something to VISIT node k
      */
      for (i = V-1; i >= 0; i--)
      { int semCount=0;
```

```
          if (adj[k][i]) {
            push(S, i);
            semCount++;
          }
          if (semCount) ReleaseSemaphore(hSem, semCount, NULL);
        }
        iWillVisit = 0;
        if (gCount == V) SetEvent(tSignal);
      }
    }
    return 0;
  }
```

The declarations shown in Example 10-5 include the global counter (gCount), the thread-safe stack (S) to hold integer indexes of graph nodes, and the data type change for the visited array to long in order to use elements with InterlockedCompareExchange(). We've declared gCount as long in order to use InterlockedIncrement() as an atomic update whenever a node is found that can be visited.

Following the template of the QuickSort() code from Example 8-17, we encase the whole computation in an infinite while loop. Each thread will use the semaphore (hSem) to determine whether there are nodes on the stack. (I'll show how hSem gets initialized in Example 10-6.) If there are items on the stack (the semaphore count is greater than 0), the WaitForSingleObject() function decrements the count. Before going on, the code checks the search termination criteria. Once all the nodes in the graph have been visited (gCount == V), there's no reason for threads to continue, so the threads will break out of the while loop and terminate.

If the search hasn't gotten to all nodes, the thread pops a node index from the stack into the local integer k. As described previously, InterlockedCompareExchange() atomically tests the state of visited[k] and updates the value to indicate that node k will be visited. If the update is made, the thread sets iWillVisit, which acts like a ticket into the code that actually performs the visit computation, and atomically increments the global counter, gCount.

If the iWillVisit flag is set, the thread does the visit computation on node k. Once this is done, the row k of the adjacency matrix (adj) is searched. Each adjacent node is pushed onto the stack with a local counter keeping track of how many new nodes are added to the stack. After all the nodes have been placed on the stack, the semaphore value is updated. By using the local counter, we need to call ReleaseSemaphore() only once, and only if there were adjacent nodes found. Finally, the iWillVisit flag is reset in preparation for the next node to be taken from the stack.

Before going back to the stack, the thread examines the value of gCount. If all nodes have been visited, a signal is sent to an external thread (likely the thread that spawned the threads for the search) to indicate that the search is done. While we could place a break here, we still need the test and break just after the WaitForSingleObject() call on the semaphore for those threads that don't handle the last node to be visited.

A little interleaving analysis

In the concurrent Quicksort algorithm, once the queue becomes empty upon completion of the sorting, threads can end up waiting for a semaphore that won't be incremented, since all the sorting threads are waiting on the semaphore. Before getting hung up on the semaphore, a signal is sent from one of the sorting threads to indicate that the sorting has been done; the receiver of that signal calls the ReleaseSemaphore() function with a count equal to the number of sorting threads. This allows the sorting threads to return from the wait on the semaphore and evaluate the termination condition test that will cause them to finish. The code in Example 10-5 is written with the similar structure, but is it really necessary?

Will the stack for depth-first search become empty at the same time the search has completed? At first glance you might say, "No." As nodes are visited, all adjacent nodes are pushed onto the stack. Once the last unvisited node is popped from the stack and visited, the search is complete and the stack will still contain many nodes that have already been visited (the last node visited adds any adjacent nodes are to the stack). Why should we care? If the stack will always have nodes, even after the search has finished, threads will pass through the wait on the semaphore in order to pop off a visited node, but will terminate because gCount has reached the number of nodes in the graph. There is no need for a signal or an external thread to load up the semaphore to free trapped threads, right?

While this might be how things play out 99 44/100% of the time, we can still create an interleaving of threaded executions where the last node to be visited is popped off the stack and the thread responsible is not allowed to execute until all other stack entries have been popped, found to be visited, and the rest of the threads are waiting on the semaphore before the last node is processed. Plus, even with new nodes being pushed onto the stack, we can always have an instance where there are fewer nodes than threads.

In contrast, if the last node is a connected component in and of itself (just the node, no edges), all processing of the rest of the graph will be done and this last node will be popped off the stack at the very end. Again, the rest of the threads will be waiting on the semaphore while the last node is visited. We had both of these possible situations with Quicksort. So, it looks like we do need the signal and semaphore loading by an external source.

Spawning the depth-first search threads

Example 10-6 shows a code fragment for creating the search threads and initializing the data structures.

EXAMPLE 10-6. Code fragment to call pDFSearch() function

```
for (i = V-1; i >= 0; i--) push(S, i);  // load up initial stack
hSem = CreateSemaphore(NULL, V, V*V, NULL);  // Initialize semaphore

for (i = 0; i < NUM_THREADS; i++)
  hThreads[i] = (HANDLE) _beginthreadex(NULL, 0, pDFSearch, NULL, 0, NULL);
```

```
WaitForSingleObject(tSignal, INFINITE);  // Wait for signal
ReleaseSemaphore(hSem, NUM_THREADS, NULL);
```

The first line pushes all the nodes onto the stack S in order to cover cases when the graph is made up of connected components. The count of the semaphore object, hSem, is initialized as V, the number of nodes on the stack, and the maximum count value is set at V^2. This corresponds to a fully connected graph with V nodes, which has the largest number of edges for the given number of nodes.

The _beginthreadex() function spawns the threads, and the returned HANDLE for each thread is stored in the hThreads array. After creating the threads, the spawning thread waits on the Windows event that will signal completion of the search. In case there are threads stalled waiting on an empty stack, ReleaseSemaphore() is called to release those threads so they can determine that the search has completed.

If you look back at Example 10-5, you might wonder why we set the tSignal event after the node had been processed, and why extra, ineffectual nodes were added to the stack. Why not put the test for completion and sending of the signal right after the InterlockedIncrement() call that results in gCount achieving the target value? This does seem like a more logical place, but it could lead to a problem in the spawning thread's use of the search results. If the signal is sent before the last node has actually been processed, the spawning thread (Example 10-6) can wake up, set the semaphore's count to ensure that the search nodes aren't ensnared by an empty stack, and then proceed to use the (incomplete) results of the search. To guarantee that all node processing has finished, the spawning thread needs another synchronization point after setting the semaphore value. By not sending the signal until after the last node is finished with the required visit processing, the spawning thread knows that all search processing is finished when the tSignal event is set and that it is safe to proceed.

Design Factor Scorecard

How efficient, simple, portable, and scalable is the concurrent version of the depth-first search code described earlier? Let's review the algorithm with respect to each of these categories.

Efficiency

Use of a modulo lock scheme should boost efficiency of threaded execution by spreading out the contention of required lock objects over multiple objects, rather than heaping it all onto a single lock. Using a finite number of locks, as opposed to a single lock for each instance of a data set, keeps the memory resource usage of your threaded code manageable and more scalable.

The maximum size of the stack needed will be V^2. A much tighter limit would be the number of 1 entries in the adjacency matrix. Rather than using a dynamically linked list implementation of a stack, it may be feasible to use a static array implementation, depending on how much space individual stack items require. If you're using a third-party thread-safe stack implementation, you're pretty much stuck with what you get.

Simplicity

The concurrent version, for the most part, is a direct translation of the iterative version of depth-first search. The code that we added to determine when the search has completed uses the same ideas and objects as the concurrent `QuickSort()`. Understanding that implementation will make it easier to understand this one.

Perhaps the most obtuse portion of the depth-first search code from Example 10-5 is the use of `InterlockedCompareExchange()` to regulate the testing and marking of elements from the visited array. In *Windows System Programming*, Third Edition (Addison-Wesley Professional, 2004), Johnson Hart demonstrates the use of this intrinsic as the implementation of a spinlock. Our use of this intrinsic mimics Hart's example, but we've only used the locking half. There is no need to "unlock" a node once it has been visited. While the use of the intrinsic and how it functions may cause another programmer to pause when reading the code, this code is much simpler (and offers better protection) than the equivalent code from Example 10-4.

Portability

Because of the use of the `InterlockedCompareExchange()` intrinsic, you can implement the code given here for depth-first search only on Windows platforms that support this intrinsic. We will need a variation on the more complex code of Example 10-4 to implement the algorithm with a different explicit threading library. Either that or include and execute assembly language code for a compare-and-swap (CAS) operation, if such an instruction is supported on the processor you are running on.

Use of Intel TBB or OpenMP for this algorithm would require the use of the explicit task interfaces from either. Rather than pushing a node onto the stack, a new task can be spawned for that node. While this would allow us to implement the algorithm without needing to find or create a thread-safe stack data structure, there are two other concerns. The first is that the task scheduling mechanism will be directly responsible for the order in which nodes are visited. This may not be a stack-based ordering, so the depth-first search may not plumb the depths of the graph as we anticipate (not to mention that a multithreaded execution with a stack data structure will likely not visit nodes in the same order as the serial code). The second concern is terminating the TBB or OpenMP threads when the search has completed; there may be more tasks (on visited nodes) "in the stack" to be considered. We could put in code to recognize the termination of the search and then simply allow the threads to finish the examination of tasks already created, quickly discard the visited nodes, and not create any new tasks.

Scalability

The amount of computation that is needed to visit a node will affect the scalability of the depth-first search code. The more computation there is, the coarser the granularity will be per thread.

This will help hide the overhead of having mutually exclusive access to the visited array and the synchronization needed to push and pop items from the thread-safe stack. Curtailing the processing of the search once all nodes have been visited will improve overall performance, too.

Modulo locks, if needed, can enhance the scalability of an algorithm by reducing the contention on a single lock object. The number of locks will depend on the time needed to perform the modulo computation and the probability of contention on a single lock in the face of multiple locks. A good rule of thumb is to use at least the same number of locks as threads, in the hopes that the worst case will be that each thread uses a different lock whenever multiple threads need a lock. Of course, you should apply the practice of having one lock per object protected (or multiple locks protecting access to elements from the same array) to ensure proper protection of diverse items (Simple Rule 7).

Breadth-First Search

Like depth-first search, breadth-first search visits all nodes within a graph. The difference is that from a given node in the graph (after that node has been visited), the algorithm next visits *all* nodes adjacent to the node. So, after visiting a node in the graph, all nodes adjacent to that node will be visited, followed by all nodes adjacent to those, and so on. If the graph is a tree, the order in which nodes are searched will be by level in the tree. That is, after first visiting the root (level 0), all children of the root (level 1) will be visited. This will be followed by visits to all the grandchildren of the root (level 2) followed by the level 3 nodes, and so on.

One "fun" problem that we can represent as a search graph is finding the sequence of moves to restore a Rubik's Cube to the original arrangement of single colored faces. In my opinion, this problem is better solved using breadth-first search. The lowest limit at the time of this writing is no more than 26 face rotations required to solve any given cube, which was proven by Daniel Kunkle and Gene Cooperman in their paper, "Twenty-Six Moves Suffice for Rubik's Cube" (*Proceedings of the 2007 International Symposium on Symbolic and Algebraic Computation*, 2007). Many situations will require fewer than 26 moves and, depending on the order of moves generated, breadth-first search could find these quicker than a depth-first search.

From a given cube configuration, there are 12 possible single moves (six faces, each with two possible rotation directions) to create another cube configuration. If one rotation does not yield the solution, we could then try any of 12 possible single moves from each of those original 12 moves. Any cycles in the search graph will denote a return to some previously created configuration and can be ignored. Eventually, after generating and searching through rotations of cube faces, a solution will be found with 26 moves or less.

CAN WE SOLVE ALL RUBIK'S CUBE CONFIGURATIONS BY BRUTE FORCE?

Before you go off and write a cube-solving application to find the minimum number of moves for a given configuration, let's look over some of the numbers. The search tree will have a depth of no more than 26 levels, 12 branches (moves) from the root, and 11 branches from each internal node (to avoid the obvious cycle generated by undoing the previous move). This gives us a worst-case grand total of $12 \times 11^{25} \approx 1.3 \times 10^{27}$ possible cube positions to examine in order to determine whether the solution has been reached. Let's assume that, on average, only half of these nodes will need to be searched, and your multicore processor platform can generate and evaluate 200 million positions per second, which is the computation rate that the 1997 version of Deep Blue achieved with 30 processors equipped with special chess hardware. See *Behind Deep Blue: Building the Computer that Defeated the World Chess Champion* (Princeton University Press, 2002) by Feng-Hsiung Hsu for details. If you have all of that, you would be able to find the correct sequence for one cube configuration in about 3.25×10^{18} seconds, or just less than 103 billion years (insert exasperated sigh here). You might want to wait for the billion-core processors to ship before attempting this.

It's all in the queue

To tackle a more tractable problem than finding the minimal solution to a Rubik's Cube configuration, the implementation of a concurrent breadth-first search algorithm will be almost exactly the same as the concurrent depth-first search code. The only difference is that a thread-safe queue is used instead of a stack to order the nodes to be searched. To initialize the queue, we should insert only one element. For a graph of connected components, the algorithm will need to load up another unvisited node when the queue is empty and there are still unvisited nodes. This change from loading up all nodes for connected components is due to the use of a FIFO queue. By placing all nodes in the queue initially, none of the adjacent nodes found would be visited in the proper order. The initialization nodes would all have been seen before those adjacent nodes get to the head of the queue.

Static Graphs Versus Dynamic Graphs

The depth-first and breadth-first search algorithms presented here both assume that the graph is defined before the search functions are called. That is, the graph is static and won't change during the execution of a search. More dynamic instances like game trees will generate the next set of adjacent nodes during the visit computation. There are game tree search algorithms specifically designed to search moves in these specialized cases. While I've never programmed a two-player, zero-sum game before, the structure of the concurrent implementations given previously appear to be adaptable for such algorithms or on searches of other dynamically generated graphs. The stopping criteria will change, depending upon the actual search algorithm and goals and limits of the search.

All-Pairs Shortest Path

Before there were online mapping applications, I would consult a paper map to find how far it was to travel from Albuquerque to Boston (2,232 miles according to Google Maps). A map or atlas of the country might have a lower triangular matrix where I could find the precomputed distance between a set of cities. Looking at the intersection of rows/columns for Albuquerque and Boston, I would find my answer. Since there isn't one single road that connects these two cities, how did the mapmakers know the shortest distance between these two places?

If you think of a map as an instance of a graph, the cities would be nodes and the roads between cities would be the edges. The length of the road is the weight of an edge. The all-pairs shortest path algorithm can compute the minimum length path (shortest distance) between all pairs of nodes within the graph. Thus, besides computing the shortest distance needed to drive from Albuquerque to Boston, you can also find the minimum driving distance between Chicago and Denver, between El Paso and Fargo, or between Georgetown and Houston.

More formally, the all-pairs shortest path algorithm takes a graph of n nodes and $n \times n$ weight matrix, W. The result is an $n \times n$ matrix, D (for distance), where the $D[i][j]$ entry holds the minimum weight of the path from node i to node j. Entries in the W matrix can be 0, positive, or negative (as long as there is no negative length cycle). This condition will assure that only simple paths are found. The weighted graph in Figure 10-2 has a negative length edge, but any cycle that includes this edge will still have a positive total weight. The "special" entries in Figure 10-2 correspond to the typical entries for a weight matrix to be used for this algorithm, i.e., the 0 entry denotes that it takes no time or distance to travel from a node to itself, and the infinity value (∞) indicates there is no direct edge between the nodes.

Floyd's Algorithm provides a simple solution to this problem. The key point to the algorithm is to find the shortest path between node i and node j that includes (or excludes) node k on the path. Each possible node k in the graph is tried in turn to find these shortest paths. The algorithm computes a series of successive D_k matrixes, one for each individual k, with the previous D_{k-1} matrix used in the computation. In mathematical notation, for all node pairs i and j, we have:

$$D_k[i][j] = min(D_{k-1}[i][j], D_{k-1}[i][k] + D_{k-1}[k][j])$$

After k iterations, the D_k matrix will hold the lengths of the shortest paths that use the first k nodes as intermediate nodes in the path. Once the algorithm has iterated over all n nodes in the graph, the D_n matrix will contain the shortest path lengths between all pairs of nodes with any other node(s) as intermediate nodes. This is the result that we are looking for.

From the description just given, we can see that there will be a nested loop pair to compute the minimum path between each i,j pair. This computation will be the body of the loop that iterates over all the choices for k. If the initial D_0 is simply the original weight matrix, W, we have the serial code in Example 10-7.

EXAMPLE 10-7. Serial implementation of Floyd's Algorithm

```
void Floyds(float **D, int N)
{
  int i, j, k;

  for (k = 0; k < N; k++) {
    for (i = 0; i < N; i++) {
      for (j = 0; j < N ; j++)
        D[i][j] = min(D[i][j], D[i][k] + D[k][j]);
    }
  }
}
```

This code uses a `float` array for both the weight and distance matrixes. The code not shown in Example 10-7 to initialize the weight matrix for computation uses the constant `FLT_MAX` from the *float.h* include file to play the role of infinity.

To convert the code in Example 10-7 to a concurrent version, the outer loop can be considered akin to a time series iteration. The algorithm must finish all updates to the D matrix entries for each k before going to the computation using $k+1$. The outer loop must be run in serial, and the two inner loops are the only possible candidates to run concurrently. The actual concurrent implementation can easily be done in OpenMP or Intel TBB. Example 10-8 shows a TBB solution. I've simply moved the nested loops into the tryK class and called the `parallel_for` algorithm using the intrinsic `blocked_range2d` range class to be able to divide up the iterations of these two loops.

EXAMPLE 10-8. Concurrent implementation of Floyd's Algorithm using Intel TBB

```
class tryK {
  const int k;
  float **D;

public:
  void operator() (const blocked_range2d<int,int>& r) const {
    for (int i = r.rows().begin(); i < r.rows().end(); i++) {
      for (int j = r.cols().begin(); j < r.cols().end(); j++)
        D[i][j] = min(D[i][j], D[i][k]+D[k][j]);
    }
  }

  tryK (const int k_, float **D_) : k(k_), D(D_) {}

  tryK (const int k_, float **D_, split) : k(k_), D(D_) {}
};
```

```
void cFloyds(float **D)
{
  int k;

  for (k = 0; k < V; k++)
    parallel_for(blocked_range2d<int, int> (0, V, rGrainSize, 0, V, cGrainSize), tryK(k, D));
}
```

This code assumes that two constants are defined, rGrainSize and cGrainSize, to set the minimum number of rows and columns into which the TBB scheduler will divide the loops. You will need to set these values, which you can find through trial and error testing to see how small the array blocks can get before performance suffers.

One thing I didn't point out in Example 10-7 is that the entire array is computed. I began this section talking about a lower triangular matrix needed to find the distance on a map between two cities. Why do we need to compute over the whole D array? On a map, roads go both ways, at least between cities. If we have a directed graph, there can be a path from node P to node Q, but there may be no path from Q to P or that path may run over edges that have a different total weight (maybe it's uphill in one direction). To compute the shortest path for all pairs of nodes in the graph, we need to work with the whole array.

What About the Data Race on the kth Row?

I don't think I need to explain the details of the code in Example 10-8. If you understand the serial algorithm and the code and understand the TBB parallel_for algorithm, it's all smooth sailing. However, before taking my word on the correctness of the concurrent implementation, can you prove that there are no adverse data races?

If you examine the serial algorithm, each iteration of the k loop accesses all entries of the D array to check for possible updates. The structure of the loops does this one row at a time, reading values from a fixed row (k). Without loss of generality, we can assume that entire row updates are assigned to individual threads. Are there interleavings of two threads, T0 and T1, where T0 is assigned some row i != k and T1 is assigned to update row k, such that T1 could update D[k][j] both before (one interleaving) and after (another interleaving) T0 updates D[i][j]? Yes, we can do that quite easily. But does it matter?

This last question is really the crux of the matter. Let's rewrite the body of the inner loop by substituting k for i to explicitly illustrate the computation that T1 would execute. This substitution gives us:

```
D[k][j] = min(D[k][j], D[k][k]+D[k][j])
```

From the original weight matrix, we know that D[k][k] will be 0. The only way to get a smaller value in a main diagonal element of the distance matrix would be to have a negative cycle from the node to itself. However, it was stipulated that the graph could have no negative cycles. The result of the operation just shown will be to find the minimum value between D[k][j] and itself, which will result in no updates to any element of the distance matrix within row k. Thus, regardless of how TBB divides up the distance matrix for updates, there will be no data race accessing elements from (the fixed) row k.

As I've mentioned before, sometimes interleaving analysis is not quite enough. Just because there appears to be a data race, you have to show that there will be actual adverse consequences from the problematic interleaving schedule.

Design Factor Scorecard

How efficient, simple, portable, and scalable is the concurrent version of the code for Floyd's Algorithm described earlier? Let's review the algorithm with respect to each of these categories.

Efficiency

Overall, the efficiency of the concurrent code will be similar to that of the serial version. By using the blocked_range2d class, we yield some of the efficiency decisions to the TBB task scheduler at runtime. If we had used the one-dimensional blocked_range class on the i loop, each iteration of the concurrent loop would access the kth row in order to update the jth row. As given in Example 10-8, the TBB scheduler would have the option of assigning work in this way, or it might carve out blocks of the distance matrix to be updated, which would be the most flexible solution.

Simplicity

Once you know that the iterations of the i loop from Floyd's Algorithm are independent, the concurrent solution practically writes itself. If we had used a single OpenMP pragma on the code in Example 10-7, the concurrent solution might even be a tad simpler than the TBB version.

Portability

It would be easy enough to use an explicit threading library to divide up the i loop iterations and assign them to threads. Implementation of a message-passing version of Floyd's Algorithm would be more difficult, since any distribution of the distance matrix D by either rows or columns would require passing data for all parts of D not held locally. There are better algorithms for this problem on distributed-memory platforms. A matrix multiplication-based algorithm or applying Dijkstra's single-source shortest path algorithm to each node in parallel would be better suited to distributed memory. These alternatives are briefly outlined in the next section.

Scalability

As the number of available threads (cores) increases, the number of rows or blocks of D to be updated per thread will be reduced. There will be some point at which the amount of computation (a number of additions and calls to the min() function) will be too small to hide the overhead of a threaded execution. This is all in direct relation to the number of nodes in the graph. More nodes in a graph yield more work and allow more threads to divide up that work.

Alternatives to Floyd's Algorithm

You may have noticed that the triple-nested loop structure of Floyd's Algorithm is very close to the linear algebra operation of matrix-matrix multiplication. Rather than using multiplication and addition, Floyd's Algorithm uses addition and minimum. In *Introduction to Algorithms*, Second Edition (MIT Press, 2001), Thomas Cormen et al. give a straightforward transformation to show the relationship between the all-pairs shortest path algorithm with the matrix-matrix multiplication algorithm using the appropriate operations. Rather than reproducing that transformation here, I will just mention the key points that demonstrate why this formulation of the algorithm works.

Let D^k be the distance matrix such that individual elements, $d^k[i][j]$, are the lengths of the shortest paths between node i and node j with $k - 1$ or fewer intermediate nodes. We can compute each term by finding the smallest sum, $d^{k/2}[i][j] + d^{k/2}[i][j]$, for all possible nodes. Going back to the map example as an illustration of this approach, to find the shortest path between Albuquerque and Boston with $k-1$ intermediate cities, by computing the sum of the shortest path of $k/2-1$ or fewer nodes from Albuquerque to CityX and the shortest path of $k/2-1$ or fewer nodes from CityX to Boston. CityX is all other possible cities (nodes) on the map (e.g., Cincinnati, Charlotte, Calgary, Chattanooga, etc.).

The initial D^1 is the weight matrix, W. To compute D^2, we simply perform matrix multiplication (using + and `min` operations) of D^1 with itself. Multiplying D^2 with itself will give us D^4, and we continue in this fashion computing D^8, D^{16}, etc., until we compute D^{n-1} (any D^k computed where $k > n - 1$ will be the same as D^{n-1}). Thus, this algorithm needs $\lceil \log_2(n - 1) \rceil$ executions of the matrix multiplication function.

You can implement the concurrent variation of matrix multiplication with an OpenMP loop worksharing construct on the outside loop or with a call to the TBB `parallel_for` algorithm on that outermost loop (there are several matrix multiplication algorithms that work in distributed memory, too). An outer loop (the fourth loop in the code) feeds the resulting matrix back into the matrix multiplication loops as the two input matrixes in the next iteration for this variation of the all-pairs shortest path algorithm.

A related graph computation is *connected components.* If you have an adjacency matrix, you can use a scheme similar to the one just described to find which nodes are in the same connected component as a given node. Another way to look at it, especially if using a directed graph, is that you will find those nodes for which there exists a path from a given node. For connected components, the matrix multiplication algorithm uses the logical and and logical or operators in place of the multiplication and addition operators, respectively.

A second alternative is to use Dijkstra's Algorithm to compute the lengths of shortest paths from a single source. The results of this algorithm are a vector (row) of the final D matrix, while the input is the original weight matrix, W. For all-pairs shortest path, then, each node in the graph is run through Dijkstra's Algorithm as the source node to fill out the distance matrix. The computation of all shortest paths from a single node is independent of the computations being performed for any other source node in the graph. So, we have a task decomposition implementation for concurrency, where each task is to apply Dijkstra's Algorithm on a node.

This variation of all-pairs shortest path is best used when the weight matrix is sparse. If the number of edges in the graph is much less than the square of the number of nodes, you can avoid examining and computing with the numerous entries of infinity within the weight matrix, W.

The details of Dijkstra's Algorithm include the use of a priority queue, sorted by (currently known shortest) distance to the source node, to find the next node to be considered in the algorithm. A heap is the typical implementation for this queue, and the heap data structure will be local to the thread executing a task. As the algorithm proceeds, original values of infinity will be updated and that new distance percolates a node up the heap. The overall concurrent algorithm is a loop over all nodes calling Dijkstra's Algorithm with the current node as the source. Any method to divide up these loop iterations and assign them to threads will work.

Minimum Spanning Tree

A *tree* is a connected (undirected) graph that contains no cycles. One node is denoted as the *root*, and this node is used as the starting point for any traversal or search of the nodes in the tree. The *spanning tree* of a connected graph is a subgraph that contains all the nodes of the original graph and a subset of just enough edges to constitute a tree. Graphs may contain many different spanning trees.

Given a weighted graph, the *minimum spanning tree* (MST) is a spanning tree that has the minimal sum of all edge weights. It is possible to have more than one MST for a graph. Looking at Figure 10-2, you can see that the minimum spanning tree for that graph is defined by the set of edges {(*A, C*) (*C, E*) (*E, D*) (*D, B*)} with a total weight of 4 (2 + 3 + 2 − 3).

The two best-known algorithms for finding the minimum spanning tree of a graph are Kruskal's Algorithm and Prim's Algorithm. I'll briefly explain each of these serial algorithms before using one as the basis for a concurrent solution to the MST code.

Kruskal's Algorithm

Kruskal's Algorithm adds edges to the partial spanning tree such that two separate connected components of subgraphs become a single connected component. At the outset of the algorithm, the partial spanning tree is made up of disconnected nodes from the graph and no edges. The edges in the graph are sorted by length. Until the tree is formed, the smallest unseen edge is considered. If this edge is between two nodes that are in different connected components, the edge is added to the partial spanning tree and the two components now form a single component. New edges are chosen until a single component is created. Figure 10-4 demonstrates how edges are added to link up separate connected components of the graph from Figure 10-2.

Notice that the main diagonal entries to the weight matrix in Figure 10-4 have been changed from 0 to infinity. If these had been left as 0 values, the "edge" between a node and itself would be part of any MST. For computing the MST, unless there is an explicit edge from a node to itself, there is no such edge in the graph. We could have retained the 0 value on the diagonal entries, but we'd need to handle these nodes as a special case to be ignored (not to mention the problems this would cause if there really were nodes with a weight of 0 in the graph). By using an infinite weight, there are no special cases and the algorithm is much simpler.

Figure 10-4 (b) starts with all nodes as separate components, and the lowest weight edge is added in Figure 10-4 (c) to create a single component from the node *B* and node *D* components. Examining the edges in sorted order adds a new edge to the partial spanning tree until the last added edge creates one connected component in Figure 10-4 (f).

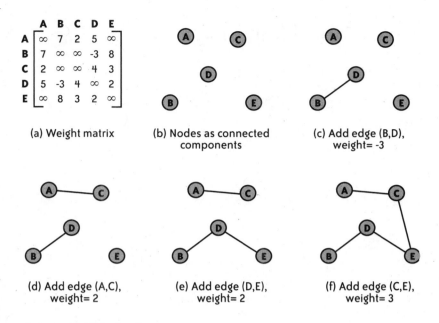

	A	B	C	D	E
A	∞	7	2	5	∞
B	7	∞	∞	-3	8
C	2	∞	∞	4	3
D	5	-3	4	∞	2
E	∞	8	3	2	∞

(a) Weight matrix

(b) Nodes as connected components

(c) Add edge (B,D), weight= -3

(d) Add edge (A,C), weight= 2

(e) Add edge (D,E), weight= 2

(f) Add edge (C,E), weight= 3

FIGURE 10-4. Example of Kruskal's Algorithm

Prim's Algorithm

Prim's Algorithm takes the almost opposite tactic to Kruskal's. This algorithm grows the MST by adding the edge that is the minimal distance from a node that is already part of the partial spanning tree. An initial node is chosen as the root of the spanning tree. For all nodes that are not currently in the partial spanning tree, each edge from the node to a node in the tree is considered, and the edge with the minimum weight is nominated. From all the nominated edges, the one with the smallest weight (ties are handled as desired) is added to the tree, which adds a new node to the partial spanning tree. The nominating and choosing process for the smallest weight edge linking a node not present in the partial spanning tree is repeated until all nodes have been added. Figure 10-5 demonstrates the order of edges added to the partial spanning tree under Prim's Algorithm on the graph from Figure 10-2.

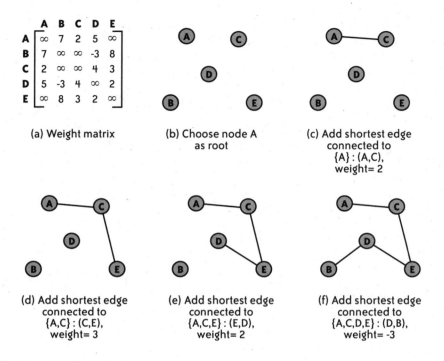

	A	B	C	D	E
A	∞	7	2	5	∞
B	7	∞	∞	-3	8
C	2	∞	∞	4	3
D	5	-3	4	∞	2
E	∞	8	3	2	∞

(a) Weight matrix

(b) Choose node A
as root

(c) Add shortest edge
connected to
{A} : (A,C),
weight= 2

(d) Add shortest edge
connected to
{A,C} : (C,E),
weight= 3

(e) Add shortest edge
connected to
{A,C,E} : (E,D),
weight= 2

(f) Add shortest edge
connected to
{A,C,D,E} : (D,B),
weight= -3

FIGURE 10-5. Example of Prim's Algorithm

Node *A* is arbitrarily chosen as the root of the spanning tree in Figure 10-5 (b). After that, the edge with the lowest weight and that is adjacent to a node in the partial spanning tree is added to the tree. The final results are the same in Figures 10-4 and 10-5. The order of the nodes added, however, is different. For example, the edge (*D,B*) is included first in Kruskal's Algorithm, but is added last in Prim's Algorithm (for the given graph and starting node). The order of nodes added to the MST by Prim's Algorithm all depends on which node is chosen as the root.

Besides the order of edge inclusion, there is one other major difference between the two algorithms. Kruskal's Algorithm needs to sort the edges by length, whereas Prim's Algorithm simply needs to keep track of the edge that has minimum distance from an unused node to some node in the partial tree. You can use a heap data structure to make the overall smallest length edge available for Kruskal's Algorithm; a pair of arrays, with an element for each node in the graph, will keep track of which is the minimal edge from each unused node and the length of that edge for Prim's Algorithm. A simple search of the arrays within Prim's Algorithm will determine the next node to be added to the tree.

Which Serial Algorithm Should We Start With?

With my eye toward a concurrent implementation, I'm going to favor Prim's Algorithm over Kruskal's. The biggest reason for this is that while edges can be sorted concurrently, the method that considers nodes from the heap needs to be serial in order to keep track of the merging of connected components. I can too easily come up with an interleaving where two threads each draw out an edge that would merge the same two components without some nontrivial synchronization. Thus, I'll use Prim's Algorithm as the basis for a concurrent MST code (as an added benefit of not using Kruskal's Algorithm as a base code, we don't have to implement a thread-safe heap—another big reason to go with Prim's). Example 10-9 is a serial implementation of Prim's Algorithm.

EXAMPLE 10-9. Serial implementation of Prim's Algorithm

```
void Prims(float **W, int **T, int N)
{
  int i, j, k;
  int *nearNode = new int[N];
  float *minDist = new float[N];
  float min;

  for (i = 1; i < N; i++) {
    nearNode[i] = 0;
    minDist[i] = W[i][0];
  }
  for (i = 0; i < N-1; i++) {
    min = FLT_MAX;
    for (j = 1; j < N; j++) {
      if (0 <= minDist[j] && minDist[j] < min) {
        min = minDist[j];
        k = j;
      }
    }
    T[i][0] = nearNode[k];
    T[i][1] = k;
    minDist[k] = -1;
    for (j = 1; j < N; j++)
      if (W[j][k] < minDist[j]) {
        minDist[j] = W[j][k];
        nearNode[j] = k;
      }
  } // for i
  free(nearNode); free(minDist);
  return;
}
```

The Prims() function in Example 10-9 assumes that there are no negative edges in the graph. If negative edges are possible, we will need to modify some of the conditional expressions to account for this. Three parameters are used: the weight matrix for the graph (W), a pointer that will return the minimum spanning tree as a vector of edges (T), and the number of nodes in the graph (N). The declarations in the function include an array to note the nearest node in the partial tree for each other node (nearNode), an array that holds the (minimum) distance from each node to the nearest node in the partial tree (minDist), and a variable to hold the overall minimum from minDist (min).

A node is chosen as the root of the partial minimum spanning tree. Just for convenience, the algorithm chooses node [0]. The initial values for elements of nearNode are set to [0], the only node in the partial tree, and the initial values for minDist will be the corresponding weights from each node to node [0] taken from the weight matrix.

The second for loop in the function iterates N−1 times. Each iteration will add an edge to the partial tree (since a tree with N nodes has N−1 edges). The code takes three steps to find the next edge to add to the tree. First, it finds the node that is the shortest distance from any node in the partial tree. Next, the associated edge is added to the partial tree. Finally, the minimum distances from the nontree nodes to the partial tree are updated in light of the newly added node.

To find the node that is the minimum distance to any node in the partial tree, the standard minimum-seeking algorithm is used. That is, the code in the first j loop examines all nontree elements of minDist in order to find the smallest value stored there (min) and the corresponding node (k) from the graph. Once the minimal distance is found, the corresponding edge is stored in the tree by saving the two nodes defining the edge (nearNode[k], k) into the tree array, T.

Note that the conditional expression used to find the minimum value includes a test to determine whether or not the node has already been added to the tree by first checking to ensure that the minDist entry for a node is nonnegative. This pretest condition is used because the element of minDist that is found to be minimal is overwritten by −1 after the new tree edge is saved. This value simply needs to be something smaller than the smallest edge weight in the graph. Thus, if we use negative edge weights, we might use a value like FLT_MIN instead.

The third step updates the minimum distance of each nonroot node from a node in the partial tree by checking to see whether the newly added tree node is closer to these nodes. The assignment of −1 to the minDist entries in the previous step will ensure that the nodes already within the partial tree do not get these updates.

N O T E

Looking to cut down on the number of conditional expressions evaluated in the code for the concurrent version, I thought to use FLT_MAX instead of −1 to note when a node had been added to the tree. This would eliminate the need for the pretest condition in the first j loop. However, since every noninfinite value in the weight matrix would be less than FLT_MAX, the test in the second j loop would have treated each node in the partial tree as if it had still not been added.

Concurrent Version of Prim's Algorithm

Edges need to be added to the partial tree one at a time to ensure that the correct edges are used. We can't just stick an OpenMP loop worksharing construct around the second i loop of the serial code in Example 10-9. So, this leaves us with the mission of trying to parallelize the steps within each iteration of the i loop. Let's look at these steps, starting from the last and moving to the first.

The final step, updating the minimum distances of nontree nodes to the partial tree, is made up of independent operations. Each node is looking at the weight of an edge from itself to the newly added tree node, and updating the corresponding element of minDist. We could use an OpenMP loop worksharing construct on this loop.

The second step, adding the chosen edge to the partial tree, must be done sequentially. If we're using OpenMP, we could do this with the single construct (the master construct doesn't have the implicit barrier we need to ensure that the tree and node updates are done before the third step commences). Since each thread will be writing the same values, we could allow all threads to update the same elements of T and minDist. There are no correctness issues for this benign data race, but there would be performance implications of multiple cores updating entries in the same cache line. To decide which method is better, we need to weigh the overhead of the single cache line being moved between cores versus the overhead of pausing threads, running code in serial, and then starting threads up again for the final step. (I'm assuming that the first step can utilize threads, which is a safe bet since I've looked ahead and know how it all turns out.)

For the first step, I presume the code can run concurrently. If this is possible, we'd need to have both min and k globally accessible, and that would mean possible synchronization at every iteration of the j loop. That's just a bit too much overhead. Rather than looking at the bits and pieces used for the computation, we should step back and look at what kind of computation is being done. Lo and behold! This is a reduction operation to find the minimum and, more importantly, the index of that minimum, which is the node of the graph that should next be added to the partial tree.

After recognizing that this first step is just a reduction, you may realize that we can't do this operation with the OpenMP reduction clause. The algorithm doesn't need the minimal value stored in minDist, but the index of the element storing that value. Even if we had a *min* operator for use in the reduction clause (which is supported in FORTRAN), there's no operator that will return the index of a minimal element. Thus, we will need to write the reduction by hand (see Chapter 7) or use the parallel_reduce algorithm from TBB. Since this computation is right out of the TBB tutorial examples, let's go with TBB. Example 10-10 has an adapted version of the tutorial example for the concurrent MST algorithm.

```
class NearestNeighbor {
  const float *const NNDist;

public:
  float minDistVal;
  int minDistIndex;

  void operator()(const blocked_range<int>& r) {
    for (int j = r.begin(); j != r.end(); ++j) {
      if (0 <= NNDist[j] && NNDist[j] < minDistVal) {
        minDistVal = NNDist[j];
        minDistIndex = j;
      }
    }
  }

  void join( const NearestNeighbor& y ) {
    if (y.minDistVal < minDistVal) {
      minDistVal = y.minDistVal;
      minDistIndex = y.minDistIndex;
    }
  }

  NearestNeighbor( const float *nnd ) :
    NNDist(nnd), minDistVal(FLT_MAX), minDistIndex(-1) {}

  NearestNeighbor( NearestNeighbor& x, split ) :
    NNDist(x.NNDist), minDistVal(FLT_MAX), minDistIndex(-1) {}
};
```

The operator() finds the minimum value and the index of that value, disregarding any −1 values, within a portion of the nearest neighbor distance array (NNDist). The join() method takes two minimum distances, from two tasks, and keeps the smaller of these along with the associated index.

The class given in Example 10-10 will support the parallel_reduce algorithm to find the node closest to the partial tree. For the rest of the concurrent Prim's Algorithm implementation, we can just as easily use the TBB parallel_for algorithm for the loop of step three. In keeping with Simple Rule 5 (to use the best method for implementation), I'm going to promote a mixed solution using TBB for the first step and OpenMP for the loop of the third step. This mixed code is shown in Example 10-11.

EXAMPLE 10-11. Concurrent version of Prim's Algorithm and helper function

```
int NodeNearestToTree(float *a, int n)
{
  NearestNeighbor Node(a);
  parallel_reduce(blocked_range<int>(0,n), Node, auto_partitioner());
  return Node.minDistIndex;
}
```

```
void cPrims(float **W, int **T, int N)
{
  int i, j, k;
  int *nearNode = new int[N];
  float *minDist = new float[N];
  float min;

  for (j = 1; j < N; j++) {
    nearNode[j] = 0;
    minDist[j] = W[j][0];
  }
  for (i = 0; i < N-1; i++) {

// Step 1
    k = NodeNearestToTree(minDist, N);

//Step 2
    T[i][0] = nearNode[k];
    T[i][1] = k;
    minDist[k] = -1;

//Step 3
#pragma omp parallel for
    for (j = 1; j < N; j++)
      if (W[j][k] < minDist[j]) {
        minDist[j] = W[j][k];
        nearNode[j] = k;
      }

  } // for i
  return;
}
```

This code uses a function, NodeNearestToTree(), to call the parallel_reduce algorithm with the current minDist array. This was part of the structure of the TBB tutorial example as well. Now, the first step in the cPrims() function is a call to this partner function, which, in turn, does the search concurrently and returns the desired node index into the variable k.

After the nearest node to the partial tree has been identified, the tree is updated with the appropriate edge and the newly added node is marked to prevent it from being considered in the future. This step is done in serial.

Finally, the distance to a node in the partial tree is updated for those nodes that are not yet included in the partial tree. For any node that has an edge to the newly added tree node, if that edge is shorter than the previously known edge connecting it to a node in the tree, an update is made to reflect the shorter connection to the MST. In Example 10-11, the loop that does this runs concurrently by using an OpenMP loop worksharing construct.

Design Factor Scorecard

How efficient, simple, portable, and scalable is the concurrent version of the minimum spanning tree code using two different threading libraries? Let's review the implementation with respect to each of these categories.

Efficiency

There is no need for mutual exclusion and synchronization objects in Example 10-11. No global data is updated in the first step, the global updates are done in serial in the second step, and the third step divides up the arrays to be updated so that elements assigned to threads will not overlap. Depending on the number of threads and loop iterations in the third step, there may be some sharing of cache lines between threads. Informed scheduling of iterations can reduce any performance hits from such sharing.

The "elephant in the room," as far as efficiency goes, is the potential for a severe penalty for switching thread models after a serial region. Would a pure TBB solution perform better than the mixed solution given here? This would be something worth testing. Your mileage may vary, so try both ways to see if the difference is significant.

Simplicity

The concurrent version is not all that different from the serial version. The OpenMP pragma keeps the serial code of the algorithm's third step intact. The biggest change is the substitution of the call to the `NodeNearestToTree()` function in place of the serial code loop. The `NearestNeighbor` class code is very straightforward in how it finds the node (index) that is minimal distance from the partial spanning tree.

Portability

You can code the loops in the first and third steps with an explicit thread library. Dividing up the iterations and assigning them to threads is an idea that we've dealt with quite a few times already. The trick is the barrier synchronization needed after each of the concurrent steps to ensure that the results of those steps are complete and available for the subsequent parts of the code to be executed. The code in Example 10-11 has the implicit barrier synchronizations built in at the end of the `parallel_reduce` algorithm (waiting for all threads to finish) and OpenMP loop worksharing construct.

You can divide the graph data by nodes across distributed processes and use a collective reduction communication to find the node nearest to the partial tree. You can then use a broadcast communication to inform all processes in the computation of the identity of the node added to the tree. The updates of the nearest nodes in the third step can be done locally, too. The message-passing and other communications provide the needed barrier synchronizations not readily available from explicit threads.

Scalability

Have you figured out that the amount of work for each iteration of the outer i loop gets smaller as execution of the code progresses? Well, actually, the number of nodes to be seriously considered each time through the loop decreases at a steady pace. As the number of nodes in the partial tree increases, the number of possible nodes that would have associated values updated in the first or third steps will decline. Threads will need to iterate through all nodes assigned by the scheduling algorithms, but fewer and fewer will generate even the chance of some computation in the first and third steps.

In an extreme arrangement, imagine nodes that are assigned to threads in a static fashion and added to the partial spanning tree in indexed order. In the midst of this situation we would have threads without any potential new tree nodes, while other threads would have all the potential nodes. Near the end, then, only one thread would even have the possibility of doing worthwhile computations and updates in the first and third steps.

The algorithm inherently contains a steady reduction in scalability. Does this decline in scalability and the load imbalance posited in the last paragraph have a noticeably adverse affect on the performance? We could alleviate the extreme cases of load imbalance by using a more dynamic scheduling of nodes to threads in each iteration of the i loop. (The TBB task scheduler should yield some modicum of dynamic scheduling automatically, so a schedule clause on the OpenMP pragma should be sufficient.) Even so, there are still scenarios that we could devise to limit the efficacy of dynamic iteration scheduling.

The cause of these imbalances is the need to look through all nodes, tree or nontree, in the first and last steps of the algorithm loop. Would a more dynamic method for keeping only nontree nodes around in the first and third steps be sensible? You might have a better idea, but the first thing I think of is to use a linked list of struct nodes containing the node number, the node in the partial tree that is closest to the node, and the length of the shortest edge between these nodes. The first step goes through all the nodes in the list to find the one that is the minimum distance from the partial tree; the second step adds the edge to the tree and removes the node from the linked list; and the third step updates the distances of the nodes remaining on the list (one way to process linked list nodes concurrently is to create a task to process each node and have those tasks placed in a queue to be accessed by threads—both OpenMP and TBB support this kind of concurrent execution).

Clearly, we would need to change the code in all steps if we adopted the linked list idea. I hope you agree that processing nodes in a linked list is going to require code that is less simple than running through an array. More importantly, will there be an adequate performance benefit possible by taking the time and trouble to implement such a solution? Again, this is something that we would need to implement and compare to the original code version for a definitive answer. With the linked list structure, we get good load balance, but we will have a very real reduction of work after each iteration of the outermost loop. For a fixed number of threads, the amount of work will eventually get to the point where each iteration is dwarfed by the threading overhead. At least with the array implementation, threads consider every assigned node, even if it is only to find that the node was already part of the tree.

There may be a crossover point in graph sizes that would favor one implementation over another. I suspect that for large graphs (e.g., thousands or tens of thousands of nodes), it is more likely that dealing with only active, nontree nodes will reap adequate performance and scalability benefits versus the original code in Example 10-11. Such a crossover point, if it exists, would need to be determined experimentally.

CHAPTER ELEVEN

Threading Tools

THIS CHAPTER MENTIONS SOME DEBUGGING AND PERFORMANCE TOOLS THAT YOU CAN USE on threaded applications. I haven't dwelled on issues of correctness or performance, except in cases that might be obvious within the development decisions made on the codes presented. As the complexity of the code increases, the use of software tools makes the tracking down and elimination of bugs and performance problems much easier.

The set of tools covered in this chapter is certainly not exhaustive. I expect many other tools to be developed and released after publication of this text. The longevity of several tools presented guarantees that they should still be available by the time you read this, though some of the names of tools may change.

To again avoid looking like a corporate shill, I've tried to give only the barest details on these tools (and keep the marketspeak to a minimum). I can't vouch for the accuracy of any of the commands or details about current versions of tools beyond the time of this writing. For more complete and up-to-date information, please refer to the individual tool manuals and other reference guides.

Debuggers

The most frequent debugging tool in use today is the `printf` statement. When trying to track down threading errors (e.g., data races, deadlock), adding such statements can cause problems to "disappear." They're not gone; they're just hiding under the altered execution order of the new application. Traditional debuggers can also mask threading errors. There are better tools to find threading errors and I've mentioned one below. However, if you don't divide up a loop just right, or if you mess up a conditional expression when transforming your serial code to a concurrent version, or if you make access a local copy of something when you should be using a global copy, you can use a standard debugging tool to locate these types of errors.

Thread-Aware Debugger

Two popular Linux debuggers, dbx and gdb, are thread-aware and can assist in tracking down logic errors that aren't related directly to the threaded implementation of the code.

In dbx, the `thread` subcommand displays and controls user threads. By itself, this command displays information about all user threads. Optionally, you can display information about specific threads by adding thread numbers as parameters. You can hold and release thread execution using `thread hold` and `thread unhold`, respectively. Both subcommands apply to all threads if no parameters are given, or to the chosen threads with the given thread numbers. To examine the current status of a thread's execution with `print`, `registers`, and `where`, set the current thread by first issuing the command `thread current <`**`threadnumber`**`>`. To print a list of the threads in the run, suspended, wait, or terminated states, use the `run`, `susp`, `wait`, and `term` flags, respectively, on the `thread` subcommand. The `mutex` and `condition` subcommands display information on mutexes and condition variables.

The gdb debugger notifies the user when a new thread is spawned during the debug session. The thread command with a thread number parameter will set the chosen thread as the current thread. All commands requesting information on the program are executed within the framework of the current thread. Issuing an info threads command displays the current status of each thread within the program. This includes the gdb-assigned thread number, the system's thread identifier, and the current stack frame of the thread. An asterisk to the left of the thread number indicates the current thread. To apply a command to other threads in addition to the current thread, use the thread apply command. This command takes a single thread number, a range of thread numbers, or the keyword all before the command that should be applied to the designated threads. You can assign breakpoints to specific threads using the break *<linespec>* thread *<threadnumber>* command.

Other debuggers that can debug multithreaded applications include the Intel Debugger (idb) and Totalview from Totalview Technologies. The Intel debugger has dbx and gdb emulation modes that implement many of the thread-specific commands available in those debuggers. Totalview can debug multiple processes that are executing within a distributed, message-passing environment through MPI (Message-Passing Interface). Also, within a chosen process, you can select, examine, and control multiple threads through the Totalview GUI.

Thread Issue Debugger: Thread Checker

Storage conflicts are the most common errors in multithreaded applications. They can also be the hardest to isolate because of the nondeterministic scheduling of thread execution by the operating system. Running a threaded code on the same system during development and testing may not reveal any problems; yet running the same binary on another system with any slight difference that could affect the order of thread execution may yield unexpected or erroneous results on the very first execution. The Intel Thread Checker is designed to identify storage conflicts, potential deadlocks, thread stalls, and other threading errors within code threaded with Intel TBB, OpenMP, POSIX, or Windows Threads. (This tool would have saved me the two hours I spent tracking down the problem with switching arrays in the straight radix sort code development.)

As a plug-in to the VTune Performance Analyzer, Intel Thread Checker runs a dynamic analysis of a running threaded application. To find storage conflicts, for example, the tool watches all memory accesses during threaded execution. By comparing the addresses accessed by different threads and determining whether or not some form of synchronization is protecting those accesses, Thread Checker can find read-write and write-write conflicts. Dynamic analysis will catch obvious errors of accessing the variables visible to multiple threads, as well as memory locations accessed indirectly through pointers.

To watch memory accesses, Thread Checker must insert instrumentation within the application for that purpose. The instrumentation can be inserted directly into the binary file (binary instrumentation) just before the analysis is run, or it may be inserted at the time of compilation (source instrumentation) if using an Intel Compiler. Regardless of how instrumentation is done, I recommend using a debug build that includes symbols and line numbers, has no optimization, and has a binary that can be relocated (for binary instrumentation). Keeping debug symbols and line numbers will give Thread Checker the chance to point directly to source lines that have possible problems; turning off all optimization will keep the application code closest to the original source order. (If there is a threading error with optimization, but no problem without optimization, the problem is more likely in the compiler and not your threading.) Also, since the code has been instrumented, there will be an increase in binary size and memory usage during execution. More importantly, though, is that the execution time will be increased. Thus, you should use a small data set that will still run through the relevant portions of the threaded code to ensure that results can be generated in a reasonable amount of time.

Performance Tools

It's all about performance. Concurrent and parallel execution, that is. If you can't get a faster execution time or compute with a larger data set in a fixed amount of time, you're spinning your wheels. Sometimes you need a little help to determine what might be causing your lack of performance. A performance problem might not be a direct outcome from some threading API function or synchronization object, but rather derived from the way data is distributed to threads or how threads are utilizing the finite resources on your execution platform. The tools in this section can point you in the right direction to where performance bottlenecks may be hampering your application or where you should begin your investigation of where to add (more) threading. It will still be up to you to decide on the best remedy, though.

Profiling

The purpose of profiling the execution of an application is to find the *hotspots* of that application. The hotspots indicate where you should focus your efforts to optimize the code to reduce the impact of negative activities. Parts of the application that take the largest percentage of execution time are good candidates for concurrency, since these hotspots are going to be the most computationally intensive portions of the serial code.

The basic Linux profiling tool, gprof, displays data that is collected during the execution of an application compiled and instrumented for profiling. The -pg flag, used in the cc command, will instrument C code. The instrumented binary will generate a profile data file (gmon.out is the default) when run. The call graph data that gprof outputs includes the amount of time spent in the code of each function and the amount of time spent in the child functions called. By default, the functions are arranged in order of execution time, from largest to smallest. This order gives you a ranked list of the functions that you should examine further for optimization or for parallelization by threads.

The Intel VTune Performance Analyzer has two primary collectors: sampling and call graph. During sampling runs of the application, the collector interrupts the processor when triggered after a number of microarchitectural events have occurred. Typically this will be ticks of the system clock, but you can set the trigger to many different architectural events. During the interrupt, the collector records the execution context, including the current execution address in memory, operating system process and thread ID executing, and executable module loaded at that address. Once execution of the target application has completed, the VTune Performance Analyzer GUI displays the sampling data for the entire system (including all the processes that were running during the sampling run). You can find hotspot data at the function and even source-line level (if you use the proper compilation and link flags when building the application).

The call graph collector in the VTune Performance Analyzer is similar to the gprof profiler. The target application is instrumented just before execution from within the VTune Performance Analyzer. Unlike the sampling collector, which can take samples from any process or module running during collection, the call graph collector will profile only the application of interest. The instrumentation records the caller of a function, how much time was spent within a function, and which child functions were called, as well as the time spent within those child function calls. The function timing results of call graph are available within a table format, but you can also view them as a graphical representation of the call tree structure resulting from the application run. You can find function execution time and number of callers or receivers by hovering the mouse over different parts of the displayed portions of the call tree. Red arcs highlight the call sequence that leads to the function with the longest execution time, known as the *critical path*. This provides a graphic indication of the flow of control of your application, including the parts you should consider for optimization or threading.

Thread Profiling: Standard Profile Tool (Sample Over Time), Thread Profiler

Besides viewing the collected sampling data as an aggregate over the course of the entire execution time that was sampled, the VTune Performance Analyzer can display the sampling results over time. That is, it can tally the number of samples taken that are associated with selected modules within discrete time units during the sampling interval. In this way, you can measure the load balance between threads of an application. If more samples are taken of some threads during a given time range than others, the former threads will have typically done more computation within that time frame. While you can deduce some load imbalances from the aggregate data, the sample over time feature allows you to find the section(s) of code— down to source lines—that are the cause.

The Intel Thread Profiler is a more general tool for identifying performance issues that are caused by the threading within an application. Intel Thread Profiler works on codes written with TBB, OpenMP, POSIX, or Windows Threads. Within the OpenMP interface, aggregate data about time spent in serial or parallel regions is given via a histogram. The histogram also represents time spent accessing locks or within critical regions or with threads waiting at implicit barriers for other threads (imbalance). The summary information can be broken down to show execution profiles of individual parallel and serial regions, as well as how individual threads are executed over the entire run. The former display is useful for finding regions that contain more of the undesired execution time (locks, synchronized, imbalance), while the latter is useful for discovering if individual threads are responsible for undesired execution.

For an explicit threading model, Intel Thread Profiler employs *critical path analysis*. This is unrelated to the critical path of call graph analysis within VTune Performance Analyzer. As the application executes, the Intel Thread Profiler records how threads interact with other threads and notable events, such as spawning new threads, joining terminated threads, holding synchronization objects, waiting for synchronization objects to be released, and waiting for external events. An *execution flow* is the execution through an application by threads where each of the events noted earlier can split or terminate the flow. The longest flow through the execution is the one that starts as the application is launched and continues until the process terminates. This is dubbed the *critical path*. Thus, if you were to make any improvement in threaded performance along this path, the total execution time of the application would be reduced, increasing overall performance.

The data recorded along the critical path is the number of threads that are active (running or able to be run if additional core resources were available) and thread interactions over synchronization objects. The Intel Thread Profiler GUI has two major divisions to display the information gathered during the threaded execution: Profile View and Timeline View. Profile View displays a histogram representation of data taken from the critical path. You can organize this histogram with different filters, including concurrency level (how many threads were active along the critical path), object view (what synchronization objects were encountered by threads), and threads view (how each thread spent time on the critical path). These filters and views can help you determine how much parallelism was available during the application execution, locate load imbalances between threads, and determine which synchronization objects were the most contended between threads. Timeline View shows the critical path over the time that the application ran. You can see the critical path switch from one thread to another and how much time threads spent executing or waiting for a synchronization object held by another thread.

Anything Else Out There?

Just going through beta testing as I was putting the finishing touches on this sentence is the Intel Parallel Studio tool. This is a parallel programming tool from Intel that plugs right into the Microsoft Visual Studio environment. The four components to Parallel Studio and their usage are:

Intel Parallel Advisor

Identifies where to insert parallelism, recognizes conflicts, and recommends solutions.

Intel Parallel Composer

Enables the incorporation of parallelism with a C/C++ compiler and threaded libraries.

Intel Parallel Inspector

Finds memory and threading errors.

Intel Parallel Amplifier

Finds multicore performance bottlenecks.

These four components blend right into the four steps of the threading methodology that I mentioned back in Chapter 1.

With the interest and desire to make parallel programming easier, there is going to be a veritable explosion of software tools made available to assist in the process of writing correct and efficient concurrent applications. I expect that those university research professors not looking to put out a new programming system are developing or have developed a software tool for analyzing concurrent codes.

Go Forth and Conquer

New tools, new programming challenges, and new ways to think about software design. It's a brave new world that we've just begun to enter. I hope you're able to join me in it and come along for the ride, and maybe take the wheel yourself every once in a while. With your gusto, new skills, and new software tools, it should be a time of excitement and wonder. Or at least, with this book, it won't be as scary as you imagined it might be.

Adjacency matrix

A graph representation method that uses a 2D array. Each row and column corresponds to a node from the graph. If an edge exists between two nodes, a 1 value is placed at the intersection of the two nodes; otherwise, a 0 is stored to show that no edge exists.

Asynchronous

Separate execution streams that can run concurrently in any order relative to each other are asynchronous.

Atomic

A type of operation that cannot be divided into smaller components or is allowed to complete execution before the operating system swaps the executing thread out of the processor.

Barrier

A synchronization object that holds all threads until every participating thread has arrived. Upon the arrival of the last thread, all threads are released to continue execution.

Benign data race

A data race that has no adverse consequences. For example, threads may write the same value into a shared location or a flag may be updated by one thread as another is reading, leading to a little extra work for the reading thread if it does not see the updated flag value.

Bus overload

A situation in which data from I/O or memory cannot be moved at the rate of the thread or process requests. This overloading of the bus capacity will cause threads to wait for memory requests to be satisfied.

Cache prefetching

Processors may have special hardware that allows them to predict which line of cache will be needed next by an executing process. The processor can retrieve (fetch) these cache lines prior to the thread requiring them.

Chunk

A portion of a larger data set that can be assigned to a thread for processing.

Compiler pragma

A programming notation that a compiler can interpret designed to provide information or hints about the code around the pragma and how to handle it.

Complete binary tree

A binary tree structure in which each level of the tree, except perhaps the deepest, is full. Leaf nodes are placed as far left as possible, if that level of the tree is not full.

Concurrency

The capability of having more than one computation in progress at the same time. These computations may be on separate cores or they may be sharing a single core by being swapped in and out by the operating system at intervals.

Connected components

A set of connected subgraphs with no shared nodes between any two subgraphs. A graph with a number of nodes and no edges is one extreme example of a graph built from connected components.

Connected graph

A graph in which there is a path from any node to any other node.

CRCW PRAM

Concurrent Read, Concurrent Write PRAM. A theoretical model of the architecture of a shared-memory machine with more than one processor. Multiple threads are allowed to read an item within the shared memory simultaneously with other threads, and are allowed to update the item at the same time as other threads. The model itself specifies the value that is written to a shared memory location by multiple threads.

CREW PRAM

Concurrent Read, Exclusive Write PRAM. A theoretical model of the architecture of a shared-memory machine with more than one processor. Multiple threads can read an item within the shared memory simultaneously, but access to update a shared location must be restricted to a single thread at any time.

Critical region

A portion of code from a concurrent algorithm where shared variables are accessed and updated. Mutual exclusion is needed for execution of a critical region by threads to prevent a data race.

Critical section

Alternate name for "critical region." Also, the name of a synchronization object type in the Windows Threads API.

Data decomposition

A method for identifying independent work that focuses on dividing large data sets that can be processed concurrently. For each chunk of data that is assigned to a thread, the computation required to process that data is assigned to that thread.

Data flow parallelism

Style of concurrency that executes an instruction when the arguments for that instruction are ready for use, as opposed to the original sequence in which the instruction was written.

Data race

The result of having two or more threads accessing the same shared resource or memory location, where at least one of the threads is attempting to update the shared resource. The threads are "racing" to deposit their value into the contended memory location or to read the memory location before or after a thread updating the value.

Deadlock

A situation in which one or more threads are waiting for an event that will never occur. The most common situation is when two threads are each holding a synchronization object that the other thread wants and there is no way for one thread to release the object it holds in order to allow the other thread to proceed.

Dependency

In a serial program, a coding sequence or property of the algorithm that may prevent parallelization of the code. There are two broad categories of dependencies: data, where reference order to the same memory location is vital to the proper execution of the algorithm; and execution, where two blocks of code must execute in the same relative order for correct execution of the algorithm. In some cases, dependencies can be removed or rewritten to be able to parallelize the affected code.

Deterministic

Given the same inputs, a deterministic application will present the same (observable) results each and every time.

Directed graph

A graph whose edges are ordered pairs of nodes; this allows connections between nodes in one direction. When drawn, the edges of a directed graph are commonly shown as arrows to indicate the "direction" of the edge.

Distributed-memory model

A configuration of processors connected to each other through a network. Memory attached to each processor is directly accessible to that processor only. Data can be shared between processors by executing processes utilizing API functions designed for moving data across the network.

Dynamic allocation

The allocation of work to threads as needed during the execution of the concurrent computation.

Edge

The part of a graph data structure that connects two nodes in the graph.

Edge weight

The real value associated with an edge in a graph.

Efficiency

A quasimetric used throughout this book to describe how well memory and other resources of the processor and platform are utilized by a concurrent implementation.

Efficiency (Speedup)

The ratio of speedup to the number of threads. This metric is expressed as a percentage that reflects on the average amount of the execution time a thread is actually doing computation.

Enchantingly parallel

The state in which decomposition into tasks does not create any dependencies between tasks. This used to be called "embarrassingly parallel" until it was pointed out that there was nothing to be embarrassed about.

ERCW PRAM

Exclusive Read, Concurrent Write PRAM. A theoretical model of the architecture of a shared-memory machine with more than one processor. A single thread can read an item within the shared memory at any time, but multiple threads are allowed to update the item at the same time. The model itself specifies the value written to a shared memory location by multiple threads.

EREW PRAM

Exclusive Read, Exclusive Write PRAM. A theoretical model of the architecture of a shared-memory machine with more than one processor. Items within the shared memory must be read and written by a single thread at any time.

Exclusive prefix scan

A prefix scan that excludes the corresponding vector item's value in the computation.

Execution stream

The portion of a process launched by the operating system that executes the instructions of the process (application).

False sharing

Updating different elements of the same cache line by different threads not sharing a cache. The updates aren't a storage conflict, but cause cache lines to be moved back and forth between the separate caches. This thrashing of cache lines will cause threads to wait for the cache to be reloaded.

Fork-join parallelism

Form of concurrency in which threads are spawned (forked), threads execute concurrent tasks, and when done, threads wait for all other threads to complete before terminating (join).

Game tree

A tree structure in which nodes are positions within the game, and edges connect nodes that can be reached by a legal move within the rules of the game. Successive levels in the tree are the alternation of moves between players.

Ghost cells

Extra array elements that surround a chunk of data. These are used to hold copies of values stored in array elements that would be in the same relative positions as the cells if the entire data array were considered as a whole.

Gustafson-Barsis's Law

A speedup metric that takes into account an increase in the data size in proportion to the increase in the number of cores. The speedup is computed as if the larger data set could be executed in serial.

Granularity

Loosely defined as the amount of computation done before synchronization is needed. The longer the time between synchronizations, the coarser the granularity will be. Fine-grained parallelism runs the danger of not having enough work assigned to threads to overcome the overhead costs of using threads. Adding more threads, when the amount of computation doesn't change, only exacerbates the problem. Coarse-grained parallelism has lower overhead costs and tends to be more readily scalable to an increase in the number of threads.

Graph

A computation object that is used to model relationships among things. A graph is defined by two finite sets: a set of nodes and a set of edges. Each node has a label to identify it and distinguish it from other nodes. Edges in a graph connect exactly two nodes and are denoted by the pair of labels of nodes that are related.

Gray code

An ordering of 2^n binary numbers such that a single bit is different between successive numbers in the sequence.

Heisenberg Uncertainty Principle

Knowing the position of something disallows the chance to measure the momentum of that thing, and conversely, being able to measure a thing's momentum precludes discovering that thing's position. This principle is typically applied to particles in small regions of space.

Helper function

A function that is threaded but calls another function to do the actual computations. A helper function can unpack the multiple parameters from the single parameter of a threaded function to be used in the call to the function doing the processing. The helper function can also provide a "waiting area" for threads in a pool and receive signals to direct the threads back to work when needed.

Hotspot

A portion of the code that has a significant amount of activity. Typically, this activity is clock cycles or execution time spent in that code portion. This activity could also be cache misses, I/O accesses, floating-point operations, etc.

Inclusive prefix scan

A prefix scan that includes the corresponding vector item's value in the computation.

Intel Threading Building Blocks

A template-based threading library for C++ programs. The library includes parallel algorithms, concurrent containers, and synchronization primitives.

Length

See Path length.

Linear speedup

A speedup curve that is drawn as a straight line on a speedup graph. This results when the speedup increases at a steady rate as more threads (cores) are utilized.

See also Perfect speedup.

Livelock

A situation in which threads are doing some computation but are unable to proceed past the current computation phase due to the actions of some other thread. This is typically caused by resource starvation where there's constant change, with no thread progressing. Two cars that meet in a narrow alley can be in livelock if there is not enough room for them to get past one another. The cars jockey back and forth and side to side, but are unable to proceed. The first meeting of Robin Hood and Little John on the log bridge is another example of livelock (solved when Little John pushed Robin off the bridge into the water).

Load balance

The measure of how the overall work is equitably divided among the threads. For best performance, each thread should be assigned the same or roughly the same amount of work. This will ensure that threads finish assigned work at the same time and threads aren't going to sit idle waiting for other threads that have been given more work.

Local variable

A variable that is accessible to only a single thread. Most common is for each thread in the application to have a copy of a variable that is given the same name.

Message-passing

A parallel programming method in which processes share data and synchronize with each other by moving data (messages) from the memory of one process to another through API calls designed for such communication operations.

Modulo locks

An algorithmic technique to associate multiple indexed objects with a single lock object. This method is a compromise between having a single lock to protect the entire set of objects and using a single lock object per object to be protected.

Mutex

Common name for a programming object that is used to enforce mutual exclusion.

Mutual exclusion

The process of allowing only one thread at a time to execute a given portion of code.

Nodes

In a graph, nodes represent the objects whose relationship is being modeled by the graph.

Nondeterministic

An application whose state of execution cannot be predicted is said to be nondeterministic. Since the operating system schedules threads for execution on processor resources and there are too many factors that influence the OS scheduling, the state of execution of a concurrent application cannot be reliably predicted. Typically, incorrect use of nondeterminism in concurrent applications will be evidenced by the application returning different results from the same inputs.

OpenMP

A directive- and pragma-based threading library. An OpenMP-compliant compiler transforms the pragmas into threaded code. A set of APIs is available to give the programmer more control over how threads execute.

Out-of-order execution

Processor technology that allows the execution of instructions to be initiated when all operands for the instruction are available.

Overhead

Additional work and execution time that was not in a corresponding serial code. In concurrent programs, this typically consists of thread management and synchronization API calls.

Parallel

Executing more than one computation at the same time. These computations must be on separate cores to be running in parallel.

Parallel region

In OpenMP, a code segment that has been prefixed with a parallel pragma, which will cause the compiler to create/use threads that will then execute the code segment concurrently.

Parallel sum

A reduction algorithm that computes the sum of all the elements within a data collection.

Path

A sequence of nodes in which successive nodes are connected by edges in the graph.

Path length

The sum of the weights of the constituent edges along a path.

Perfect speedup

The speedup that is equal to the number of threads applied to the parallel execution. Graphically, this is a 45° line on a speedup curve. This is typically the maximum achievable speedup, and is the execution goal of every concurrent application.

POSIX threads

The explicit threading library available on UNIX and Linux platforms.

Portability

A quasimetric used throughout this book to describe how easily a concurrent algorithm could be translated from the given threading library to an alternative.

PRAM

Parallel Random Access Machine. A theoretical model of the architecture of a shared-memory machine with more than one processor. Execution of instructions is done in lockstep fashion (SIMD) across all processors that are defined for the model.

Prefix scan

An algorithm that computes all partial results of an associative operation applied to all elements of a vector that precede the position in the vector that stores the result. For example, if the operation is addition, the sum of all items with a lower index value is computed for each item in the vector.

Private variable

A variable that is accessible to only a single thread. Most common is for each thread in the application to have a copy of a variable that is given the same name.

Process

The operating system's spawned and controlled entity that encapsulates an executing application. A process has two main functions. The first is to act as the resource holder for the application, and the second is to execute the instructions of the application.

Pthreads

See POSIX threads.

Quicksort

A recursive sorting algorithm that first partitions the elements to be sorted such that the lesser elements are found to the left and greater elements to the right of a pivot element. Each subset is then sorted recursively.

Race condition

A flaw in a concurrent application in which the result is dependent on the timing or sequence of multiple threads' execution.

Readers/writer lock

A synchronization object that allows either multiple threads to read the data in a critical region or a single thread to update the data within the critical region.

Reduction

A computation that takes a large data set and computes a value based on the data. Typical reduction operations include addition, multiplication, minimum, and maximum. The operation involved with a reduction computation executed concurrently must be associative and commutative.

Reentrant code

Code that multiple threads can execute concurrently without any adverse side effects. The most common way to ensure that a function is reentrant is to not update shared variables.

Removable dependence

A dependence that can be eliminated by rewriting the serial code. Examples of potential removable dependencies include recurrences and induction variables.

Rendezvous

A "meeting" of two threads to exchange data or information.

Reordering buffer

A location where instructions wait for other instructions to complete so that they can be retired in the proper order. When instructions start and execute out of order, they will wait in the reordering buffer for the completion of the instructions that originally precede them.

Round-off error

The truncation of floating-point result accuracy to fit a result into a fixed-sized data type. With concurrent execution, the order of arithmetic computations can be different, which can lead to different results than the serial code due to round-off error.

Scalable

The capability of a process or application to smoothly handle changes in the number of threads and size of data without adverse performance side effects. For example, if you add threads to execute an application and the speedup increases, that is a scalable application. If the speedup decreases, the application is not considered scalable.

Scalability

A quasimetric used throughout this book to describe an application's capability to handle changes, typically increases in system resources (e.g., number of cores, memory size, bus speed) or data set sizes.

Scaled speedup

See Gustafson-Barsis's Law.

Semaphore

A synchronization object that has an associated nonnegative count. Two operations that are defined on a semaphore are known as *wait* (if the count is nonzero, decrement count; otherwise, block until count is positive) and *post* (increment count).

Separable dependence

A dependence that can be eliminated by rewriting the serial code to move the dependence outside of the code to be parallelized. Reduction computations are examples of a potential separable dependence.

Simple path

A graph path that has no repeated nodes.

Sequential consistency

The property of parallel and concurrent programs to obtain the same results as an equivalent sequential application on the same input data.

Shared-memory

A configuration of processors or cores that can read and write into the same memory address space without any special functions or APIs.

SIMD

Single Instruction, Multiple Data stream. This is a category of parallel hardware that executes the same instruction on all processors in lockstep fashion. The processors will all have different data on which to apply that instruction. The most common parallel programming model for SIMD processors is data parallelism.

Simplicity

A quasimetric used throughout this book to describe how much or how little a concurrent implementation resembles the original serial code.

Speedup

The ratio of serial execution time of the best serial algorithm to the parallel execution time for a given number of threads.

Starvation

A condition of execution in which a thread is not allowed to proceed with assigned computations. This term applies to threads that are blocked from being scheduled into a processor by the operating system due to execution of higher priority threads.

Static allocation

Allocation of all the work to threads at the outset of the concurrent computation.

Storage conflict

A situation in which two or more threads access the same memory location and at least one of the threads attempts to update the shared memory location.

Streaming SIMD execution (SSE)

An instruction set and built-in, special hardware that can execute the same instruction on multiple arguments at the same time.

Superlinear speedup

Speedup of an application that is higher than the number of threads used. This atypical speedup is only achieved through some artifact of parallel execution, for example, splitting the data into chunks that easily fit into cache, which cannot be duplicated by the serial application.

Synchronization

Coordination in the execution of multiple threads. The most common cases of synchronization occur when you provide mutually exclusive access to shared resources or gather all threads at a point in the code before they are allowed to proceed.

Synchronization object

A programming object that can control how threads execute in relation to each other or how they interact with shared resources. Locks, mutexes, and semaphores are examples of synchronization objects.

Task decomposition

A method for identifying independent work that focuses on the computations to be performed by threads. At the time a task is assigned to a thread, the data for that task needs to be available to the thread.

TBB

See Intel Threading Building Blocks.

Thread

The operating system object that executes the instructions of a process.

Thread-local storage (TLS)

An API available within explicit threading libraries that creates private storage per thread, which will persist across function call boundaries.

Thread monkey

A programmer with wicked mad skills, capable of designing multithreaded, concurrent, and parallel software, as well as grinding out correct and efficient code to implement those designs.

Thread pool

A group of threads that are typically spawned once and assigned work as the need arises. When not needed, threads in the pool are blocked, waiting for some "wakeup" signal. By recycling threads in the pool, the overhead of repeatedly spawning and terminating threads every time they are to be used is avoided.

Thread-safe

The characteristic of a function that can execute correctly when two or more threads call that function concurrently.

Undirected graph

A graph in which the nodes of an edge are unordered. This implies that the edge can be thought of as a two-way path.

Vertices

An alternate name for nodes in a graph.

Wavefront algorithm

A parallel algorithm method that allows threads to proceed with computations at regular intervals. Typically, some large data structure is the basis for using this technique, and threads sweep across the structure one after the other like waves washing up on shore.

Weight

See Edge weight.

Weighted graph

A graph that has a value assigned to every edge. These values can represent some measure of the relationship between the nodes connected by the edge. When speaking about weighted graphs, it is normal to refer to the weight in terms of a distance.

Windows Threads

The explicit threading library available on Microsoft Windows platforms.

Worksharing

In OpenMP, a construct that distributes the computation of the associated region to the members of the thread team.

PHOTO CREDITS

Preface, Jeffrey D. Gallagher, Brighton Railway Station, Brighton, England

Chapter 1, Jeffrey D. Gallagher, Giant Dipper, Santa Cruz, California

Chapter 2, Jeffrey D. Gallagher, Street view from rue de Grenelle, Paris, France

Chapter 3, Jeffrey D. Gallagher, Big Ben, London, England

Chapter 4, Lorna Breshears, A binary game of Go

Chapter 5, Jeffrey D. Gallagher, Bath Cathedral, Bath, England

Chapter 6, Jeffrey D. Gallagher, Jin Mao Tower, view from the 88th floor, Shanghai, PRC

Chapter 7, Jeffrey D. Gallagher, The Giant's Causeway, County Antrim, Northern Ireland

Chapter 8, Jeffrey D. Gallagher, Souvenir cart outside Wat Pho, Bangkok, Thailand

Chapter 9, Jeffrey D. Gallagher, Street market radish bin, rue Cler, Paris, France

Chapter 10, Jeffrey D. Gallagher, The Eiffel Tower at night, Paris, France

Chapter 11, Jeffrey D. Gallagher, Work bench, Scotts Valley, California

INDEX

T

U

About the Author

Dr. Clay Breshears has been with Intel Corporation since September 2000. He started as a senior parallel application engineer at the Intel Parallel Applications Center in Champaign, Illinois, implementing multithreaded and distributed solutions in customer applications. Clay is currently a courseware architect, specializing in multicore and multithreaded programming and training. Before joining Intel, Clay was a research scientist at Rice University helping Department of Defense researchers make the best use of the latest High Performance Computing (HPC) platforms and resources. Clay received his Ph.D. in computer science from the University of Tennessee, Knoxville, in 1996, but he has been involved with parallel computation and programming for over 20 years; six of those years were spent in academia at Eastern Washington University and the University of Southern Mississippi.

Colophon

The cover image is an aerial view of wheat-harvesting combines from Getty Images. The cover fonts are Akzidenz Grotesk and Orator. The text font is Adobe's Meridien; the heading font is ITC Bailey.